On Irreconciliation

T0373144

Journal of the Royal Anthropological Institute Special Issue Series

The *Journal of the Royal Anthropological Institute* is the principal journal of the oldest anthropological organization in the world. It has attracted and inspired some of the world's greatest thinkers. International in scope, it presents accessible papers aimed at a broad anthropological readership. All of the annual special issues are also available from the Wiley-Blackwell books catalogue.

Previous special issues of the *JRAI*:

ON IRRECONCILIATION

EDITED BY NAYANIKA MOOKHERJEE

JRAI Associate Editors: Narmala Halstead and Geoffrey Hughes

Registered Office
John Wiley & Sons Ltd, The Atrium, Southern Gate, Chichester, West Sussex PO19 8SQ, UK

Editorial Offices
350 Main Street, Malden, MA 02148-5020, USA
9600 Garsington Road, Oxford OX4 2DQ, UK
The Atrium, Southern Gate, Chichester, West Sussex PO19 8SQ, UK

For details of our global editorial offices, for customer services, and for information about how to apply for permission to reuse the copyright material in this book, please see our website at www.wiley.com/wiley-blackwell.

Library of Congress Cataloging-in-Publication Data

CIP data requested

9781119933267

A catalogue record for this book is available from the British Library.

Journal of the Royal Anthropological Institute.
Incorporating MAN
Print ISSN 1359-0987
All articles published within this special issue are included within the ISI Journal Citation Reports® Social Science Citation Index. Please cite the articles as volume 28(Supp) of the Journal of the Royal Anthropological Institute.

Cover image: Front Cover: Base of the Colston statue lying in the M Shed Museum, Bristol, UK, copyright: @ProfDanHicks, Twitter.

Back Cover: Empty pedestal where the Colston statue stood in Bristol, UK, copyright: @ProfDanHicks, Twitter.

Cover design by Ben Higgins

Set in 10 on 12pt Minion by Aptara Inc.

Printed in the UK by Hobbs the Printers Ltd.

1 2022

Contents

Notes on contributors

Bjørn Enge Bertelsen is Professor of Social Anthropology at the University of Bergen and his research revolves around politics, protest, violence, egalitarianism, and urban Africa. His publications include *Violent becomings: state formation, sociality, and power in Mozambique* (Berghahn Books, 2016), several edited volumes, and edited special issues and articles in international journals. *Department of Social Anthropology, University of Bergen, Fosswinckelsgate 6, 5020 Bergen, Norway. Bjorn.Bertelsen@uib.no*

Vindhya Buthpitiya is an Associate Lecturer in Social Anthropology at the University of St Andrews and a member of the PhotoDemos Collective. Her current research, focused on war, photography, and civilian resistance in northern Sri Lanka, considers the local and global aftermaths of civil conflict through the making and moving of images. *Department of Social Anthropology, University of St Andrews, 71 North Street, St Andrews, Fife KY16 9AL, UK. vlb9@st-andrews.ac.uk*

Kamari Maxine Clarke is a Distinguished Professor of Transnational Justice and Sociolegal Studies at the University of Toronto. Her research explores issues dealing with the increasing judicialization of international justice, social inequality, race, and globalization. She is the author of nine books and over sixty book chapters and articles in peer-reviewed journals. *University of Toronto, Centre for Criminology & Sociolegal Studies, Canadiana Gallery, 14 Queen's Park Crescent West, Room 205, Toronto, Ontario M5S 3K9, Canada. Kamariclarke1@gmail.com*

Lisette Josephides, Emeritus Professor at Queen's University Belfast, trained in philosophy and anthropology. She conducted fieldwork in the Highlands of Papua New Guinea, publishing on gender, politics, the self and self-narratives, human rights and cosmopolitanism, ethics, morality, and knowledge creation. Her current interests include the imagination and world-building in ethnography and science fiction. *School of History, Anthropology, Philosophy and Politics, Queen's University Belfast, 25 University Square, Belfast BT7 1PB, UK. l.josephides@qub.ac.uk*

Nayanika Mookherjee is Professor of Anthropology and Co-Director of the Institute of Advanced Study at Durham University. She researches public memories of violent pasts and aesthetic practices of reparative futures through gendered violence in conflicts, memorialization, and adoption. She is the author of *The spectral wound: sexual violence, public memories and the Bangladesh War of 1971* (Duke University Press, 2015) as well as *Birangona: towards ethical testimonies of sexual violence during conflict* (with Najmun Nahar Keya; Durham University, 2019), which is available as both a graphic novel and an animation film. *Department of Anthropology, Durham University, Dawson Building, South Road, Durham DH1 3LE, UK. Nayanika.mookherjee@durham.ac.uk*

Ronald Niezen is Distinguished James McGill Professor of Anthropology and Associate Member of the Faculty of Law at McGill University. He has carried out research on an Islamic reform movement in West Africa, justice campaigns in indigenous communities in Canada, and in a variety of international organizations, including the World Health Organization, the Arctic Council, and the United Nations Permanent Forum on Indigenous Issues. His most recent book is *#HumanRights: the technologies and politics of justice claims in practice* (Stanford University Press, 2020). *Department of Anthropology, McGill University, Stephen Leacock Building, 855 Sherbrooke Street West, Montreal, Quebec H3A 2T7, Canada. ronald.niezen@mcgill.ca*

Sara Shneiderman is Associate Professor in the Department of Anthropology and School of Public Policy & Global Affairs at the University of British Columbia. She is a sociocultural anthropologist with long-term ethnographic commitments in the Himalayas and South Asia, and emerging research engagements in British Columbia, Canada. Her current work focuses on the relationship between post-conflict and post-disaster transformation. *Department of Anthropology, University of British Columbia, 6303 NW Marine Drive, Vancouver, British Columbia V6T 1Z1, Canada. sara.shneiderman@ubc.ca*

Noa Vaisman is a sociocultural anthropologist with over a decade and a half of ethnographic research experience in Buenos Aires. Her research has led her to engage with a diverse set of themes, including justice, truth, subjectivity and new scientific technologies, temporality, and psychoanalysis in Argentina. She is an Associate Professor in the Anthropology Department at Aarhus University. *Department of Anthropology, School of Culture and Society, Aarhus University, Moesgaard Allé 20, 8270 Højbjerg, Denmark. noa.vaisman@cas.au.dk*

Jacco Visser is a research assistant at the School of Communication and Culture, Aarhus University. He wrote his Ph.D. (2020) on the memorialization of the Bangladesh War in London. His research interests include transnational politics of memory, especially in and between Britain and South Asia, commemoration, nationalism, and decolonization in history education. *School of Communication and Culture, Aarhus University, Langelandsgade 139, 8000 Aarhus C, Denmark. jvisser@cc.au.dk*

Richard Ashby Wilson is the Associate Dean for Research and Professor of Anthropology and Law at the University of Connecticut. He is the author or editor of eleven books on human rights, legal anthropology, and international justice institutions. His current research is on online hate speech and digital authoritarianism in Colombia and Guatemala. *School of Law, University of Connecticut, 65 Elizabeth Street, Hartford, Connecticut 06105, USA. richard.wilson@uconn.edu*

Preface and acknowledgements

Khomite parilam na je khawmo he mawmo deenota. [That I could not forgive,
please pardon the poverty of my forgiveness.]
Rabindranath Tagore, *Shyama* (2009 [1936]: 22)

This special issue of the *Journal of the Royal Anthropological Institute*, related to 'On
irreconciliation', is a selection of essays presented (with the exception of chap. 10) in
an American Anthropological Association executive panel titled 'The Time of Justice:
Explorations through the Debates of Irreconciliation', organized by myself and held
in Vancouver in November 2019. While there exists an anthropological critique of
reconciliation, the panel ethnographically explored how irreconciliation has not been
reflected on as both a social and a political position. We sought to examine the need
to not forgive, not reconcile, as a political stance and to think through the ideas and
aspirations of justice embedded in it. In spite of the normative prevalence of forgiveness
and reconciliation, as scholars studying post-conflict contexts, we were coming across
the position of non-reconciliation in different ethnographic settings.

The theme of irreconciliation also corresponds poignantly with events in the last two
years (2020-2). This special issue has been written in a time marked by contradictions.
In the quote above with which I began this preface, and which I take from Nobel laureate
Rabindranath Tagore's dance drama *Shyama*, written in the context of the Second World
War and anti-colonial movements in India, the character Bajrasen's inability to forgive
is seen as a flaw, deemed to be a poverty of the soul. However, in the last two years it
has been difficult to forgive and forget the loss of so many lives as a result of COVID.
And yet it has been two years which have seen the goalposts of allowable speech shift
around bullying, racism, and discrimination, triggered by the death of George Floyd,
the resistance to racism through Black Lives Matter, and institutional pushbacks at anti-
racist mobilizations.

I would like to thank the anonymous reviewers, *JRAI* Editors and Publications
Committee, and two reviewers who waived anonymity, Allen Feldman (chap. 11) and
Matan Shapiro (chap. 9), as well as the contributors to this special issue. Thanks

Journal of the Royal Anthropological Institute (N.S.) **28**, *9-10*
© Royal Anthropological Institute 2022.

particularly to Jessica Turner for all the administrative help, Preetirupa Saikia for the cover layout, and Justin Dyer for the copy-editing. I am grateful to Regina H. Boone/Richmond Free Press and Dan Hicks for giving me permission to use their photographs for the cover and within the volume. I hope the collection as a whole might provide an assessment of the scholarship on forgiveness, reconciliation, apologies, transitional justice, nation, aesthetics, and emotions and be of interest to anthropologists, historians, philosophers, critical legal and political theorists, and peace, conflict resolution, and transitional justice scholars. This volume was formulated and prepared under the arc of COVID and is dedicated to the many loved ones several of the contributors have lost.

Nayanika Mookherjee, March 2022

REFERENCE

TAGORE, R. 2009 [1936]. *Shyama*. London: Createspace Independent Publishing Platform.

1

Introduction: On irreconciliation

NAYANIKA MOOKHERJEE *Durham University*

Most post-conflict reconciliatory exercises make it incumbent upon survivors to forgive, and seek closure as a demonstration of 'moving on'. Various anthropologists have criticized reconciliation and related forms of 'alternative justice' extensively but within the framework of maintaining social bonds and the rule of law. In this introduction, I reflect critically on the interdisciplinary scholarship on reconciliation, apology, and forgiveness, and theorize irreconciliation as a less examined lens of analysis. Rather than being in opposition to 'peace', irreconciliation allows us to interrogate the status quo by refusing to forgive endemic impunities, particularly in the aftermath of staged processes of justice and the absence-presence of the rule of law. In this special issue of the *JRAI*, I ethnographically explore irreconciliation's links with law, aesthetics, temporality, resistance, and control to locate its multiple analytical manifestations. Irreconciliation allows an important examination of the rule of law within processes of unresolved genocidal injustices and debates relating to slavery, Black Lives Matter, and institutional responses.

> As a Bangladeshi I can tell this is never possible until 1971 events are faced, discussed and resolved through justice. Genocide took place there and it is a daydream to think that Bangladeshis will just forget or bypass that.
>   Comment by Arman Hossein, cited in Kamran Yousaf, 'Pakistan in diplomatic push to reset ties with Bangladesh' (2020)

In an 1882 lecture, 'Qu'est-ce qu'une nation?' ('What is a nation?'), French historian Ernest Renan (1896: 165) famously proclaimed that forgetting past acts of violence was essential for the future of the nation. Jacques Derrida extends this discussion to argue that, by hiding this fundamental destruction through amnesia, the narratives of a nation are made (2001: 57). This 'apparent amnesia' (Forty 1999: 8),[1] or long-term unacknowledgement of and impunity for those who have perpetrated violence, has been prevalent in various historical and political contexts. 'That' in the above quote by

Journal of the Royal Anthropological Institute (N.S.) **28**, 11-33
© 2022 The Authors. *Journal of the Royal Anthropological Institute* published by John Wiley & Sons Ltd on behalf of Royal Anthropological Institute.

Hossein refers to a similar non-recognition of the widespread violence perpetrated by the Pakistani army and its Bengali and non-Bengali collaborators against East Pakistanis during the Bangladesh War of 1971,[2] which also led to the formation of Bangladesh.[3] In contrast to Renan's argument about forgetting and apparent amnesias, Hossein (as evident in the opening quote) refuses to forgive and forget until the events of 1971 are 'faced' through justice. As Jacco Visser (this volume) shows, for Bangladeshi activists, it is impossible to move forward until the past is tackled. This is because they feel the injustices rooted in the violence of the Bangladesh War continue in the present. This is the focus of this special issue: the various ethnographic instances of refusal to forgive in response to persistent impunity for those who have perpetrated past injustices, and particularly in the face of selective processes of justice that claim to seek redress. The rule of law plays a vital role in sometimes questioning, but predominantly sustaining, the status quo. As contributors to this volume have noticed, the ethnographic instances of refusing to forgive remain less examined within the academic literature, which has paid more attention to the dominant debates and languages of transitional justice.

Transitional justice has been identified by the United Nations Security Council (2004) as the official policy for post-conflict societies (Wilson 2020: 18). It has been taken up by various states, particularly in response to endemic impunities of perpetrators of past violence. Following the Truth and Reconciliation Commission in post-apartheid South Africa in 1994, debates on reconciliation, practices of apology and forgiveness, expressions of 'regret' or 'remorse' have had a particular currency in addressing violent pasts, seeking 'closure' and 'moving forward'. The idea of 'national reconciliation' emerged from a particular set of historical and political experiences, namely the transitions to liberal democracy that occurred at the end of the Cold War (Wilson 2003: 368). Embedded in the idea of reconciliation is the idea of the role of historical research and memory in helping to build sustainable peace and stability in new nations – and, conversely, the idea that ignoring violent pasts undermines peacebuilding efforts. So, two ideas are central here. The first is that reconciliation is an attempt to address/confront a violent past which would in turn lead to a departure from that violence in the future. It is thereby seen as a counterpoint to retributive justice. Second, the processes of reconciliation can often involve a process of accountability – through international and domestic prosecutions and a search for truth through tribunals and Truth and Reconciliation Commissions (TRCs).

Notable among the transitional justice processes are the instances of apologizing for past injustices, which have become significant speech acts (Mookherjee 2019; Mookherjee et al. 2009)[4] and are often strategic in their timing, context, and geopolitical concerns (Nobles 2008). Richard Wilson (2003: 383) refers to reconciliation as a "'thick' sense of forgiveness", practices which aim to go beyond the rhetoric and can strengthen social movements seeking to combat impunity, creating in the process new forms of political agency and sociality (Wilson 2020: 8-9; 18; see also this volume). In most of these instances of reconciliatory and apologetic exercises, there is 'commanded forgiving' (Josephides, this volume). It is often incumbent upon survivors to forgive, reconcile, and seek closure as a demonstration of peacefulness. This is also suggested in instances where there is persistent unacknowledgement of and impunity for past injustices.

Reconciliation as the 'positive' and 'normative' way forward, however, fails to capture the feelings of injustice felt by survivors when processes claiming to seek justice end up serving the powerful and the status quo. In 2015, after Justin Trudeau came

Journal of the Royal Anthropological Institute (N.S.) **28**, 11-33
© 2022 The Authors. *Journal of the Royal Anthropological Institute* published by John Wiley & Sons Ltd on behalf of Royal Anthropological Institute.

to power, he made reconciliation the cornerstone of his government and sought to address the long-term injustice towards the First Nations people in Canada through the publication of the final report of the Canadian Indian Residential Schools (CIRS) Truth and Reconciliation Commission. However, the Canadian TRC ensured impunity for the perpetrators by only allowing the victims to articulate their experiences (Niezen, this volume). That the template of reconciliation can be an instrument in support of the status quo is brought out in the complex trajectories of Bangladesh. Bangladeshi civil society has long campaigned to highlight the effects arising from the unacknowledged genocidal events of the 1971 war and the impunity of perpetrators (Pakistani authorities; Bengali and non-Bengali collaborators). A dominant cross-section of citizens and current state authorities also support this activism. Since 2009, through a Bangladesh-based state-led international crimes tribunal (ICT), juridical redress has been meted out through death penalties for well-known collaborators (mostly opposition party leaders). Bangladesh's complex case of seeking accountability is an attempt to keep the irreconciled wounds of 1971 open. In response to Bangladesh's demand for an apology for the killings and rapes of East Pakistanis in that year, Pakistani governments have expressed 'regret', but have also suggested that Bangladeshis should bury their past, show 'magnanimity' (McCarthy 2002), abandon their deep 'grudge' towards Pakistanis, and move on. The Bangladeshi ICT has also faced international criticism for its lack of transparency, flouting the rule of law, and its exhibition of vengeance through its use of death penalties. In Bangladesh, however, the ICT was considered significant among a large proportion of the electorate and its death penalties were largely popular (*Economist* 2013).[5] Pakistan has, however, referred to the trials in the tribunal as demonstrating a 'politics of revenge' and called for 'reconciliation' (*Tribune* 2015).

There is no doubt that forgiveness and reconciliation are the normative aspirations in public life as well as among many transitional justice theorists, who often frame forgiveness as 'Christian'. However, the role of Islamic mercy and the enforced right to forgiveness has also been explored by some scholars (Osanloo 2020). In Pakistan, under the Islamic law of Qisas and Diyat (meaning retribution and blood money), in instances of serious crimes/murder the law prescribes the need to be 'reconciled' to a form of material 'justice' for the victims' family as determined by the perpetrators, while the latter evade any punitive action. In 2016, an amendment tried to close this loophole of forgiveness and consequent impunity with mixed success.[6] This amendment proposed to the forgiveness law differs profoundly from our examination of the refusal to forgive on the part of survivors.

Undoubtedly, the need for social harmony in our daily lives is driven by varied reasons beyond that of religion, and the focus of this special issue is not on the discourses of forgiveness in different religions. My ethnographic insights from Bangladesh resonate with the various contributions to this volume, which highlight the need to examine the position of non-forgiveness on the part of survivors. Of particularly novel and analytical significance here is the response of survivors in response to juridical processes which selectively seek to address justice but, in the end, do so mostly in support of the status quo and sometimes of the perpetrators. Debates from the recognition of Aboriginal sovereignty further illuminate how calls for 'reconciliation' also serve a shield for those who are perceived to be the cause of violent forms of injustice. Paul Muldoon and Andrew Schaap (2012: 536) show that liberals in Australia distinguish themselves from the culture war of social conservatives to support what they deem to be the progressive reconciliation movement. However, this does not recognize that reconciliation was brought in as a measure to thwart the campaign for treaty by Aboriginal people in the 1970s and 1980s. Similar to the Australian call are Pakistan's call for reconciliation over 1971 and Donald Trump's call for 'a moment of reconciliation' after the Capitol Hill attacks on 6 January 2021 (Woodward 2021). Similar calls for 'temporary reconciliation' were also made by Indian public intellectuals so that Indian Prime Minister Narendra Modi could lead the nation despite widespread criticism of the Indian government in the face of its catastrophic failure to address the dystopic realities of COVID-related deaths in India in April-May 2021 (Mehta 2021). The call for reconciliation in these and various other instances enables what Allen Feldman refers to as 'exclosure': 'the self-defacement of this appearing non-appearance of violence' (2015: 12). Exclosure makes the violence inherent in these calls for reconciliation illegible as it secures and re-establishes the same violence through the process of reconciliation.

In this special issue, I wish to make a theoretical and ethnographic case for irreconciliation as both a social and a political phenomenon. My aim is not to further critique the goals and technologies of 'reconciliation', but to propose an understanding of the past based on a positive commitment to 'irreconciliation' as a position in its own right. Hence, irreconciliation is not violent and vengeful and not against the aspirations of peace and reconciliation. In contrast to Renan's and Derrida's positions on amnesias, this volume seeks to examine the phenomenon of refusal to forget and forgive, particularly in the face of unacknowledged injustices, and more specifically in the aftermath of selective, staged, compromised, failed processes claiming to address injustice.

Hannah Arendt (2002), writing from 1950 to 1973 in her *Denktagebuch* (*Thought diary*), poses three questions in her judgement of Nazi war criminal Adolf Eichmann. Ought one to reconcile himself to Eichmann and his wrongs? Or, barring such an active reconciliation, ought one to bypass these wrongdoings? Or, finally, ought one to say that such crimes are irreconcilable, and that the world in which such crimes exist must be rejected in the face of unacknowledged injustices? Arendt's call to reject this world questions not just the 'wrongs' but also the structures within which such wrongdoings are enabled. This might seem utopian, but the very idea of reconciliation to her is an acceptance of our limited humanity and hence is a compromise with the imperfect world. She writes: '[O]ne cannot reconcile himself to and that about which one ought also to neither be silent about or to pass by' (Arendt 2002: 7, as translated by Berkowitz 2011: 3). The defiance in the phrases 'just forget or bypass that' (Hossain's comment in the opening epigraph) and 'neither be silent about or to pass by' (Arendt) is well encapsulated by Audra Simpson's 'refusal' (2017: 19) or what Kamari Clarke (2019) refers to as 'reattribution'. It is a stance for producing and maintaining alternative structures of thought, politics, and traditions apart from and in critical relationship to states. Simpson ethnographically examines how indigenous communities in North America and Australia resort to refusal (instead of recognition) as deliberate actions. And for Clarke, reattribution is the act of reassigning culpability using different logics, histories, and tools. Thus, in this volume, irreconciliation undertaken by a collective/individual is an act of boundary-making and what is bounded is the legitimate political community.

One of the few ethnographies which has focused on the refusal to forgive and which links the discussion with apology, betrayal, abandonment, revenge, and retaliation is

Vincent Crapanzano's *The Harkis: the wound that never heals* (2011), which I expand on later (see also Crapanzano 2012). The work of Thomas Brudholm and Valérie Rosoux (2009) and of Walter Reich (2006) also provides us with various illustrations of the refusal to forgive by survivors. Writing on the politics of remorse in South Africa, Nancy Scheper-Hughes (1998: 131) notes two instances of refusal to forgive. In February 1998, the mother of Sidizwe Kondile, a victim of a police-orchestrated murder, rejected the TRC-imposed 'duty' to reconcile and told Scheper-Hughes that 'I am not ready to forgive'. Scheper-Hughes also notes that the advice she heard in her childhood catechism class – 'it is impossible to undo the damage caused by malicious acts' – was counterintuitive to 'the romance with remorse and healing … which has emerged as a master narrative of the late 20th century as individuals and nations struggle to overcome legacies of suffering' (1998: 126).

Following Arendt, Simpson, Clarke, Crapanzano, and the contributors to this special issue, our departure in this volume is not only to interrogate this 'romance with remorse and healing'. We also seek to focus on those who refuse to forgive, and specifically on those who do so in response to various unjust processes of justice (including transitional justice). Hence, what are the various instances of not forgiving, not reconciling, remaining irreconciled to past, unresolved injustices? What forms does this position of not reconciling manifest in, apart from refusing to forgive? We explore the work of irreconciliation in three instances: first, when past historical injustice has not been addressed; second, when historical injustices have been symbolically addressed – virtue-signalled – without structural changes (like 'a cut-price apology' given to the stolen generation by the Australian government without any reparation) (Mookherjee *et al.* 2009); and, third, when highlighting the forms of continuous protests against this virtue-signalled and performative reconciliation.

In the following sections, I examine the interdisciplinary debates on reconciliation and the refusal to forgive. This leads to a discussion of irreconciliation through semantics, temporality, law, aesthetics, and the self by means of ethnographically informed interdisciplinary contributions in the context of Papua New Guinea, Mozambique, Bangladesh, Canada, Argentina, Sri Lanka, Colombia, Northern Ireland and the wider United Kingdom. The protests around Black Lives Matter in 2020-1 and the subsequent institutional pushbacks against anti-racist resistance (Mookherjee, this volume) highlight the need for irreconciliation, the need for dissent and affective work against continuing impunities. Visibilizing irreconciliation across different geographical spaces and temporalities in the Global North and South is significant so as to move away from the simplistic binaries where 'peaceful' societies are deemed to be forgiving while 'violent' ones are deemed to be more vengeful. As outlined above, in numerous instances, processes of reconciliation come to stand in for the maintenance of the status quo. For the contributors to this special issue, irreconciliation is indistinguishable from an anthropological examination of and search for truths along with acknowledgements of the realities of injustice.

Reconciliation, 'we are back to that cup of tea'[7]: anthropological and other disciplinary perspectives

This special issue proposes a conceptualization of irreconciliation which engages with and departs from the debates within the fields of peace and conflict resolution studies, what has been referred to as the continuum of the 'peaceandconflict system' (Mac Ginty 2019), critical legal and political theory, and anthropological critiques of the

Journal of the Royal Anthropological Institute (N.S.) **28**, 11-33
© 2022 The Authors. *Journal of the Royal Anthropological Institute* published by John Wiley & Sons Ltd on behalf of Royal Anthropological Institute.

transitional justice literature. The foundations of peace studies are often attributed to Johan Galtung's conceptualization of 'negative' peace, which was defined as the absence of direct, individual violence, and 'positive' peace, which was theorized as the absence of structural violence and framed initially as integration and co-operation. Galtung (1968: 190) acknowledges the status quoist perspective of this lens on peace following criticism by Herman Schmid (1968: 221) and reframes positive peace as social justice which refers to 'vertical development, of participation, decentralization, codecision' (Galtung 1968: 186). The existing scholarship has critiqued reconciliation in an attempt to improve it but within its prescribed framework of the rule of law. However, for critical and progressive theorists, reconciliation is inherently politically conservative and morally contestable as it entails problematic compromises of justice (Lu 2017: 15). Irreconciliation, the way we define it, instead aims to highlight the struggles against any violence of 'peace' (Buthpitiya, this volume) which seeks to camouflage an unjust status quo in the name of seeking reconciliation.

The status quoist attributions to peace studies have also been applied to the concept of reconciliation which is central to processes of transitional justice. The idea of reconciliation has an inherent linearity of transitioning from authoritarian/military to liberal democratic structures (e.g. Argentina and Bangladesh) as a solution, the need to look forward at the cost of closing the problematic debates about the past for those most affected. Reconciliation is thus meant to enable 'renewal of applicable relations of persons who have been at variance' (Gallimore 2008: 251), or, in this instance, the collective of persons standing in as nations. The three steps of reconciliation involve acknowledgement of injury; contrition, responsibility, and the seeking of forgiveness; and the granting of forgiveness by the victim who is also joined by bystanders. The dialogical therapeutic process of giving and hearing testimonies is also deemed to be intrinsic to reconciliation for audiences, as in the case of the International Criminal Tribunal for Rwanda (Eltringham 2019). In instances where past injustices have not been acknowledged and addressed, juridical means like TRCs and War Crimes Tribunals are deployed to bring the issues to the fore (Rosoux 2009). In other instances, when states and institutions are willing to engage with past injustices beyond the juridical, history rewriting processes, aesthetic representations, apologies, forgiveness, and reparations become the means through which reconciliation is attempted. Ironically, the need to apologize which compels nations to confront their pasts runs counter to current official, national self-images of tolerance and pluralism (Hage 1994, as cited in Mookherjee et al. 2009: 347).

Initially, juridical structures can be set up in response to laws enabling amnesty and as forums which are tasked to address injustice. Richard Wilson (2001), in critiquing reconciliation, has focused on the need for post-conflict state legitimacy and accountability through retributive justice (via bureaucratic and legal processes) as reconciliation is deemed to undermine the rule of law. Others, meanwhile, have focused on everyday reconciliation (e.g. Doughty 2016). Along with Fiona Ross (2003), Wilson (2003; 2020) has also critiqued reconciliation for its emphasis on positivism while excluding certain kinds of survivor narratives. He also identifies multiple competing discourses and moral systems around justice and reconciliation. Drawing on the TRC in South Africa, he shows how it brought together wider transnational notions of human rights and moral notions of forgiveness and redemption. The banner held at the TRC by the survivors read: 'Reconciliation through Truth' (Wilson 2020: 18), highlighting the need for transparency (i.e. truth telling and reparations from the TRC), which was

Journal of the Royal Anthropological Institute (N.S.) **28**, 11-33
© 2022 The Authors. *Journal of the Royal Anthropological Institute* published by John Wiley & Sons Ltd on behalf of Royal Anthropological Institute.

eventually not addressed. Instead, the TRC only recognized suffering and rendered the grief morally equal. It assumed that by encouraging forgetting and forsaking feelings of revenge among survivors, the nation would be liberated. As a result, feelings of resentment (Mihai 2010; Schaap 2005) among those wronged remained unaddressed. Instead, individual suffering was thus brought back to the public space and shared – it became part of a narrative of national redemption. Wilson (2003) shows that with the collectivization of suffering, a new identity – that of a national victim – was created.

The various juridical structures of reconciliation could be set up by the United Nations, national governments, local mediation, and community courts with complex power dynamics and geopolitics at play (Anders & Zenker 2014; Wilson 2020: 2-4). The role of international organizations like the International Criminal Court has, however, been rightly criticized for primarily indicting male African rather than European and American leaders for their war crimes, with the aim to 'shield the west and pursue the rest' (Clarke 2019: 105). As a result of this imbalance, various national courts have been set up to carry out trials. The Bangladesh ICT is such an example. These national tribunals have, however, been criticized for reiterating hierarchies of patriarchy and patronage (like the *gacaca* courts in Rwanda – see Clark 2010) and for flouting the rule of law to achieve justice. This legitimizes Laura Nader's (1991) account of the aspiration towards a 'harmony ideology'.[8] For decades, therefore, anthropologists have extensively criticized reconciliation and related forms of 'alternative justice' (Anders & Zenker 2014; Branch 2014; Clarke 2019; Eltringham 2019; Niezen 2017; Thiranagama 2013; Wilson 2003; 2020). They have emphasized its coerciveness and even theorized it as an alternative modality of social control, discipline and instrumentalization in pursuit of a liberal framework (Branch 2014: 611-12).

Political and legal theorists have argued that a readiness to forgive is, however, important so that members of a divided polity can be engaged in a mode of agonism: a back-and-forth contestation which can challenge each other's version of the violent past (Schaap 2005). Recognizing the significance of resentment on the part of a collective who have been wronged, scholars (e.g. Mihai 2010; Schaap 2005) invoke a third-party mediated retribution to recuperate 'negative emotions for democracy' (Mihai 2010: 183), to address this anger, and to acknowledge this injustice. In the 'triad of conflict' response framework (of management, resolution, and transformation), the study of the peaceandconflict continuum is today more cognizant of complexities, but with a focus on accommodation, co-existence, 'conflict calming' (Mac Ginty 2019: 269), and an 'adaptive peacebuilding approach' (de Coning 2018) focusing on the cohesion and resilience of local and national institutions. This laudable pro-peace perspective needs to make reconciliation effective by including calls for criminal prosecutions, civil reparations for violations, and structural analysis of conditions of violation (Lu 2017; Wilson, this volume). For these theorists, the role of law becomes foundational for this purpose of recognition and retribution, setting up parameters within which the contestation needs to be resolved. This, however forecloses further debate on political issues, arriving thereby at the impossibility of the process of reconciliation, which always remains deferred (Turner 2016: 40-1).

The prevalence of the framework of reconciliation as the raison d'être of conflict resolution in the face of these various social scientific critiques is intriguing. This narrative of reconciliation can be found in the prevalence of the positive uplifting story from trauma to hope and renewal: what has been described as the 'Schindlerization of Holocaust testimony' (Reich 2006: 466). This entails the need to have feel-good, upbeat endings which the framework of reconciliation readily provides, and which often run counter to the negative experiences and emotions of survivors. In the process, such upbeat 'healing' accounts control and foreclose the survivors' emotions of injustice. Since 2002, Rwandan President Paul Kagame has emphasized the need for forgiveness for the sake of the country's future. Yet, as the contributions in this special issue show, a move away from these legal and political structures highlights that people are often forced to forgive against their will and, when asked, participants in reconciliation are often quite scathing about it. This is evident in Rwandan sociologist and psychotherapist Esther Mujawayo's account of 'the interest in post-atrocity forgiveness as an "obsession" – not on behalf of the survivors, but on behalf of the authorities, NGOs, and other agents of reconciliation' (Brudholm & Rosoux 2009: 43) – what Wilson calls a 'global reconciliation industry' (2003: 383). Similarly, Innocent Rwililiza notes that humanitarian organizations 'are importing forgiveness in Rwanda, and they wrap it in lots of dollars to win us over. There is a Forgiveness Plan as there is an Aids Plan' (Hatzfield 2009: 18; also cited in Brudholm & Rosoux 2009: 44).

Similar positions of refusal to reconcile (Shneiderman, this volume; Simpson 2017) were evident in a First Nation Panel on Reconciliation at the American Anthropological Association (AAA) conference in Vancouver in November 2019. 'Thou shall reconcile' was one of the phrases I heard being mentioned by panellists to highlight the compulsion to reconcile in the context of Canada's relationship with its First Nation communities, particularly in the light of the horrific accounts of the missing children of the residential schools (Niezen and Shneiderman, both this volume). In May-June 2021, the remains of over 1,000 Indigenous children – students of some of Canada's largest residential schools – were found in unmarked graves near the cities of Kamloops, Cranbrook, and Saskatchewan (Honderich 2021). Running between 1874 and 1996, these government-run boarding schools were part of a policy to attempt to assimilate Indigenous children and destroy Indigenous cultures and languages.

If acknowledgement of the moral truth of wrongdoing is not a precondition for reconciliation, but rather reconciliation makes possible a collective remembrance of past wrongs (Schaap 2005: 140), in the words of a First Nation panellist (which were reiterated later by other panellists) on the AAA panel, such a renewal of reconciliation would be 'like a tape on a bleeding wound, how would that help?' This is similarly expressed by Sara Ahmed: '[W]e are back to that cup of tea' (2019: 188): the reconciliatory processes often suggested by human resources (HR) departments of organizations when dealing with complaints. Attending the AAA conference in 2019 in Vancouver, referred to as the city of reconciliation, I was cognizant that our executive panel on irreconciliation felt antithetical to the reconciliatory trend. However, attending this First Nations panel, where similar criticisms of reconciliation and forgiveness were taking place, the theme of this issue – irreconciliation – became even more pertinent to address the injustices of the past and present and map the reality on the ground. Since those 'who will not forgive might be mentioned, admonished, or received with expressions of understanding or even respect' (Brudholm 2008: 35-6), the contributions in this special issue seek to examine their motivations and reflections, which are seldom seriously and ethnographically investigated. This would enable an understanding of the long-term impact and social effects of the various processes of transitional justice (Wilson 2020: 18). In the following section, I explore the interdisciplinary scholarship which is a precursor to what we are referring to as irreconciliation.

Journal of the Royal Anthropological Institute (N.S.) **28**, 11-33

Irreconciliation and its manifestations

> There is no reconciliation without truth. These 215 children brought out the truth.
> Geraldine Lee Shingoose as cited in Holly Honderich, 'Why Canada is mourning the deaths of
> hundreds of children' (2021)

Shingoose's powerful statement above of the abuses she faced in the Canadian residential school system she was sent to as a child powerfully resonates with the urgency with which we are arguing for irreconciliation as a prevailing phenomenon and a concept to grapple with ethnographically. If reconciliation is about coming to terms with what is fated (Arendt 2002; Berkowitz 2011: 8),[9] the position of Shingoose and various other children in the Canadian residential schools refuses such conciliation. The normative position within the social sciences and much classical anthropological scholarship (e.g. Gluckman 1955) has predominantly highlighted the role of agreement and conciliation, showing in the process how conflict and harmony are modes of maintaining social control. Yet, as explored in various examples in and contributions to this special issue, the ethnographic realities on the ground also highlight the refusal to reconcile in the face of continuing injustice. Here, ethnographies of feuding among the Bedouins (Peters 2007) and the Glendoits in Crete (Herzfeld 1985) show that the conflicts they discuss are not 'anti-social'. They in fact constitute alternative grounds for human relationships. I elaborate on these ethnographies below to carve out a formulation of irreconciliation as a social good which is interrogating the compulsion and control intrinsic to the prescriptions of reconciliation.

For Emrys Peters (2007), feuding between Bedouin groups is about the control of resources and cannot be explained by Evans-Pritchard's (1940) mechanical fission and fusion model. Referred to as *fitna*, it is about an act which causes an impasse in relationships, creates chaos among a small group of related people, produces internal calamity (Peters 2007: 62), and enables a settlement of hostilities over proprietary rights in land and water. *Fitna* necessitates the need to form a collective to guard resources against others. Michael Herzfeld (1985) shows how the villagers in Glendi, Crete, negotiate their multiple conflicting identities and tensions with the Greek bureaucratic state over the endemic practice of herd theft. Here, re-narration of vengeance killing across groups over herd theft generates *simasia*, meaning manly selfhood. *Simasia* is hinged on a patrilineal ideology such that the deaths of one's agnates are deemed to be wounds of the self. Describing various *eghoismos* (aggressive self-regard related to male concerns articulated by men and women), Herzfeld argues that the Glendoits have 'more aggressively poetic expectations of social life' (1985: 49). The focus on these feuds and revenge killings brings out the complexity of conflictual identities among the Bedouins and the Glendoits, within and beyond their communities and in relation to external actors like the state or opposing groups.

I discern strands of irreconciliation in the mnemonic manipulation or strategic remembering deployed by the villagers of Ambodiharina, Madagascar, to take note of their colonial past and postcolonial present (Cole 2001: 276). Similarly, Greek villagers describe events of the Ottoman occupation, which they could not have experienced, and yet they do not talk of the experiences during the Greek national and civil wars of 1940-50. Anna Collard (1989) shows how this not talking enables the communities to avoid addressing their ambiguous moral complicities during this period. Reflections among the Greek left on the unaddressed and unfinished repercussions of the civil wars could be read as irreconciliation (E. Kirtsoglou pers. comm., July 2021). The rift between

Journal of the Royal Anthropological Institute (N.S.) **28**, 11-33
© 2022 The Authors. *Journal of the Royal Anthropological Institute* published by John Wiley & Sons
Ltd on behalf of Royal Anthropological Institute.

Euro-remainers and 'No' supporters in the Greek referendum was seen by many as another expression of the unacknowledged dynamics of these civil wars (Kirtsoglou 2020: 161-4).

Vincent Crapanzano's (2011; 2012) moving ethnography on the Harkis is one of the few extensive anthropological explorations discussing the refusal to forgive. The Harkis are the Algerians now living in France numbering around 260,000 and are 'history's forgotten' as they were ignored by both journalists and scholars. During the Algerian War of Independence, they sided with the French and were demobilized at the end of the conflict by the French government. On returning to their villages in Algeria unarmed, they were then attacked by locals and also by the Front de Libération Nationale (FLN) for their support of the French army. Despite appeals for help, the French government at first did nothing to protect them. When it did finally allow them to settle in France, they were kept interned in camps amid miserable conditions. Being thus humiliated, the Harkis have adopted a 'haunting silence'. The children of the Harkis are affected by their parents' silence and also by their own experience of discrimination in France. They have been campaigning to claim compensation and seek apology from France for betraying and abandoning their parents. As Crapanzano puts it poignantly:

> For forgiveness to occur, the wrongdoers and their victims have to acknowledge the wrongdoing, appreciate each other's perspective and recognize the role it has played in the way they have each configured their individual and collective lives (as, for example a central trauma, an excuse for inaction, a source of resentment) (2012: 199).

Scholars also point out that, as with the Harkis, no comprehensive study has been undertaken to assess whether or not the victims of the Rwandan genocide 'feel vindicated or that their injuries or grievances have been redressed by the outcome of the trials' (Gallimore 2008: 240). The main concern for the prosecutor's spokesperson was the cathartic effect of testifying, which was meant to release the hurt, and enable the testifiers to forgive and reconcile with those who had harmed them. While Rwandan psychotherapist Esther Mujawayo, mentioned above, refuses to forgive, she sees forgiveness as easy and 'tempting'. Innocent Rwililiza also finds forgiveness strange and constraining. This precisely highlights how difficult it is for many survivors (whose injury has not been – and will never be – redressed) to forgive.

The prevalence of such legitimate resentment among survivors is also explored by the psychiatrist Walter Reich (2006), exploring Holocaust narratives in America, and the philosopher Thomas Brudholm (2008; Brudholm & Rosoux 2009), exploring group forgiveness in the cases of three examples of atrocities: the Holocaust, the killing of Tutsis by Hutus in Rwanda, and the murder of black South Africans by the apartheid government. He shows how both the Holocaust survivor Jean Améry and Rwandan Esther Mujawayo consider resentment to be something deeply human which victims have a right to not rise above (Brudholm & Rosoux 2009: 45). If the corresponding counterpoint to reconciliation is the averted look – to be silent and pass by (Arendt 2002; Berkowitz 2011: 13) – it is worth reflecting on the role of silence as irreconciliation. Silence here is a site of mourning and dignity, a place from which to make the demands of acknowledgement, the demands for retribution (not revenge and amnesty). A politics of refusal (rather than recognition) thereby marks out a quiet confrontation (Selimovic 2018) born out of an unwillingness to participate in and hence legitimize the transitional justice process (Shaw 2007; Turner 2016: 45). The following section explores the relationship of irreconciliation with semantics and temporality.

Journal of the Royal Anthropological Institute (N.S.) **28**, *11-33*
© 2022 The Authors. *Journal of the Royal Anthropological Institute* published by John Wiley & Sons Ltd on behalf of Royal Anthropological Institute.

Civilizing tropes of reconciliation and semantic temporalities of irreconciliation

The paucity as well as relative invisibility of the ethnographic references to non-forgiveness might suggest that anthropologists were guided by the prevailing paradigms of their times aligning with a harmonic 'nostalgia for synthesis' (Nader 1991: 319). Within a normative framework, non-forgiveness comes across as non-peaceful and discordant. Or we could ask with Nancy Scheper-Hughes (1998) if these concepts are semantically *deemed to be* modernist, individualized, and Western and hence unimaginable for 'non-Western' societies and ethnographies. It is important to examine the semantic terrains of reconciliation and irreconciliation to decentre these Orientalizing discourses that are intrinsic to the framework of reconciliation. The civilizational undertones in reconciliation can be identified through the binaries of forgiving (often associated with Christianity and 'peaceful' societies) and avenging (associated with conflict-ridden societies) collectives. These constructions are akin to a form of Occidentalism – 'the essentialist rendering of the west by westerners' (Carrier 1995: 199). Further, as we noted, forgiveness in Christianity is deemed to grant humanity while Islamic law is deemed to be about sovereign control and making deals for impunity through the process of forgiveness. Arzoo Osanloo (2006: 587) has astutely shown how the granting of mercy in the case of death penalties in both Iran and America can be about sovereign control. Yet the consensus and compromise of daily life are not guided by religion alone. Crapanzano (2012) shows how the French, in thinking of themselves as a forgiving society and the Algerians as vengeful, were quick to seize on this Algerian stereotype in their attempt to understand why villages were often split between the FLN and the Harkis. Conversely, ethnographies on victim rights in Iran (Osanloo 2020) have highlighted the role of the juridical system and the prevalence of forbearance and spaces for victims to forgive within it. This raises questions about the prevalent stereotype of Iran as vengeful in its practice of the death penalty. The use of the death penalty by the Bangladesh War Crimes Tribunal towards its collaborators has enabled the configuring of Bangladesh as vengeful, 'complex and problematic' by many human rights organizations as well as some anthropologists (pers. comm.) working on TRCs. Rahnuma Ahmed (2013), a critically acclaimed Bangladeshi anthropologist, however, shows that demands for the death penalty/*fashi* 'feed on long years of betrayal, both manifest and hidden', by Bangladeshi elites and institutions. This feeling of betrayal is a consequence of the political and social rehabilitation of collaborators that has continued in Bangladesh under military rule. It refers to the contemporary 'deals' made between democratic governments and political parties supporting collaborators. This is similar to the 'rehabilitation' of the law in Argentina (Vaisman, this volume), which would likely have resulted in the release of most convicted perpetrators of human rights crimes in the country had it not been amended to exclude those guilty of crimes against humanity. Perpetrators were not released eventually, although many are serving their sentence under house arrest.

In spite of the established criticism of reconciliation, policy circles seem impervious to these realities and 'commanded forgiving' (Josephides, this volume) appears to be the norm. The focus on 'Africa' for restorative justice ('cultural' forms of legal pluralism) (Minow 2000) driving supposedly African transitional justice mechanisms has been critically examined (Anders & Zenker 2014; Branch 2014: 613; Feldman 2015). That structural adjustment proposed in various African countries by the World Bank and International Monetary Fund (Clarke 2019: 104) was conditional on including the

© 2022 The Authors. *Journal of the Royal Anthropological Institute* published by John Wiley & Sons Ltd on behalf of Royal Anthropological Institute.

ratification of the Rome Statute is telling of the multiple contradictions that are intrinsic to the civilizational and liberal frameworks of reconciliation. In this special issue, we are exploring juridical and aesthetic manifestations of irreconciliation in three instances: first, when past historical injustice has not been addressed: Mozambique (Bertelsen), Bangladesh and the United Kingdom (Visser, Mookherjee); second, when historical injustices have been symbolically addressed – virtue-signalled – without or with insufficient structural changes: Northern Ireland (Josephides), Canada (Niezen), Sri Lanka (Buthpitiya), Colombia (Clarke), and the United Kingdom (Mookherjee); and, third, in highlighting the forms of continual protests against this virtue-signalled and performative reconciliation (all essays). Additionally, Vaisman shows that in Argentina symbolic changes have been accompanied by structural changes through ongoing trials as a result of persistent protests against impunity.

Writing in response to the South African TRC, Jacques Derrida (2001) emphasizes the need for unconditional forgiveness on the part of those forgiving, which is not based on the expectation of atonement on the part of those who need to be forgiven. This unconditional forgiveness, according to him, also needs to be delinked from sovereign power: state power or a top-down forgiveness. Paul Ricoeur (2004), on the other hand, emphazises the significance of taking responsibility on the part of those seeking forgiveness. Josephides (this volume) provides us with a valuable theoretical and ethnographic starting point in juxtaposing Derrida's and Ricoeur's positions on forgiveness with the experiences of *ressentiment* felt by the Holocaust survivor Jean Améry, the refusal to forgive oneself among Turkish Cypriots, and the letting go of resentment in Northern Ireland and among the Kewa in Papua New Guinea. I cite Josephides' extensive parsing of the semantic terrain of irreconciliation. She groups the various concepts as those of fault, trauma, and resentment, which can follow each other sequentially. Responsibility, accountability, and imputability are the next set of closely connected concepts, followed by apology, atonement, repentance, and remorse. Forgiveness and forgetting are linked but do not necessarily follow each other. It thereby becomes important to think through the relationship between irreconciliation and temporality.

Citing the example of Northern Ireland, Josephides shows that when there are grievances on all sides, there is a tendency to apportion blame. As a result, the way out of this impasse in Northern Ireland is to take a chance on the future and move forward. Yet at the same time, such moving forward can get blocked, as in the case of the report of the 'Consultation Group on the Past' of 2009, which recommended monetary compensation of £12,000 to the families of all those who died in the Troubles, irrespective of whether the victims were IRA members, security forces, or civilians. This moral equivalence was greeted with anger as this equalizing position derecognized the suffering of families of victims. It highlighted the limited role of the sovereign in trying to easily address long-standing grievances, somewhat reflecting Derrida's position about the importance of unconditional forgiveness without sovereignty. So, for Derrida, the primary onus of forgiveness falls back on the victim.

In Bangladesh and its diasporic contexts in the United Kingdom (Visser, this volume), this onus not to forgive has been taken on by activists. For them, addressing the unaddressed past through the death penalty for those who collaborated with the Pakistani army is of utmost importance. Mala's explanation of the death penalty and the role of law in ensuring this execution is highlighted in her quote:

Journal of the Royal Anthropological Institute (N.S.) **28**, 11-33

On the day they executed Quader Mollah, I was thinking, am I cherishing the death of Quader Mollah? No. I was celebrating the justice that the victims got. I never had anything to do with politics, I don't want to kill him, but I don't want anything less punishment for Quader Mollah than that what is in my law (Interview with Mala, 24 September 2017, as cited by Visser, this volume).

Bertelsen (this volume) shows how Mozambique, like Bangladesh, defies the global linear templates of so-called reconciliation processes. By examining how Mozambicans understand and relate to the prevalence of the violence of the civil war and the era of popular justice, he understands it as a form of irreconciliation which is non-chrononormative. Hence, the past and the prospects of a post-war future have been called off. The non-linear and spatiotemporal perpetuity of war has also made it unwitnessable, thereby co-producing the rise of irreconciliation as a result of a postcolonial betrayal (as we see among the Harkis in Crapanzano). This enables critical readings of contemporary war as elite accumulation or rehashes/repurposes notions of popular justice into politics as irreconciliation.

Compared to Bertelsen's 'futureless chronocracy', Niezen (this volume) shows how in the survivor-centred TRC in Canada, there was no pre-conflict state to be returned to as the harm was ongoing. In Buthpitiya and Clarke's contributions, temporality can be found in the idea of reattribution (Clarke 2019), through which culpability is reassigned using different logics, histories, and tools. Vaisman (this volume) shows how chronological time is skewed as the past might be lurking everywhere with the prospect of finding either a sibling or the body of a disappeared parent. Through films and the everyday, the past is felt in the present, as an ongoing experience which disallows the books to be closed. This itself determines the visions of the future of Argentina. In my essay, the problematic past lurks in the presence of statues of slave owners while the history of slavery continues to be absent in pedagogical texts. The Black Lives Matter movement of 2020-1 has also impacted on the contours of conversation taking place in organizations around various transgressions. Its call for a change is about the vision of the future. In the following section, we unravel irreconciliation's complex relationship with law.

Legal (im)possibilities and irreconciliation

The essays in this special issue seek to make a case for developing irreconciliation through three paradoxical aspirations of justice. First, I explore the practices of sovereign law (Derrida 2001: 59) as enabling and working with the state, leading to judgements which have predominant national support, as in Bangladesh. This enables the wounds of a past to be kept open as irreconciliation. Second, we explore the role of law as disabling, as violence, working with the sovereign (states or organizations mentioned in my essay) to showcase the performance of justice in order to limit and derail truth. Irreconciliation emerges among non-state actors against such sovereign practices to maintain continued vigilance against the reinscription of continued impunity (Canada, Argentina, Sri Lanka, Colombia, the United Kingdom). Third, law is also empowering when it is distinct from executive power, working against the sovereign to demand justice, and can be a protagonist in the claims of irreconciliation (as in contemporary Argentina).

To explore the role of sovereign law as enabling, Derrida's position about the victim's ability to forgive as the test of humanity becomes particularly challenging in various contexts. As a result, in instances of long-term impunities, for victims, 'law's possibilities can be found in emotional aspirations for social change' (Clarke 2019: 264). Visser (this volume) shows that through the ICT in Bangladesh, the solution to long-term political impunity of collaborators in the Bangladesh War of 1971 can be seen to be a form of retributive violence but is also conscious irreconciliation. This is achieved by Bangladeshi human rights activists in the United Kingdom and Bangladesh through the invocation of global human rights tropes as well as the contradictory demand for the death penalty for wartime collaborators – a demand they would not support in other instances. But this demand redraws the line of ethnic exclusion in Bangladesh by disregarding the role of Bengali chauvinism and its militarized relationship with ethnic minorities (R. Ahmed 2013). It is here that the limitations and exclusions of irreconciliation are worth noting. The coming together of the state and law, victim and executive, results in a regime of extra-judicial repression. Visser (this volume) has shown how the violence of the Bangladesh War of 1971 is addressed in London in the light of increasingly 'authoritarian victimhood' (Mookherjee 2020) in Bangladesh and the way the framework of reconciliation and transitional justice is unable to address contestations over the war. Here the colonial legacies and the evocation of 'territorial integrity' (as in Sri Lanka)[10] to sustain 'national reconciliation' is only possible through state violence seeking to contrive the imaginaries of the nation project.

Second, we explore the disabling and violent capacities of law and irreconciliation. In instances where attempts have been made to put institutions and processes in place, to showcase transitional justice, 'exclosure' works 'by making the violence inherent in these calls for redressal illegible, as it secures and re-establishes the same violence through the process of reconciliation' (Feldman 2015: 12). Instead of Benjamin's law-making and law-preserving violence, here Derrida's commentary on Benjamin's theorization on violence – that 'force is essentially implied in the very concept of justice as law (*droit*)' (Derrida 1992: 5) – helps me to further formulate the violence of this showcasing of justice. The Canadian TRC is a case in point (Niezen 2017 and this volume). In 2015, just after Justin Trudeau came to power, the CIRS TRC released its final report, marking perhaps the culmination of reconciliation talk in the national public sphere. Since then, the federal government has apologized and has claimed that the relationship with the First Nation communities is its cornerstone and will impact on all policy-making. The Canadian TRC, however, decided to focus on the experience of the victims and not on the perpetrators, thereby enabling impunity for the latter. So it gave voice to the marginalized but kept out of focus those who had stolen the lives and dignity of the victims. It is this impunity which is theorized as irreconciliation.

The technicolour absences of the disappeared (Buthpitiya, this volume) are evocatively rendered in each of the essays by Vaisman, Buthpitiya, and Clarke. Vaisman's essay shows how in Argentina reconciliation was used by the armed forces in the 1980s first through a decree, promptly annulled by the democratically elected government, and, later, through an attempt to fashion a narrative of heroism that ensures closure of the unresolved injustices, enacting a form of 'exclosure'. In response, human rights organizations established by family members of the disappeared demanded both truth and justice. The trials taking place since the mid-2000s have, in part, answered some of these demands, although, as noted above, their outcome was threatened when the Supreme Court attempted to 'rehabilitate' a law that would have released convicted perpetrators of human rights crimes.

In Sri Lanka (Buthpitiya, this volume), the LTTE's demand for political self-determination, in response to decades of Sinhala systemic discrimination and violence against the minority Tamil community, took the form of an aspirant Tamil homeland.

Journal of the Royal Anthropological Institute (N.S.) **28**, 11-33
© 2022 The Authors. *Journal of the Royal Anthropological Institute* published by John Wiley & Sons Ltd
on behalf of Royal Anthropological Institute.

It has been estimated that from September 2008 to May 2009, between 40,000 and 70,000 civilians were killed, with both the government and the LTTE credibly accused of war crimes and crimes against humanity. There has been a call by the Tamil diaspora to formally recognize the events of 2008-9 as a genocide which has been denied by the Sri Lankan government. Above all, the state has enabled a process of invisibility by concerted 'acts of erasure, silencing, spatial (re)organization, and embellishment that relied on not only infrastructure development, heritage construction, and cultural production, but also state violence, terror, and suppression aimed at contriving a consensus of "peace"'. As international pressure to address wartime atrocities mounted, a conciliatory government inquiry took place in the guise of the 2011 performative (Thiranagama 2013) 'Lessons Learnt and Reconciliation Commission' (LLRC), the recommendations of which have yet to be taken up.

A similar remorse-driven Truth Commission was set up in Colombia (Clarke, this volume) following the peace agreement between the Colombian government and the Revolutionary Armed Forces of Colombia (FARC). However, with the focus on individual perpetrators, the lack of a commitment to unveiling state complicity[11] and the distinction of victimhood made between victims and their surviving families, we see demands for a rethinking of the framework of reconciliation in contexts of mass atrocity. The newly instituted Victims' Law defined judicial and administrative actions aimed at assisting the victims and repairing harm using economic means. Yet many victims refused this overture as they argued that there was no accountability as the implementation of these measures was slow and insufficient due to the lack of political will, limited resources, and legal gaps. Thus, a politics of irreconciliation emerged.

In May 2020, the killing of George Floyd in America by a policeman reignited the Black Lives Matter (BLM) movement. I map a politics of irreconciliation in the call to reckoning on issues of memorialization of slavery, race, and history, along with institutional responses to BLM, bullying, and harassment. While these are not equivalent, the institutional pushback against anti-racist protests, particularly in 2020-1, makes it essential for us to draw the connections between these events and analyse them on the basis of our experiences as ethnographers of memory and post-conflict contexts. This aligns with theorists (e.g. Lu 2017) who are calling for reparative justice for injustices linked to colonialism and slavery as the transitional justice scholarship is focused only on Nuremberg and thereafter. There are similarities between the legal processes through which redress related to genocidal injustices has been stalled and the way in which the debate around statues has been curtailed by law. In January 2021, a new law was passed in the United Kingdom to ensure that historic statues should be 'retained and explained' for future generations. The issue of 'due process' is also invoked in various institutional complaints relating to bullying and harassment.

The rule of law is meant to be present and enforced in all these instances, but is marked by its unofficial, palpable absence-presence, thereby enabling the continuation of status quo and corruption. At the same time, the force of law decides the boundaries of the cases, which, at the outset, shuts down, forecloses, the possibilities of truth and justice. In short, 'the rule of law', the instruments of law, do not always build impunity. There are many instances when they have enabled long-term impunity, sometimes double impunity, for perpetrators in the United Kingdom, Bangladesh, Canada, Sri Lanka, and Colombia. In the United Kingdom (including Northern Ireland), Mozambique, Sri Lanka, Argentina, and Colombia there has been a process of 'equalizing' blame where violence was carried out on both sides, thereby problematically

Journal of the Royal Anthropological Institute (N.S.) **28**, 11-33
© 2022 The Authors. *Journal of the Royal Anthropological Institute* published by John Wiley & Sons
Ltd on behalf of Royal Anthropological Institute.

equating executive powers and victims. In Bangladesh, Argentina, and Canada, the perpetrators are primarily deemed to be on one side, though the violence of the other side is also invoked. In both Bangladesh and Mozambique, there has been no language of reconciliation, but it is this long-term impunity for the perpetrators in Bangladesh that has led to the establishment of the national ICT. To redress past impunities, various investigative committees (as in Argentina and the United Kingdom), presidential commissions of inquiry (like the LLRC in Sri Lanka), and TRCs (as in Canada and Colombia) have been set up, which, as we discussed, have resulted in further institutionalization of impunity and irreconciliation. In thinking through instances when law is empowering, is distinct from executive power, works against the sovereign to demand justice, and can be a protagonist in the claims of irreconciliation, we turn to contemporary Argentina. Here, the amnesties through the presidential decree lasted just over a decade and thereafter the trials have become the forum where information about the newly discovered disappeared is updated. While the debate rages over past and continuing ideologies in Northern Ireland, some structural changes have occurred since the Good Friday Agreement.

In the enabling and disabling processes of law, Bangladesh's rejection of the International Criminal Court (ICC) is also linked to how global powers have not highlighted the genocidal ramifications of the Bangladesh War of 1971, given the subcontinental politics (India and Pakistan engaging with the Bangladesh War as part of its arsenal of propaganda against each other) and Cold War dynamics of the period (with the United States and China supporting West Pakistan and the Soviet Union and India supporting East Pakistan). While Bangladesh has rejected the ICC in the past (as it doesn't trust in getting a fair hearing from it given the Cold War dynamics of 1971), on 14 November 2019 the court's Pre-Trial Chamber III authorized the Prosecutor to initiate an investigation into crimes within the People's Republic of Bangladesh/Republic of the Union of Myanmar (International Criminal Court 2019). The call for accountability and impunity within the rule of law of the human rights framework disregards the need to critique the framework itself, which has been perceived to be skewed by many in the Global South like Bangladesh and the sub-Saharan African states (Clarke 2019). Irreconciliation, in all the instances we have discussed, is linked to the role of Cold War politics, big/regional superpowers, and contemporary geopolitics; a continuation of neo-colonialism by various colonial settler states, like the United Kingdom (Northern Ireland), Russia and China (Mozambique), the United States (Bangladesh, Argentina, Colombia), Canada (First Nations), and India (Sri Lanka). Various forms of irreconciliation are also displayed through different aesthetic manifestations in the next section.

Aesthetic (im)possibilities and irreconciliation

In *The art of forgetting* (1999), Adrian Forty shows how Italy, Greece, France, and Germany have all undergone radical programmes of 'apparent amnesia' for the sake of relative stability. In contrast to Forty's idiom of forgetting, all the cases discussed in this special issue demonstrate how a vibrant memory culture and a strong human rights community supported by grassroots and political mobilization have worked to keep irreconciliation and active remembering present in the public sphere (similar to what Vaisman has portrayed about Argentina in this volume). The role of memorials in each instance demands 'recognition of what was done, to whom, and by whom' (Rowlands 1999: 130), generating ambivalence and/or collective validation of loss, coming together

Journal of the Royal Anthropological Institute (N.S.) **28**, 11-33

through loss rather than victory (Renan 1896: 165). This is because these aesthetic structures might be capable of reflecting a nuanced and emotional account of the violent experiences (Mookherjee & Pinney 2011). Martha Minow (2000) highlights the therapeutic dimensions of reconciliation and opposes them to the limitation of legal processes which cannot address the injury of survivors. However, this does not highlight the irreconciliatory functions that aesthetic practices can perform in the face of endemic failure and impunity enabled by these juridical structures.

In Sri Lanka, Colombia, Argentina, Canada, and Bangladesh, the processes of multiple impunities enabled by the legal processes set up to address such impunity make it imperative for the expression of gendered victim visibilizations (Clarke, this volume) in demonstrations and commemoration sites. Through the exhibition and circulation of photographs, silhouettes, children's shoes (in Canada), and other aesthetic artefacts of subversion and surveillance of the disappeared, the past is made present. It enables 'new kinds of juxtaposition and seriality' (Pinney 2015: 28) as irreconciliation. Here, censorship is maintained in the face of state terror while also pointing out the role of the violent sovereign and the positions of discontent and irreconciliation about it. Aesthetics (the original Greek form *aisthetikos* denotes 'perception by feeling') here refers to an affective domain, a sensibility through which various objects and phenomena animate and perform the unresolved genocidal injustices. In post-war Sri Lanka, where 'reconciliation' has been concretized in the form of shiny infrastructure, heroic memorials, and roads, the noticeable sites of civilian protests where the technicolour absences of the disappeared endure as photographs constitute the evocative vision of irreconciliation which counters the state's narrative of 'peace'.

In Argentina, the documentary film *70 y Pico* (2016) (Vaisman, this volume) brings out the complicated history of civilian complicity in supporting state terrorism and its repressive apparatus. Rather than equalizing blame – what is known as the 'two-demon theory' in Argentina – the film shows the multi-layered nature of repression, silence, affect, and complicity. The film becomes an illustration of irreconciliation among many Argentinians in its capacity to keep the past alive and contentious so that these questions can always be asked, even if, and especially because, they are not, and cannot be, resolved. Clarke shows how irreconciliation as an affective sentiment is taking shape in Colombia through *victim visibilizations* of 'false positives': those civilians misrepresented as guerrilla fighters, killed in combat, and reported on from 2000 to 2010. The home galleries and memorializations – '*Memoria en casa*' (Memory at home) – enabled surviving family memories as they feared the state would erase these remembrances through false representations. This extended the memory of the missing into the concerns of the contemporary moment and enabled the material transference of the deceased to the bodies of the living. 'Affective attribution' (Clarke 2019), manifesting through embodied, emotive refusals, is what unfolded as irreconciliation. These gendered, emotive refusals disallowed the obfuscation of the disappeared.

The bringing down of statues linked to slavery and residential schools in Canada is an act of irreconciliation (Mookherjee, this volume) as they 'may be a necessary embodiment of reconciliation in action, beyond intent' (Shneiderman, this volume). These publicly visible acts of defacement are highlighting the obfuscated and public secret of slavery and racial injustice which is foundational to these 'philanthropists', embodied in these statues, towering over cities. Aesthetically, these interventions are highlighting irreconciliation through the felled monuments and graffities. As

Journal of the Royal Anthropological Institute (N.S.) **28**, 11-33
© 2022 The Authors. *Journal of the Royal Anthropological Institute* published by John Wiley & Sons
Ltd on behalf of Royal Anthropological Institute.

Shneiderman puts it powerfully in this volume: '[T]he affective power of publicly visible acts and words may provide political cover of sorts for the mundane everyday work of transforming intent into action within the institutional structures that govern our lives'.

In this context, the genocidal cosmopolitan trope of 'never again' (Mookherjee 2011) emerges in many of the contributions. This global trope and aesthetic artefacts enable a connection to a global, diasporic audience. The 'emancipatory' possibilities of aesthetic registers in representing violent past injustices should not consign to oblivion the processes of standardization therein, particularly when the civil society and sovereign are in congruence. Nations caught in an image of self-certainty can depend on a reiterated aesthetic of performance, only to find themselves incarnated differently, remaining unfulfilled and always questing. In interrogating the production of a national affect (Mookherjee 2011), it is important to remember that the process is neither productive nor straightforward.

Conclusion: The self and irreconciliation

A dominant strand of transitional justice scholarship has considered a lack of reconciliation to be dysfunctional, a rupture which can apparently be addressed by properly designed legal institutions. Irreconciliation is precisely the move away from violence and the inequalities that foster such violence (Wilson, this volume). The various cases discussed in this volume show the lived reality, effects, and limitations of transitional justice through semantics, temporalities, critique of civilizing frameworks, and the juridical and aesthetic (im)possibilities of irreconciliation. To contributors, irreconciliation is accountability and grievance (Josephides); politics (Bertelsen); enforced political accountability (Visser); a conscious irreconciliation (Niezen); an agentive act of social reconstruction, affective ambivalence, a vigilance against impunity (Vaisman); victim visibilization, reattributive irreconciliation from the dead to the living (Clarke); technicolour absence through photographs (Buthpitiya); and an injunction against institutional 'window dressing' (Mookherjee). The volume covers ethnographies from a heterogeneity of fieldsites manifesting irreconciliation which is transitional/restorative, reparative apparatuses of justice and/or governmentality. We are, however, cognizant of the tensions that can exist between local histories of each ethnography, and any attempts to generate a global, comparative, universal language of irreconciliation (Shneiderman, this volume) might reiterate the criticisms we have posed about reconciliation. I agree with Shneiderman's argument in this volume that rather than bestowing subjectivity on the perpetrator through the debate of intentionality, we are also calling into question the structures which enabled such intent – echoing Arendt's (2002) claim that 'this ought never to have happened' (see also Berkowitz 2011: 3). Irreconciliation is a necessary tactic to enable the deep work of addressing impunity; structural transformation embodied in institutional processes (Shneiderman, this volume). As a result, in enabling civic education, vigilance, and action, the everyday meanings of irreconciliation – the mundane practices and experiences of time, embodiment, memory, collective guilt, victimhood, responsibility, and social relations – are crucial. Irreconciliation is thus a vigilance against impunity, against a 'window-dressed', symbolic performance of redress.

Critiques of reconciliation have stopped short at noting the exclusions and compromises within the transitional justice processes. What are the limits of irreconciliation if the sovereign legal and aesthetic registers work together to create admissible memories? Our redoubling of vigilance is also meant for instances when

Journal of the Royal Anthropological Institute (N.S.) **28**, 11-33
© 2022 The Authors. *Journal of the Royal Anthropological Institute* published by John Wiley & Sons Ltd on behalf of Royal Anthropological Institute.

irreconciliation itself leads to new forms of exclusion, blame, culpability, power, subjectivation, and governmentality on the part of survivors. Theorization of the self and irreconciliation is significant in this context. The essays highlight how survivors are often compelled to inhabit this forgiving, corrosive subjectivity in spite of their vulnerabilities. Following the ethnography among the Kewa (Josephides, this volume), it is worthwhile noting that this critical positionality can emerge outside politics and the state in relationship to one's sense of self. While politicization can generate some redress for the suffering, the position of irreconciliation often emerges outside the realm of the sovereign. Josephides shows the perils of neglecting the self, and suggests that being held accountable is a necessary aspect of a mature, enlightened self.

Scholars have argued for the idea of political reconciliation whereby the self of communities of victims and perpetrators might live through an agnostic clash of worldviews within the context of a community that is 'not yet' (Schaap 2005: 4). Such a political potential based on contestation of views does not, however, address how 'reconciliatory work' involves working on the self and is chronic illness management – one of the poignant points made at the AAA panel in Vancouver in 2019. The long-term physical and psychological impact of fighting against injustice or fighting for the acknowledgement of such injustice is viscerally known by survivors/victims. Derrida's call to recognize humanity through forgiveness has no place for this vulnerability felt by individuals as a consequence of unacknowledged injustice.

Audra Simpson's (2017) idea of 'refusal' (rather than resistance, resilience, revenge) as a generative alternative political and existential practice captures our essence of irreconciliation. The ethnographic realities also reiterate the collectivism of individual refusals, which needs to be harnessed for juridical and social changes. Following Clarke (this volume), we need to rethink the idea of the social itself.

> [Irreconciliation] involves moving beyond notions of individual subjectivity and interrogating personhood through a unity of collective being. That unity combines the disappeared and contemporary personhood with the practices of representation. To miss this cycle of interconnection as a progression to retributive justice is to miss the philosophical tenets that undergird the radical aspirations that drive it. For as the argument of the introduction to this special issue suggests, irreconciliation emerges from the lack of recognition and acknowledgement of a harm, the lack of truth telling that allows for the assignment of responsibility for wrongdoing, and the absence of an explanation for that wrongdoing.

Josephides (this volume) has shown us how the concern for humanity (of the one forgiving for Derrida and of the guilty for Ricoeur) is crucial for the development of the self of both the victim and the perpetrator. The self, however, also needs acknowledgement, accountability to flourish as a person in the aftermath of injustice. In such contexts, the continuing demand for accountability, acknowledgement, and truth in post-conflict complexities through social movements is what makes irreconciliation significant.

Acknowledgements

Thank you for the comments and feedback received for this introduction from the anonymous reviewers, Editors (particularly Hannah Knox), Associate Editors (particularly Narmala Halstead and Geoffrey Hughes), and publication committee of the *JRAI* as well as the contributors to this special issue. I am also thankful for Ronald Niezen's translation of the German version of Hannah Arendt's *Denktagebuch*

(*Thought diary*). The foundation for this introduction was laid in a panel I organized on irreconciliation at the 2019 AAA conference in Vancouver.

NOTES

[1] For discussions on various forms of forgetting, 'remembering to forget', and 'knowing what not to narrate', see Mookherjee (2006; 2019) and Rowlands (1999).

[2] I have used Bangladesh War of 1971 instead of liberation war or war of independence to avoid semantic and party political attachments.

[3] For varied accounts of the Bangladesh War, see Akhtar, Begum, Hossein, Kamal & Guhathakurta (2001); Bass (2013); Mascarenhas (1971); Mookherjee (2015); Muhith (1992).

[4] See Derrida (2001) and Nobles (2008) for extensive discussion on apologies.

[5] An opinion poll in Bangladesh by AC Nielsen in April 2013 showed that though nearly two-thirds of respondents said the trials were 'unfair' or 'very unfair', 86 per cent wanted them to proceed regardless. Annual opinion polls show that the war crimes trials ranked among the top three 'positive steps that the government has taken', but they consistently fail to make the top ten list of 'issues that need the greatest attention of the government' (*Economist* 2013).

[6] Thanks to, Kamran Ali, Sadaf Aziz, Angbeen Atif Mirza, and Ali Usman Qasmi for their advice about the Qisa and Diyat laws (Wasti 2008). See also Kermani (2020) and Khan (2020), who show how in practice the 2016 amendments to bar the inclusion of forgiveness have been unable to stop cases which slip in such pardons. This has occurred through the pleas of sudden and grave provocation which are frequently used as a mitigating circumstance in order to reduce sentences in instances of honour killings, to the disadvantage of victims. When brought under anti-terror legislation, cases, however, cannot be forgiven.

[7] S. Ahmed (2019: 188).

[8] Nader (1991) shows that among villagers in southern Mexico, harmony ideology (introduced during Spanish colonialism by missionaries), while being a mode of counter-hegemonic resistance against the government, disallowed weaker members from seeking legal redress. This shows how hierarchies within communities can hamper processes of redress. This ideology manifested in the United States as alternative dispute resolution (ADR).

[9] I am drawing on Ronald Niezen's translation.

[10] Thanks to Vindhya Buthpitiya for this comment.

[11] See Pettigrew, Shneiderman & Harper (2004) for a discussion of complicity in Nepal.

REFERENCES

AHMED, R. 2013. Reclaiming Ekattur (71): Fashi, Bangali [hanging, Bengali]. Alal o Dulal, 14 February (available online: *https://alalodulal.org/2013/02/18/rahnuma-ahmed-shahbagh/*, accessed 10 March 2022).

AHMED, S. 2019. *What's the use? On the uses of use*. Durham, N.C.: Duke University Press.

AKHTAR, S., S. BEGUM, H. HOSSEIN, S. KAMAL & M. GUHATHAKURTA (eds) 2001. *Narir ekattor o juddhoporoborti koththo kahini* [Oral history accounts of women's experiences during 1971 and after the war]. Dhaka: Ain-O-Shalish-Kendro (ASK).

ANDERS, G. & O. ZENKER (eds) 2014. Transition and justice: negotiating the terms of new beginnings. Special Issue *Development and Change* **45**: 3.

ARENDT, H. 2002. *Denktagebuch*, vol. 1: *1950-1973* (eds U. Ludz & I. Nordmann). Munich: Piper Verlag.

BASS, G. 2013. *The blood telegram: Nixon, Kissinger, and a forgotten genocide*. New York: Alfred A. Knopf.

BERKOWITZ, R. 2011. Bearing logs on our shoulders: reconciliation, non-reconciliation, and the building of a common world. *Theory & Event* **14**, 1-16.

BRANCH, A. 2014. The violence of peace: ethnojustice in northern Uganda. *Development and Change* **45**, 608-30.

BRUDHOLM, T. 2008. *Resentment's virtue: Jean Améry and the refusal to forgive*. Philadelphia: Temple University Press.

——— & V. ROSOUX 2009. The unforgiving: reflections on the resistance to forgiveness after atrocity. *Law and Contemporary Problems* **72**: 2, 33-50.

CARRIER, J. 1995. Occidentalism: the world turned upside down. *American Ethnologist* **19**, 195-221.

CLARK, P. 2010. *The gacaca courts, post-genocide justice and reconciliation in Rwanda: justice without lawyers*. Cambridge: University Press.

CLARKE, K. 2019. *Affective justice: the International Criminal Court and the pan-Africanist pushback*. Durham, N.C.: Duke University Press.

Journal of the Royal Anthropological Institute (N.S.) **28**, 11-33

© 2022 The Authors. *Journal of the Royal Anthropological Institute* published by John Wiley & Sons Ltd on behalf of Royal Anthropological Institute.

COLE, J. 2001. *Forget colonialism? Sacrifice and the art of memory in Madagascar*. Berkeley: University of California Press.

COLLARD, A. 1989. Investigating social memory in a Greek context. In *History and ethnicity* (eds) E. Tonkin, M. McDonald & M. Chapman, 89-103. London: Routledge.

CRAPANZANO, V. 2011. *The Harkis: the wound that never heals*. Chicago: University Press.

——— 2012. The contortions of forgiveness: betrayal, abandonment and narrative entrapment among the Harkis. In *The interview: an ethnographic approach* (ed.) J. Skinner, 195-210. London: Berg.

DE CONING, C. 2018. Adaptive peacebuilding. *International Affairs* **94**, 301-17.

DERRIDA, J. 1992. Force of law: the 'mythical foundation of authority'. In *Deconstruction and the position of justice* (eds) D. Cornell, M. Rosenfeld & D. Carlson, 3-67. London: Routledge.

——— 2001. *On cosmopolitanism and forgiveness* (trans. M. Dooley & M. Hughes). London: Routledge.

DOUGHTY, K.C. 2016. *Remediation in Rwanda: grassroots legal forums*. Philadelphia: University of Pennsylvania Press.

ECONOMIST 2013. Bangladesh's war-crimes trials: final sentence. 17 September 2013 (available online: *https://www.economist.com/banyan/2013/09/17/final-sentence*, accessed 10 March 2022).

ELTRINGHAM, N. 2019. *Genocide never sleeps: living law at the International Criminal Tribunal for Rwanda*. Cambridge: University Press.

EVANS-PRITCHARD, E.E. 1940. *The Nuer: a description of the modes of livelihood and political institutions of a Nilotic people*. Oxford: Clarendon Press.

FELDMAN, A. 2015. *Archives of the insensible: of war, photopolitics and dead memory*. Chicago: University Press.

FORTY, A. 1999. Introduction. In *The art of forgetting* (eds) A. Forty & S. Kuchler, 1-18. Oxford: Berg.

GALLIMORE, T. 2008. The legacy of the International Criminal Tribunal for Rwanda (ICTR) and its contributions to reconciliation in Rwanda. *New England Journal of International and Comparative Law* **14**: **2**, 239-66.

GALTUNG, J. 1968. Violence, peace and peace research. *Journal of Peace Research* **6**, 167-91.

GLUCKMAN, M. 1955. *The judicial process among the Barotse of Northern Rhodesia*. Manchester: University Press.

HAGE, G. 1994. Locating multiculturalism's other: a critique of practical tolerance. *New Formations* **24**, 19-34.

HATZFIELD, J. 2009. *The strategy of antelopes: living in Rwanda after the genocide* (trans. L. Coverdale). London: Serpent's Tail.

HERZFELD, M. 1985. *The poetics of manhood: contest and identity in a Cretan mountain village*. Princeton: University Press.

HONDERICH, H. 2021. Why Canada is mourning the deaths of hundreds of children. *BBC News*, 15 July (available online: *https://www.bbc.co.uk/news/world-us-canada-57325653*, accessed 10 March 2022).

INTERNATIONAL CRIMINAL COURT 2019. Bangladesh/Myanmar: Situation in the People's Republic of Bangladesh/Republic of the Union of Myanmar. ICC-01/19. Investigation (available online: *https://www.icc-cpi.int/bangladesh-myanmar*, accessed 10 March 2022).

KERMANI, S. 2020. Pakistan's forgiveness laws: the price of getting away with murder. *BBC News*, 6 January (available online: *https://www.bbc.co.uk/news/world-asia-50716694*, accessed 10 March 2022).

KHAN, A. 2020. 'Honour' killings in Pakistan: judicial and legal treatment of the crime: a feminist perspective. *LUMS Law Journal* 7, 74-104.

KIRTSOGLOU, E. 2020. Anticipatory nostalgia and nomadic temporality: a case study of chronocracy in the crypto-colony. In *The time of anthropology: studies of contemporary chronopolitics* (eds) E. Kirtsoglou & B. Simpson, 159-86. New York: Routledge.

LU, C. 2017. *Justice and reconciliation in world politics*. Cambridge: University Press.

MAC GINTY, R. 2019. Complementarity and interdisciplinarity in peace and conflict studies. *Journal of Global Security Studies* **4**, 267-72.

MCCARTHY, R. 2002. Musharraf faces storm on mission to Bangladesh. *Guardian*, 30 July (available online: *https://www.theguardian.com/world/2002/jul/30/pakistan.bangladesh*, accessed 10 March 2022).

MASCARENHAS, A. 1971. *The rape of Bangladesh*. Calcutta: Vikas Publications.

MEHTA, P.B. 2021. We need temporary reconciliation, a national action plan. PM must take lead. *Indian Express*, 7 May 2021 (available online: *https://indianexpress.com/article/opinion/columns/we-need-temporary-reconciliation-a-national-action-plan-pm-must-take-lead-7304954/?fbclid=IwAR3N2dxOpZkBitPbsZpWWJh7K43Z3vQ2FK93veLlZK6UM-dWeYQZfZs66Ls*, accessed 10 March 2022).

Journal of the Royal Anthropological Institute (N.S.) **28**, *11-33*
© 2022 The Authors. *Journal of the Royal Anthropological Institute* published by John Wiley & Sons Ltd on behalf of Royal Anthropological Institute.

MIHAI, M. 2010. Transitional justice and the quest for democracy: a contribution to a political theory of democratic transformations. *Ratio Juris* **23**, 183-204.

MINOW, M. 2000. *Between vengeance and forgiveness: facing history after genocide and mass violence*. Boston: Beacon Press.

MOOKHERJEE, N. 2006. 'Remembering to forget': public secrecy and memory of sexual violence in Bangladesh. *Journal of Royal Anthropological Institute* (N.S.)**12**, 433-50.

———— 2011. 'Never again': aesthetics of 'genocidal' cosmopolitanism and the Bangladesh Liberation War Museum. *Journal of the Royal Anthropological Institute* (N.S.)**17**: **S1**, S71-91.

———— 2015. *The spectral wound: sexual violence, public memories and the Bangladesh War of 1971*. Durham, N.C.: Duke University Press.

———— 2019. 1971: Pakistan's past and knowing what not to narrate. *Comparative Studies of South Asia, Africa and the Middle East* **39**, 212-22.

———— 2020. Affective Justice Symposium: law's emotional (im)possibilities. *Opinio Juris*, 26 May (available online: *https://opiniojuris.org/2020/05/26/affective-justice-symposium-laws-emotional-impossibilities/*, accessed 10 March 2022).

———— & C. PINNEY (eds) 2011. Aesthetics of nations: anthropological and historical perspectives. *Journal of the Royal Anthropological Institute* (N.S.)**17**: **S1**.

————, N. RAPPORT, L. JOSEPHIDES, G. HAGE, L.R. TODD & G. COWLISHAW 2009. Ethics of apology: a set of commentaries. *Critique of Anthropology* **24**, 345-66.

MUHITH, A.M.A. 1992. *Bangladesh: emergence of a nation*. Dhaka: University Press.

MULDOON, P. & A. SCHAAP 2012. Aboriginal sovereignty and the politics of reconciliation: the constituent power of the Aboriginal Embassy in Australia. *Environment and Planning D: Society and Space* **30**, 534-50.

NADER, L. 1991. *Harmony ideology: justice and control in a Zapotec mountain village*. Stanford: University Press.

NIEZEN, R. 2017. *Truth and indignation: Canada's Truth and Reconciliation Commission on Indian Residential Schools* (Second edition). Toronto: University Press.

NOBLES, M. 2008. *The politics of official apologies*. Cambridge: University Press.

OSANLOO, A. 2006. The measure of mercy: Islamic justice, sovereign power, and human rights in Iran. *Cultural Anthropology* **21**, 570-602.

———— 2020. *Forgiveness work: mercy, law and victims' rights in Iran*. Princeton: University Press.

PETERS, E.L. 2007. *The Bedouin of Cyrenaica: studies in personal and corporate power*. Cambridge: University Press.

PETTIGREW, J., S. SHNEIDERMAN & I. HARPER 2004. Relationships, complicity and representation: conducting research in Nepal during the Maoist insurgency. *Anthropology Today* **20**: **1**, 20-5.

PINNEY, C. 2015. Civil contract of photography in India. *Comparative Studies of South Asia, Africa and the Middle East* **35**, 21-34.

REICH, W. 2006. Unwelcome narratives: listening to suppressed themes in American Holocaust testimonies. *Poetics Today* **27**, 463-72.

RENAN, E. 1896. What is a nation? In *The poetry of the Celtic races and other studies* (trans. W.G. Hutchinson), 163-76. London: Walter Scott Ltd.

RICOEUR, P. 2004. *Memory, history, forgetting* (trans. K. Blamey & D. Pellauer). Chicago: University Press.

ROSOUX, V. 2009. Reconciliation as a peace-building process: scope and limits. In *The Sage handbook of conflict resolution* (eds) J. Bercovitch, V. Kremenyuk & I.W. Zartman, 543-60. London: Sage.

ROSS, F. 2003. On having voice and being heard: some after-effects of testifying before the South African Truth and Reconciliation Commission. *Anthropological Theory* **3**, 325-41.

ROWLANDS, M. 1999. Remembering to forget: sublimation as sacrifice in war memorials. In *The art of forgetting* (eds) A. Forty & S. Kuchler, 129-46. Oxford: Berg.

SCHAAP, A. 2005. *Political reconciliation*. London: Routledge.

SCHEPER-HUGHES, N. 1998. Undoing: social suffering and the politics of remorse in the new South Africa. *Social Justice* **25**, 114-42.

SCHMID, H. 1968. Peace research and politics. *Journal of Peace Research* **5**, 217-32.

SELIMOVIC, J.M. 2018. Time to listen to silence. *Leuven Transitional Justice Blog*, 17 December (available online: *https://blog.associatie.kuleuven.be/ltjb/time-to-listen-to-silence-3/*, accessed 10 March 2022).

SHAW, R. 2007. Memory frictions: localizing the Truth and Reconciliation Commission in Sierra Leone. *International Journal of Transitional Justice* **1**, 183-207.

SIMPSON, A. 2017. The ruse of consent and the anatomy of 'refusal': cases from indigenous North America and Australia. *Postcolonial Studies* **20**, 18-33.

Journal of the Royal Anthropological Institute (N.S.) **28**, *11-33*
© 2022 The Authors. *Journal of the Royal Anthropological Institute* published by John Wiley & Sons Ltd on behalf of Royal Anthropological Institute.

THIRANAGAMA, S. 2013. Claiming the state: postwar reconciliation in Sri Lanka. *Humanity: An International Journal of Human Rights, Humanitarianism, and Development* **4**: **S1**, 93-116.

TRIBUNE 2015. Pakistan voices anguished concern at Dhaka hangings. 22 November (available online: *https://tribune.com.pk/story/996561/flawed-war-crimes-trial-pakistan-voices-anguished-concern-at-dhaka-hangings*, accessed 10 March 2022).

TURNER, C. 2016. *Violence, law and the impossibility of transitional justice*. London: Routledge.

UNITED NATIONS SECURITY COUNCIL 2004. The rule of law and transitional justice in conflict and post-conflict societies. Report of the Secretary General. S/2004/616 (available online: *http://www.un.org/Docs/sc/sgrep04.html*, accessed 10 March 2022).

WASTI, T. 2008. *The application of Islamic criminal law in Pakistan: Sharia in practice*. Leiden: Brill.

WILSON, R. 2001. *The politics of truth and reconciliation in South Africa: legitimizing the post-apartheid state*. Cambridge: University Press.

——— 2003. Reconciliation. *Anthropological Theory* **3**, 367-87.

——— 2020. Justice after atrocity. In *The Oxford handbook of law and anthropology* (eds) M.-C. Foblets, M. Goodale, M. Sapignoli & O. Zenker, 1-22. Oxford: University Press.

WOODWARD, A. 2021. Trump turns on his supporters after inciting Capitol riot and tries to call for 'healing and reconciliation'. *Independent*, 8 January (available online: *https://www.independent.co.uk/news/world/americas/us-politics/trump-video-twitter-capitol-riot-b1784218.html*, accessed 10 March 2022).

YOUSAF, K. 2020. Pakistan in diplomatic push to reset ties with Bangladesh. *Tribune*, 19 July (available online: *https://tribune.com.pk/story/2255657/pakistan-in-diplomatic-push-to-reset-ties-with-bangladesh&fbclid=IwAR2WRst29HDlGiSJekZmL_CT56h4eRGeLwNp-L5f9lKSxohrB1NEbb3hF28*, accessed 10 March 2022).

Introduction : de l'irréconciliation

Résumé

La plupart des exercices de réconciliation engagés à l'issue d'un conflit imposent aux survivants de pardonner et de chercher une manière de résolution pour « aller de l'avant ». Divers anthropologues ont formulé des critiques de la réconciliation et des formes apparentées de « justice alternative », sans sortir du cadre du maintien des liens sociaux et de l'État de droit. Dans cette introduction, l'autrice pose un regard critique sur les travaux interdisciplinaires étudiant la réconciliation, l'excuse et le pardon, et elle théorise un prisme d'analyse moins usité : celui de l'irréconciliation. Au lieu de s'inscrire en opposition à « la paix », l'irréconciliation permet d'interroger le statu quo en refusant le pardon des impunités endémiques, notamment au terme de procédures judiciaires mises en scène et en l'absence-présence de l'État de droit. Dans ce dossier, elle propose une exploration ethnographique des liens entre l'irréconciliation et le droit, l'esthétique, la temporalité, la résistance et le contrôle, afin d'en localiser les multiples manifestations analytiques. L'irréconciliation est un moyen important d'analyse de l'État de droit dans les procédures sur les injustices génocidaires irrésolues et les débats sur l'esclavage, Black Lives Matter et les réponses des institutions.

2

Being held accountable: why attributing responsibility matters

Lisette Josephides *Queen's University Belfast*

Debates over reconciliation, atonement, forgiveness, and forgetting involve political and personal elements, with substantial investments and commitments. I contrast two perspectives: one stresses unconditional forgiveness independent of atonement; the other reflects on the importance of moral responsibility for the formation of the person. Being held accountable, for Ricoeur, matters for the development of the self. For Derrida, forgiveness is a defining aspect of being human, becoming debased when seen as a legal form of justice. I use philosophical arguments and ethnographic writings from Papua New Guinea, Cyprus, and the Holocaust to examine reconciliation and irreconciliation as strategies for either reaffirming or reimagining a common world.

My experience of living in Northern Ireland with its history of sectarianism (known as the Troubles) first alerted me to the intricacies of reconciliation as a real and pressing issue for a viable peace process. Several terms were used alongside reconciliation in the political exchanges that tore through the community: apology, atonement, repentance, remorse, forgiveness, forgetting. Were these prerequisites for reconciliation? Other terms were thrown up in the process of analysis: fault, trauma, resentment, responsibility, accountability, imputability. I define my use of some of these terms to minimize analytical elision, and arrange them in groups to allow a nuanced range of meanings to emerge.

Fault, trauma, and *resentment* follow each other sequentially. *Fault* is the offence (evil deed, wrongdoing, atrocity), the act that causes the *trauma* (a life-changing effect for a group or person) which leads to resentment. *Resentment* is a feeling of having been violated, experienced as having one's humanity and identity denied or demeaned.

Apology, atonement, repentance, and *remorse* are linked by a family resemblance. *Apology* is the blandest instrument (saying sorry denotes regret on a more personal level). *Repentance* and *remorse* (the second being stronger) indicate a real change of heart at the emotional level. *Atonement* presages or promises an act of penance.

Journal of the Royal Anthropological Institute (N.S.) **28**, 34-49
© 2022 The Authors. *Journal of the Royal Anthropological Institute* published by John Wiley & Sons Ltd on behalf of Royal Anthropological Institute.

Responsibility, accountability, and *imputability* are closely connected concepts. *Responsibility* is to accept/own up to one's part in the fault. We see in the ethnography of Yael Navaro-Yashin (2009) how ignoring the trauma of responsibility leads to a state of abjectness, ruination, and melancholia. *Accountability* is the acknowledgement that the responsibility for a fault requires 'making good' in some way. *Imputability* is the general acceptance of fault in the broadest sense – the capacity by virtue of which actions can be held to someone's account (Ricoeur 2004).

Forgiveness and *forgetting* are quite different things; one does not follow naturally from the other. *Forgetting*, just like remembering, is a moral and identity-building act of memory (Lambek 1996). It can be pathological repression following trauma or a conscious decision of non-reconciliation in order to re-form the world into a better common world (Arendt 2002, as cited in Berkowitz 2011: 3-4). Arendt also adopts a seemingly contradictory position, arguing that forgiveness comes from a claim of absolute superiority ('only God can forgive') and so is not humanly possible, but at the same time it is what enables human action. What serves a similar function in politics is called reconciliation (Berkowitz 2011: 12). I offer some pointers rather than a definition for *forgiveness*, which is discussed extensively throughout the essay. Is it a political or human act? Can it be stretched to encompass extreme acts? And would granting it unconditionally be tantamount to accepting evil in the house of good (insofar as forgiveness suggests the creation of a space of goodness and goodwill, into which an unexpiated wrongdoing is accepted as part of a common cultural world)?

I begin my discussion by contrasting two philosophical perspectives which engage with forgiveness and reconciliation, but see them as fulfilling different functions. Jacques Derrida stresses unconditional forgiveness that is not contingent on repentance or atonement; such expectations would debase the act of forgiveness. Paul Ricoeur, by contrast, reflects on the kind of moral responsibility that is important in the formation of the person. Being held accountable, in his view, matters for the development of the self. To the aims of reconciliation and reparation he adds the necessity to restore the victim's damaged humanity, in an act of redemption that will also strengthen the self of the perpetrator.

For Derrida, pure forgiveness is a defining aspect of being human. Attaching conditions to forgiveness degrades it into a legal form of justice, subject to the logic of exchange as a political-economic transaction based on negotiation and calculation. Thus Derrida's call for unconditional forgiveness is concerned with enacting the humanity of the one forgiving, while Ricoeur's expectation of an admission of guilt shows a concern with redeeming the humanity of the guilty person. The act of reconciliation, or the attempt to reconcile, is not the beginning of the debate for either philosopher; their concern, rather, is with the pre-existing requirements of humanity.

How helpful are these philosophical perspectives in ethnographic contexts like Northern Ireland and among the Kewa in Papua New Guinea which highlight the impact on the sense of self as manifestations of political responses and people's humanity? What if we cannot forgive others, choose not to reconcile, as Thomas Brudholm (2008) argues in his discussion of the *ressentiment* felt by the Holocaust survivor Jean Améry? What if we cannot forgive *ourselves* and suffer moral degradation, as in Navaro-Yashin's (2009) ethnography of Turkish Cypriots? And, conversely, how can Kewa persons let go of their resentment to reconcile with those whose acts have diminished their sense of self-worth (Josephides 2005)?

Journal of the Royal Anthropological Institute (N.S.) **28**, 34-49
© 2022 The Authors. *Journal of the Royal Anthropological Institute* published by John Wiley & Sons Ltd on behalf of Royal Anthropological Institute.

To examine the usefulness of these philosophical perspectives, I consider case studies that demonstrate the perils of neglecting the self, and suggest that accountability is a building of the self. In the first section, I explore Derrida's and Ricoeur's positions on forgiveness along with that of Hannah Arendt. I juxtapose the ethnographic context of Northern Ireland and Papua New Guinea to elaborate on my own work on 'resentment as a sense of self', which is further examined through the work on Brudholm and Améry. Following Navaro-Yashin's ethnography on accountability as abjectness and ruination, I move to a juxtaposition of my own work on 'resentment as a sense of self' and Brudholm's arguments on *ressentiment* as a legitimate moral sentiment expressed as a refusal to forgive. My argument throughout, and most specifically as developed in the section on accountability, is that being held accountable is a necessary aspect of a mature, enlightened self. Subsequent sections show how self-formation as an ethical project is linked to what is valued beyond the self, moving to mutual evaluation when respect for the sense of self of the guilty person means to treat that person as someone who can take responsibility.

Repentance or unconditional forgiveness? Derrida versus Ricoeur[1]

In his major work on memory and forgetting, philosopher Paul Ricoeur (2004) refers to amnesty as 'commanded forgetting'. Can reconciliation at the political level be seen as 'commanded forgiving'? A commanded amnesia, Ricoeur writes, would deprive private and collective memory of something precious: 'the salutary identity crisis that permits a lucid reappropriation of the past and of its traumatic charge'. Instead, 'the institution of amnesty can respond only to the need for urgent social therapy, in the nature not of truth but utility' (2004: 456).

Here Ricoeur recalls Derrida's (2001) distinction between pure forgiveness and pragmatic forgiveness: the former being a truly human act announcing our freedom from the sovereignty of the state, the latter being mere procedural justice controlled by the state and contributing to its smooth running. For Derrida, human forgiveness is unconditional and directed to the unforgivable. He distinguishes two types of forgiveness: unconditional purity, as in Kant's moral law (1972 [1785]) or Levinas's (1969) sense of infinite responsibility, and forgiveness for pragmatic, legal, or political reasons, when a form of reconciliation is desired. The second type of forgiveness is part of the complex of apologies offered by governments and other public or corporate bodies. If apology is to be effective in these cases, reparation and restitution must go hand in hand. These state apologies, one may deduce from Derrida, lead to an 'impure' kind of forgiveness.

Derrida develops his argument by posing a fourfold question: who is to forgive whom about what, and who is to arbitrate the process? As to the 'what', there is no merit in forgiving what is forgivable, either because the perpetrator intended no harm or because she or he has already done penance. The sort of crime that requires forgiveness is the unforgivable crime, which can only be a crime against humanity, against what makes us human ('that which makes of man a man' [Derrida 2001: 34]); and this is the power of forgiveness itself. Not to forgive, then, would be that ultimate crime against humanity. Concerning who is to do the forgiving, Derrida diffuses blame by asking who among us, by proxy or otherwise, is not guilty of such a crime. Hannah Arendt (2002) makes a similar point in her discussion of 'levelling down' by accepting that 'everyone … could have done the wrong done by the wrongdoer' (cited in Berkowitz 2011: 8). Anthropologist James Laidlaw, as we shall see below, argues for shared responsibility and uses ethnographic examples to demonstrate its practice in many cultures. My concern is that the two arguments – 'to forgive is human' and 'we all share the guilt' – leave no room for action to resolve post-conflict predicaments.

The most important question for Derrida is: 'who is forgiven?' If forgiveness requires penance, expiation, and the transformation of the perpetrator, then the perpetrator is no longer guilty and there is nothing to forgive. Forgiveness worthy of the name, Derrida concludes, must be unconditional, given while there is still something to forgive. Repentance cannot be part of apology, because what is forgiven is unforgivable. Nonetheless, although Derrida does not acknowledge this, the act of forgiveness implies a fault. In the following sections, I elaborate on the two ethnographic contexts of Northern Ireland and Papua New Guinea to explore the impact of deep loss on the sense of self.

The case of Northern Ireland

In Northern Ireland, with all sides nursing grievances, reconciliation was more a question of amnesties, taking chances on the future, and working towards integrated lifestyles. The two sides (loyalist/unionist and republican) had come a long way, with the leaders of the Democratic Unionist Party and Sinn Féin sitting shoulder to shoulder as first and second ministers. But at a crucial stage of the negotiations, attempts at resolution, whether at government or community level, had tended not to stress apology or even forgiveness, but rather a forgetting, a forging ahead and conciliating, such as establishing integrated schools. Conciliation, as reconciliation's more pragmatic sibling, was concerned with building the future rather than atoning for the past. It resembled Arendt's non-reconciliation in its attempt to re-imagine and re-form a new common world (Berkowitz 2011: 14). Now again, in 2021-2, the Northern Ireland protocol following the United Kingdom's exit from the European Union contributed to the suspension of Stormont and ushered in further uncertainties for the future.

Throughout these events, unremitting calls for inquiries into past atrocities continue apace, with an unsated appetite for apportioning blame. The emotionally charged scenes in May 2021 following the coroner's report on the events in Ballymurphy in 1971 attested to the power of rightful resentment that continues to hold strong sway. As part of Operation Demetrius, the British army had rounded up 'hundreds of suspects without trial in the hope of snuffing out the IRA's campaign' (Carroll 2021). The operation, which left ten people dead in chaotic circumstances, was found to be based on poor army intelligence resulting in the killings of innocent unarmed civilians. The scenes following the publication of the report demonstrate that exoneration is a powerful fillip for a violated sense of self.

There have been personal cases of forgiveness closer to Derrida's first type of unconditional purity. For two days in 2008, a 'mini' Truth and Reconciliation session was held in Belfast, with Archbishop Desmond Tutu presiding. Though local feelings about its efficacy were mixed, some participants reported therapeutic effects, and even a burgeoning understanding of the motives of those who had maimed them or killed their relatives. But as the event clearly attracted the participation of people who desired such reconciliation, the feelings reported might not have been representative of the broader population.

Another initiative provoked open public outcry. In January 2009, eighteen months after being set up, the 'Consultation Group on the Past' launched its report. One recommendation was to offer a monetary compensation of £12,000 to the families of all those who died in the Troubles, irrespective of whether the victims were IRA members, security forces, or civilians.

According to the BBC Ulster News (from 28 January 2009, 18.30), the report was greeted with anger by some sections of the Northern Irish community. There should be no 'moral equivalence', they argued, between the deaths of civilians and members of the security forces, on the one side, and paramilitaries, on the other. 'Perpetrators of murder' cannot be treated the same as 'victims of murder'. A spokesman for a victims' group insisted that people wanted recognition for their suffering, not money, but implied that extending recognition to the suffering of the families of paramilitaries debased the quality of that recognition. The first minister of the Assembly was reported as saying that the Commission (i.e. Consultation Group) damaged itself and compromised its findings by making this recommendation. One of the Commission's two chairmen (a cleric) was at pains to explain that the figure of the monetary compensation was immaterial – there could be no compensation for a person's life. What members of the Commission had learned while listening to the bereaved was that the present judicial institutions were not answering their concerns: for justice, the truth, and recognition. The work of Kamari Clarke (2019; this volume) on the International Criminal Court and research by Nigel Eltringham (2019) on the Rwandan tribunal attest to similar failures of the judicial institutions. The system, said the Commission's chairman, had to combine the need for reconciliation with other strands in order to bring order out of chaos and restore balance. The security forces could not respond to these needs. To deal with the legacy of the past, it was necessary to develop a system that blended the needs for justice, truth, and reconciliation. What was apparent in this debate was the limited effect of legal and state actions, for the laudable reasons of peace-making, to achieve psychological repair or even appease a sense of long-standing outrage for perceived ills suffered.[2] As I discuss below, those who feel they have been wronged experience traumatic loss of integrity of the self. The human response in such cases is one of resentment.

Resentment as a sense of self

Early on in my fieldwork in Papua New Guinea,[3] I became acutely aware of how the Kewa in their everyday lives allocated responsibility to others, making each other accountable for any perceived personal affront (Josephides 2005). People were always trying to fathom each other's thoughts through elicitation, a form of questioning akin to the Socratic method, with the intention of bringing to the fore hidden grudges that might cause illness or even death. Using the same method, they negotiated acceptance of their own understanding of the state of affairs before making that understanding explicit (Josephides 2008). Kewa 'covered up' their thoughts, not because they were private and unspeakable (Keane 2015: 126-7), but because they wished to ascertain how the thoughts would be received before revealing them. Their elicitations were invitations to agree about the state of the world, in a strategy of drawing forth the other's thoughts through a process of negotiation and willingness to compromise.

But resentment, the emotional response I encountered most commonly, was beyond reconciliation, negotiation, agreement, and compromise. It required acknowledgement of the hurt caused and compensation for causing it, even if only by taking back the words or reversing the action responsible for the resentment. People felt resentment at being slighted, cheated, deceived, exploited, singled out for blame, prevented from participating equally in distributions, and more generally from exercising a controlling

Journal of the Royal Anthropological Institute (N.S.) **28**, 34-49
© 2022 The Authors. *Journal of the Royal Anthropological Institute* published by John Wiley & Sons Ltd on behalf of Royal Anthropological Institute.

influence over affairs that concerned them. The cumulative effect of such perceived slights was the feeling that respect had been withheld and one's opinions had been ignored. This was experienced as an arrow to the heart and drew an immediate response, often violent and resulting in considerable physical injury. Resentment was such a strong emotion that, if left unexpressed, it could kill the person whose words or actions had caused it. Everybody was constantly on the lookout for possible neglect, lack of appreciation, or offences against one's person. Local concepts of what was due to a person (whether male or female) provided a powerful incentive for such fears, keeping in check more open expressions of contempt and disdain (Josephides 2005).

Insights from my fieldsite suggested that resentment is less an emotion that defines the structure of people's culture and identity than it is the mode of constructing the self everywhere; it is a manifestation of what Kant (2015 [1788]) has described as respect for the self as the origin for respect for the law, which shrinks from disparaging the hero in one's soul. Resentment is the feeling of not being acknowledged. What gives rise to the feeling, as action, is the (psychological) need for such acknowledgement in order to flourish as a person. Resentment is close to anger but differs from it in being specifically concerned with perceptions pertaining to one's sense of self and self-worth. The examples of resentment in my ethnography were responses to real situations in which Kewa persons felt unappreciated and disadvantaged, at risk of losing respect and suffering damage to their position in society. Resentment interprets an act of omission or commission as being injurious to oneself. It is a judgemental emotion on the lookout for a slight or an offence, but it is also experienced as deep personal pain.

The Kewa ethnographic example of resentment shows no support for Derrida's position. Unconditional forgiveness is not a response that occurs to Kewa people, who always insist on acknowledgement of their personhood and their pain. In their strong stand to be compensated for a perceived injury, Kewa persons demonstrate Ricoeur's understanding of forgiveness, as a response that requires a form of 'making good' to reinstate an injured person's humanity and place in the community. They will not willingly accept a world in which they are treated disrespectfully. Although the Kewa live in a nation-state, the basis of local community organization is tribal and generally free of any strong awareness of being subject to the sovereignty of state power. This relatively weak presence of the state in local communities enables me to argue that resentment is a mode of construction of the self that is more fundamental than a response to the sovereignty of the state. Instead, I make a distinction between political responses and responses from the font of people's humanity and sense of self.

Acknowledgement and a sense of self

The Northern Irish and Papua New Guinea examples bring to the fore an important aspect of the apology left untouched in Derrida's discussion: the effect of the acknowledgement of a wrong on a person's sense of self. To the aims of reconciliation and reparation must be added the need to return people's humanity. As mentioned earlier, Derrida sees pure forgiveness as a defining aspect of being human, not a political-economic transaction. But when he insists that forgiveness is the aim of apology, he is focusing on the responsibility of the victim to forgive, rather than the acknowledgement of the violation of her or his humanity. His concern is thus with humanity in its collective sense, rather than the personal trauma suffered. The acknowledgement of harm done to a particular person's sense of self is quite different from a concern with the state of grace of the perpetrator. Though Derrida sees the victim's ability to forgive as the test of humanity, this is a heroic humanity whose test consists in overcoming personal vulnerability.

Derrida does not stop there. Unconditional forgiveness is mad, he concedes, but if humanity is to act beyond the sovereignty of the state, forgiveness must remain a madness of the impossible. Being given freely and without conditions (for apology, remorse, or atonement), forgiveness escapes the sovereignty of the state, for which everything is based on negotiation and calculation. Unconditionality then becomes dissociated from sovereignty. That is, when forgiveness is not part of the function of political power, enforced, mediated, or enabled by the state, the quality of unconditionality is not linked to the sovereignty of the state. This independence from the state announces that humanity has an aim beyond its sovereignty. Though the chairman of the Consultation Group on the Past (in Northern Ireland) might not have intended his words to be taken this way, his call for a response to people's grievances that went beyond the powers of the judicial institutions may be read in Derrida's terms: beyond the pastoral state performing its duty, people must turn to their own humanity if they hope for forgiveness.

Ricoeur's different perspective on forgiveness and accountability is developed in his magnum opus *Memory, history, forgetting*, where he seeks, through the work of memory, to preserve a boundary between amnesty and amnesia. This work of memory, which would follow mourning, must be guided by the spirit of forgiveness: 'If a form of forgetting could then be legitimately invoked [after mourning and forgiveness], it would not be as duty to silence evil, but to state it in a pacified mode without anger' (Ricoeur 2004: 456). This is 'difficult forgetting', and Ricoeur outlines the philosophical problems it encounters. He begins with the problem of the representation of the past on the plane of memory, and of history at risk of forgetting (2004: 457). There are two issues: the fault that paralyses action, and the forgiveness that lifts this paralysis or 'existential incapacity'.

First, the power to act is an existential capacity (we are all presented with situations that call for our action), but the trauma of the fault causes paralysis by robbing the victim of the freedom to act. (For 'fault' we may read offence, evil deed, act of terrorism, atrocity, genocide, etc.) The person I am called upon to forgive in the process of reconciliation may have killed my sister, my brother, my father, my mother, my life's partner, my child, part of my own self. These are the 'effects of the fault'; together with the effects of forgiveness, they work through memory and history and place 'a mark on forgetting' as a possible next step.

But there is a disproportion between the pole of fault (or offence) and the pole of forgiveness. Ricoeur uses the metaphor of difference in altitude, a vertical disparity: 'below, the avowal of fault; above, the hymn to forgiveness' (2004: 457). These are different speech acts. The first comes from experience and names a failure. The moral accusation is audible and transgressors hold themselves accountable.

The second issue is expressed in the second speech act: the forgiveness that lifts the paralysis or 'existential incapacity', which belongs to the sort of poetry that celebrates love and joy. Watching the news on various television channels on the 'mini' Truth and Reconciliation hearings in Northern Ireland in 2008, I felt that the victims seemed to have put themselves in the place of the perpetrator. I add here an observation I had from watching these hearings:

As part of these hearings, a policeman injured by IRA action in England met with his would-be killer. In their exchanges he reflected that he might have done the same thing in his attacker's place. This sort of understanding and forgiveness is based on finding justice in the 'fault' – something Ricoeur does not discuss. In this and another instance, of the daughter whose father was killed, victims felt the need to come to terms with what had happened, to understand it as human action which they themselves might have undertaken in similar circumstances.

Would such reconciliation constitute self-alienation, in the face of the impossibility of forgiveness as a response to 'the unpardonable nature of moral evil' (Ricoeur 2004: 458)? That is, did the daughter/victim repress part of herself/himself in accepting as somehow legitimate the action that did them so much harm? This question is part of the discussion of resentment and 'neglect of self'.

What must be kept in mind is that for Ricoeur this (empathetic) understanding ('if I were in your shoes …'), which is a prerequisite for reconciliation, is not to be gained without the imputability of the offending act and the acceptance of responsibility by the offending party. This is diametrically opposed to Derrida's perspective. It requires a realization of unequal exchange which is then carried back to the 'heart of selfhood' as imputability, where 'the paradox of forgiveness is laid bare' (Ricoeur 2004: 459). Thus at this stage there is a journey of forgiveness from criminal guilt to 'political and moral guilt inherent in the status of shared citizenship'. Forgiveness is to be found in 'gestures incapable of being transformed into institutions', designating 'the ineluctable space of consideration due to every human being, in particular to the guilty' (2004: 458). Ricoeur situates forgiveness at the margins of institutions, if justice is to be done. In this, he is in agreement with Derrida, who writes that forgiveness is not to be found in institutions, but rather it is tied to freedom from the sovereignty of the state. Forgetting is not part of Derrida's brief and it does not enter the debate; nor does Derrida call for acknowledgement of guilt or for penance.

Ricoeur (2004: 460) cites Karl Jaspers' argument that fault, or culpability, is a 'boundary situation'. By that, Jaspers meant a non-fortuitous situation that is always 'already there' (such as death, suffering, struggle). Culpability is implied in every contingent situation – somebody will always blunder because the possibility in action is always open to blunders, as the experience of fault 'gives rise to thought' (Ricoeur 2004: 460). Imputability is the capacity by virtue of which actions can be held to someone's account. It is an integral dimension of the capable human being: not only imputing to others, but having imputed to oneself. This was established by Jaspers in his book *The question of German guilt* (1947), where he identified four types of guilt as responses to the following questions: What is the category of fault? Before what court can it be brought? What are its effects? What is its justification, exoneration, or sanction?

Ricoeur responds with his own three questions. First, 'Can one forgive someone who does not admit his fault?' Yes, if forgiveness is unconditional in Derrida's sense. But Ricoeur has a different answer. It is a matter of respecting the sense of self of the guilty person, he argues, to expect an admission from her or him (Ricoeur 2004: 479). To expect nothing would amount to withholding from her/him consideration as a person who can take responsibility.

On the one side, Derrida calls for unconditional forgiveness. This call is concerned with the humanity of the one forgiving. On the other side, Ricoeur expects an admission from the guilty person. This expectation reveals a concern with the humanity of the wrongdoer. I side with Ricoeur, even though I am attracted to Derrida's thesis on the madness of forgiveness. But his forgiving victim recalls Heidegger's first type of

Journal of the Royal Anthropological Institute (N.S.) **28**, 34-49
© 2022 The Authors. *Journal of the Royal Anthropological Institute* published by John Wiley & Sons Ltd on behalf of Royal Anthropological Institute.

solicitude, where one 'leaps in and dominates' under the pretence of taking away 'care' from the Other, instead of 'leap[ing] forth and liberat[ing]' by handing to the Other back its burden (Heidegger 1962 [1927]: 158-9).

Ricoeur then asks a second question: 'Must the one who pronounces forgiveness himself have been offended?' (2004: 478). To what degree of kinship, friendship, or other forms of affiliation must the offence be extended? Ricoeur is disturbed to note that the victims' list continues to grow and regrets the 'excesses in the contemporary tendency toward victimization' (2004: 479). For instance, is it reasonable for a political leader to request forgiveness on behalf of members of a community when they did not themselves suffer from the offence?

The third question is whether one can forgive oneself. The immediate response is that 'Only another can forgive, the victim' (Ricoeur 2004: 479). But Ricoeur adds a decisive reservation: 'the difference of height between forgiveness and an admission of fault' (following his earlier characterization of the two as existing on different planes) disappears 'in a relation in which the vertical structure [the fact of difference in height] is projected onto a horizontal relation' (2004: 479). The horizontal relation is the 'assimilation of forgiveness to an exchange defined by reciprocity alone', or extending 'the problematic of forgiveness to a model of exchange tied to the model of the gift' (2004: 479). Such assimilation is overhasty, to Ricoeur's mind, yet it is found in the etymology and semantics of several languages: *don-pardon*, *Geben-Vergeben*, give-forgive.

Here Ricoeur offers a novel account of Mauss's *The gift* (Mauss 1974 [1925]). He makes the valid point that Mauss does not oppose 'gift' to 'exchange', but to a 'market form of exchange, to calculation and self-interest' (Ricoeur 2004: 480). If forgiveness is simply aligned with the circularity of the gift, the model no longer permits a distinction between forgiveness and retribution, thus completely equalizing the partners (2004: 481). In these circumstances, a horizontal relation is created and we may be enjoined to forgive and love unconditionally; even the enemy who has not asked for forgiveness must be loved as he is. But this breaks the Golden Rule which is supposed to reject retaliation: 'Don't do to someone else what you would not want him to do to you' (2004: 481). 'The commandment to love one's neighbours begins by breaking the rules of reciprocity [giving, obliging return, and giving back] and requiring the extraordinary' (2004: 482).

Ricoeur turns to the deliberations of the Truth and Reconciliation Commission (TRC) in South Africa. As opposed to the Nuremburg Trials, the TRC motto was 'understanding, not revenge. Neither amnesty nor collective immunity' (2004: 483). Responses to this reparative justice may have been less positive on both sides than at first painted (see Wilson 2000). Perpetrators may not have felt political guilt even as they spoke of the atrocities they committed. Ricoeur comments on the rejoicing of the victims of some transgressors who were not granted amnesty (2004: 484). When amnesty was granted to others, this did not amount to forgiveness from the victims. As far as the accused were concerned, some cravenly confessed and informed on their accomplices, while others maintained a haughty refusal to ask for forgiveness. Ricoeur is led (with regret) to the viewpoint that people do not forgive (2004: 485), while others do not regret. Many people rejected the TRC's report.

To sum up on the process of the inquiry into forgiveness: it began with the analysis of the admission of fault, internalizing an accusation which then pointed to the author behind the act: '[W]hat the codes disavow are violations of the law; but what the courts punish are persons' (Ricoeur 2004: 489). Accepting a thesis that affirms the inseparability of the act and the agent then led to the unforgivable character of the guilty self and established the requirement of impossible forgiveness. Ricoeur now returns to the unbinding of the agent from the action through the concept of the gift. He asks: 'What force makes one capable of asking, of giving, of receiving the word of forgiveness?' (2004: 486). Forgiveness dissociates the debt from its burden of guilt, but it does (or should do) more: '[I]t should release the agent from his act' (2004: 489).

Ricoeur now introduces a new concept: repentance (2004: 490). Forgiveness and repentance are joined in the inexorable affect of the one upon the other:

> Under the sign of forgiveness, the guilty person is to be considered capable of something other than his offences and his faults. He is held to be restored to his capacity for acting, and action restored to its capacity for continuing. This capacity is signalled in the small acts of consideration in which we recognize the *incognito* of forgiveness played out on the public stage. And, finally, this restored capacity is enlisted by promising as it projects action towards the future. The formula for this liberating word, reduced to the bareness of its utterance, would be: you are better than your actions (Ricoeur 2004: 493).

Brudholm (2008, to be discussed in a later section) may interpret this formula as the Christian motto of 'love the sinner, hate the sin'. But I would argue that it does something more. It recognizes the self in its fundamental moral capacity, imputability. That is, that action for which it has been responsible can be imputed to it. It has been imputed by the other, who forgives while calling into question (imputing). So the victim does not let the perpetrator off the hook, and accepting responsibility makes the perpetrator human. We leave the culpable there, hoping they will access responsibility. After all, they are all of us.

Distributing responsibility or diffusing the issue?

In order for someone to be held accountable, culpability must be assigned. The difficulty here, some diffusionist scholars argue, is that responsibility is rarely assignable to one individual. James Laidlaw (2014) cites ethnographic examples of, among others, Azande witchcraft. On the heels of arguments from the moral philosopher Bernard Williams, Laidlaw stresses the distinction between intention and the state of mind in determining responsibility. Azande beliefs and practices created and distributed responsibility, and were balanced by others, such as the notion that witchcraft was hereditary and its practices unconscious, which softened and dispersed the weight of responsibility (Laidlaw 2014: 207). But it is also known that Azande witchcraft does not account for all instances of wrongdoing (e.g. it is not blamed for adultery). Moreover, witches who are not consciously aware of their acts of witchcraft still take responsibility and apologize for having caused suffering. The fact that there is a social strategy for maintaining social relations does not mean that such acts do not cause ill-feeling resulting in enmity, as we see from witch killings and revenge killings among the Azande.

Laidlaw also engages with Kenneth Read's writings on the Gahuku-Gama, who recognize moral obligations only 'distributively'. Indeed, he argues that distribution of responsibility is what we all do (Laidlaw 2014: 215). The scenario he outlines on the relevance of one's state of mind at the time the offence is committed is similar to that of a current-day barrister pleading extenuating circumstances because of temporary insanity (2014: 189). While the Gahuku-Gama and other groups may hold these views of distributive responsibility, this does not usually stop one person in specific cases

Journal of the Royal Anthropological Institute (N.S.) **28**, 34-49
© 2022 The Authors. *Journal of the Royal Anthropological Institute* published by John Wiley & Sons Ltd on behalf of Royal Anthropological Institute.

from holding another person accountable for offences against herself or himself, as I discussed in the section on resentment.

Accountability experienced as abjectness and ruination

An earlier question was about who would hold whom accountable. The response suggested in Navaro-Yashin's ethnography from Northern Cyprus is that even if there is no one around to hold you accountable, you may do so yourself. Accountability here is experienced as abjectness and ruination.

Navaro-Yashin (2009) begins the debate by considering two different problems: the ethnographic problem of Turkish Cypriots' relations to material objects left by Greek refugees and the theoretical problem of managing affect and subjectivity. She clarifies, through a reading of Spinoza (and Thrift), that affect refers to emotion extending through space, beyond the scope of individual subjectivities. Navaro-Yashin makes good use of the concepts (and metaphors) of abjectness and ruination as developed in the work of Julia Kristeva, Gilles Deleuze and Félix Guattari, and Bruno Latour. The abject, for Kristeva, is situated outside the symbolic order, built on the back of an inherently traumatic experience. It is an object violently cast out of the cultural world.

Abject belongings in this case are those things left behind by fleeing Greek Cypriots and appropriated by Turkish Cypriots, but considered ill-gotten and ruined through acts of violation. As spoils of war, 'loot', they are seen as being outside the cultural world of normal material acquisition. The Turkish Cypriots who must use them feel alien to them and experience melancholy, leading to a loss of moral integrity. Being looted objects, they constitute internal psychic violence. This melancholy is reproduced by ongoing relations with these materials, whose ubiquity means they cannot be escaped.

One suggestion is that Turkish Cypriots attribute shame to themselves because they empathize with the owners of these ruined objects, and they affect loss because they cannot mourn them (since they are the enemy). So they allow the houses, the clothes, and the orchards to fall to rack and ruin, and their decay reflects the Turkish Cypriots' experience of loss of moral integrity. Mary Douglas's (1966) theory of 'matter out of place' in debates on pollution does not need to be taken literally. Defilement marks the boundaries of the social system in more than a physical or geographical sense. Those items are 'out of place' because they were acquired illegitimately. Even if there is no outsider to hold them accountable, Turkish Cypriots hold themselves accountable. Even if the fault giving rise to this abject situation may be on both sides, it is not distributed but its legacy is suffered individually by those politically, socially, and geographically living in these impossible spaces.

A more general point that this ethnography underlines is that social groups – and governments – may find all sorts of ways to keep the political peace, and even keep a lid on explosive social relations. But this does not deal with people's personal or psychological responses, which continue to hold them in thrall or abjection.

Accountability as building of the self

I return to the discussion of the difficulty of assigning responsibility to one particular individual for any practice or action, with this comment: nowhere does the writing on this topic address the question of how being held accountable can build the self. Yet this effect on the self, not only morally but also psychologically, is part of the debate that sees ethics as self-formation (Laidlaw 2014: 216). This is the reason why the title of this essay – 'being held accountable: why responsibility matters' –turns not on the outcome desired (as one reader perceptively asked), but on the building of the self as a mature and respected person. This self-building is the desired outcome. In this understanding, the self – both of the one forgiving and of the one being forgiven – is harmed if forgiveness simply discounts the question of responsibility for an action.

Thus 'being held accountable' does more than impute guilt; it reflects on responsibility. Webb Keane (2015: 4) argues that 'humans are inevitably evaluative creatures' whose important actions are motivated by ethics rather than self-interest (2015: 8; see also Williams 2006 [1985] on ethics as a manner of life). Value judgements, Keane continues, 'commit one to certain forms of self-assessment', revealing a 'crucial link between one's sense of self-worth and what one values beyond the self' (2015: 21). This self-evaluation is linked to responsibility as 'mutual evaluation', and, I would add, acts against an inclination to 'let ourselves off' by evading accountability. As Ricoeur has argued, accepting responsibility makes the perpetrator human; as Navaro-Yashin demonstrates with her ethnography, ignoring the trauma of responsibility leads to a state of abjectness, ruination, and melancholia. Diffusing responsibility does not save those who have benefited from looted objects from experiencing loss of moral integrity. This value judgement as self-evaluation is double-edged: while it will not tolerate ill-treatment of one's self by another, it will also resist the evasion of responsibility. But crucially for our debate, value judgement as 'mutual evaluation' must balk at the expectation of forgiveness without accountability and in the absence of atonement.

Améry and *ressentiment*

Without doubt, there is a world of difference between the Kewa case and the appearance of resentment in conditions of genocide and mass violations of human rights, as described in the work of Thomas Brudholm (2008). Nonetheless, there are similarities in that in both cases resentment is seen as a legitimate moral sentiment (Brudholm 2008: 44) that 'stands as emotional testimony that we care about ourselves and our rights' (2008: 10). The refusal to forgive may thus reflect a moral protest 'as permissible, admirable, or humane as the willingness to forgive' (2008: xiiv).

Brudholm's arguments are anchored in two case studies: the TRC in South Africa and the Holocaust as experienced by Jean Améry. In both cases, Brudholm seeks to demonstrate that forgiveness and conciliation are not the best strategies, but on the contrary can 'reduce the victims' anger to trauma' (2008: 16). This is especially so in the use of therapeutic language in exhortations to overcome the anger felt following traumatic experiences, such as Archbishop Tutu's plea that 'to forgive is the best form of self-interest' (2008: 47). Brudholm considers Tutu's radical rejection of anger in favour of social harmony and a truly human life and attributes this to his Christian background, then pronounces him to be a Stoic (2008: 48). But this is to ignore ethnographic analyses of law in face-to-face societies, where consensus and the achievement of social harmony guide conflict settlement. Here, as elsewhere, there are different strategies and priorities for achieving peace and compensating persons by acknowledging hurt and restoring their humanity. As Brudholm states, trivializing suffering can never be a quick fix (2008: 8). But Brudholm himself trivializes Ricoeur's work when he uses a partial excerpt from him as an example of Christian responses to the TRC (2008: 21). My earlier discussion gives a fuller and more considered account of Ricoeur's response to the findings and influence of the TRC. Arguments critical of the rhetoric of catharsis of TRC hearings have value and are well taken, but it is also worth considering to what extent the lack of follow-up actions to deal with the injustices suffered, rather than just the 'catharsis' of

Journal of the Royal Anthropological Institute (N.S.) **28**, 34-49
© 2022 The Authors. *Journal of the Royal Anthropological Institute* published by John Wiley & Sons Ltd on behalf of Royal Anthropological Institute.

testifying, made people feel worse. Regrettably, it is an expected psychological response to feel worse when bad experiences are being relived, and more longitudinal studies would help us understand the situation better.

Through a close reading of Jean Améry's essay on *ressentiment*, Brudholm distinguishes two meanings of the term as Améry used it: an unforgiving response to the inexpiable horror of the Nazi past and the result of the faulty German *Vergangenheitsbewaltigung* ('struggle to overcome the negatives of the past'), which is more about an indifferent present than an atrocious past (Brudholm 2008: 80, 81). Brudholm declares his intention to cut across this split. The problem with this aim is that the two meanings of *ressentiment* do not represent a split for Améry, but a possible progression. Améry characterizes his refusal to let go of his *ressentiments* as 'a protest against forgetfulness and shallow conciliatoriness', rather than a failure of moral virtue. It is a 'struggle to regain dignity' (Brudholm 2008: 151). This sentiment is very much in line with Brudholm's earlier argument and indeed my findings from Kewa ethnography. For Améry, it incorporates a vision of the rehabilitation of the German people: if they rejected everything that was carried out in their name during the years of the Third Reich, it would be 'a redeeming act' which would eventually make his *ressentiment* 'subjectively pacified' and 'objectively unnecessary' (Brudholm 2008: 153, citing Améry). For Améry, writing in 1966, the Nazi past is not dead, yet he still hopes, believing in the moral value and historical validity of his *ressentiments* (Brudholm 2008: 156). What he resents is that he 'can be treated this way, and that such treatment is acceptable'. 'Resentment, then, is a protest' (Brudholm 2008: 157, citing Hieronymi). Améry himself expresses frustration at the failure of the aggressors to recognize 'the moral truth of their crimes'. He wishes his *ressentiment* could be overcome, but the onus is not on the victim to forgive; it is for others 'to provide the long-awaited response' (Brudholm 2008: 158). This perspective is 'part of a stance of holding others responsible' (2008: 173). Brudholm refers to Strawson and Wallace, but as I argued earlier, Ricoeur shares this radical notion of responsibility.

Despite Brudholm's disparagement of what he describes as Ricoeur's high praise for the TRC and its achievement of forgiveness and restorative justice in South Africa, in his discussion of Améry on resentment he ends up adopting a Ricoeurian position. The anger/rage of the victim centres on the lack of punishment of murderers, while victims continue to suffer. This is reminiscent of Ricoeur's discussion of 'the difference in height between forgiveness and an admission of fault', which precludes reciprocity in a consideration of this relationship. This is why both acts – admission of fault and forgiving – must reach beyond perpetrator and victim to the restoring of the humanity of each of them. Thus, Brudholm somewhat misrepresents Ricoeur's understanding of the South African situation by ignoring his critical points and his perspective on accountability in general.

Conclusion

In this essay, I have forged a conversation between the philosophical reflections on forgiveness (by Derrida and Ricoeur), non-reconciliation (by Hannah Arendt), my ethnographic observations and accounts from Northern Ireland and Papua New Guinea, Yael Navaro-Yashin's research among the Turkish Cypriots, and Thomas Brudholm's exploration among Holocaust survivors like Jean Améry. The aim was to explore the varied positions of non-forgiveness and irreconciliation, accountability, responsibility, and the effect of acknowledgement of a wrong on a person's sense of

Journal of the Royal Anthropological Institute (N.S.) **28**, 34-49

self. This exploration has linked irreconciliation to various key concepts, such as *fault, trauma*, and *resentment*; *apology, atonement, repentance*, and *remorse*; *responsibility, accountability*, and *imputability*; *forgiveness* and *forgetting*. The result provides new and nuanced ways of looking at these concepts.

The discussion has revealed some unexpected convergences, though other issues remain unresolved. Is there less resistance to forgiveness if the harm is only to an individual in the course of everyday, normal human life (as in the Kewa case) than when a whole group suffers mass atrocities and genocide? Does 'resentment' mean something different in the different cases? How important to the resolution is the degree and scale of the harm for which forgiveness is sought? And what is the significance of the cause behind atrocities? In the case of historical IRA bombings, some victims said they might have behaved like the perpetrators in similar circumstances. A similar point is made by Derrida and Arendt, as elaborated earlier.

Brudholm deals with forgiveness in the aftermath of mass atrocities, arguing that 'negative' emotions and attitudes also 'possess a moral component', ignored when the stress is on healing and reconciliation. The refusal to forgive may reflect a moral protest 'as permissible, admirable, or humane as the willingness to forgive' (Brudholm 2008: xvvi). It seems to me that Améry describes *ressentiment* as a sense of self, in the way it is for the Kewa, but also reaching beyond, as a sense of the humanity of others. *They* (the Germans) must right themselves, correct their 'impossible attitudes' (Brudholm 2008: 157). In a similar vein, Arendt found it impossible to pass by when a crime was so heinous, and could not reconcile with Eichmann, who must be banished from the earth for a common world to emerge (Berkowitz 2011: 14).

Though Améry is full of justifiable anger, his *ressentiment* is not immovable. In fact, its demands are modest and reasonable: a 'moralization of history' to awaken a political community 'willing to assume responsibility for its Nazi past', collectively and intergenerationally (Brudholm 2008: 147); 'an obligation to include the Nazi past as an inalienable and indelible part of the collective political-ethical identity and memory'; in other words, an *overcoming* of the negative legacy of the past for a better present (Brudholm 2008: 112). Although Améry may not choose to 'wait for better times', as Ricoeur (1996: 11) counsels, his refusal to let go of his *ressentiment* is still not a principled stand for all times. It can fall into irrelevance when certain conditions are met (such as a 'redeeming act' of 'moral rehabilitation'), and, as Ricoeur writes, the offender has attained 'full understanding of the crimes that he or she has committed' (1996: 11). Between Derrida's call for 'pure forgiveness' and Ricoeur's requirement of accountability, Améry would follow Ricoeur.

Thus the path to reconciliation is always *theoretically* open and awaiting certain conditions of varying stringency to be met, but in practice this may not happen for several generations after the 'fault'. It comes down to a question of understanding and acknowledging the fault, accompanied by repentance, atonement, and the assumption of responsibility. It cannot be Derrida's 'pure' or unconditional forgiveness, which removes responsibility and imputability and ignores the trauma that paralyses action. Améry argues that forgiving without acknowledgement of fault would dehumanize the victim; Ricoeur talks about imputability as part of self-formation; and Navaro-Yashin's ethnography demonstrates that people who consider themselves at fault can be so full of remorse that they are paralysed. For Ricoeur, too, the fault paralyses action until forgiveness releases the agent from her/his act and allows her/him to imagine new futures. For Arendt, great crimes offend nature by violating a metaphysical balance and

Journal of the Royal Anthropological Institute (N.S.) **28**, 34-49
© 2022 The Authors. *Journal of the Royal Anthropological Institute* published by John Wiley & Sons Ltd on behalf of Royal Anthropological Institute.

thus demand vengeance (Berkowitz 2011: 2). While Arendt argues that no action is possible without mutual forgiveness (Berkowitz 2011: 12), she leaves room for non-reconciliation. Reconciliation is desirable as it reaffirms a common world, but when this world has been shattered following the actions of people like Eichmann, non-reconciliation can re-imagine and re-form its replacement (Berkowitz 2011: 14).

A final word on forgiveness and state power: what interests me is how to account for forgiveness and non-reconciliation in societies without a strong presence of state power. To sum up on four positions on the necessity for forgiveness: we are all potential wrongdoers (Arendt); it is an act of empathy (Ricoeur); somebody will always blunder (Jaspers); it's being human (Derrida). These positions, though having different emphases, all come from outside the state.

Much evidential research has demonstrated that reconciliation as 'commanded forgiving' can never provide a lasting or meaningful resolution. The course to pursue, then, must be through imputability, responsibility, and accountability. Both perpetrators and victims need to be accountable for their humanity to flourish. This is the work of human persons, not of politics or the state, though the latter can do much to hinder it.

NOTES

[1] The discussion in this section and the next was started in Josephides (2009).

[2] For comparison, see Wilson (2000) on the Truth and Reconciliation Commission in South Africa.

[3] I began fieldwork in 1979 and continued living in Papua New Guinea until 1986, travelling widely within the region and teaching at the University of Papua New Guinea. My last visit to PNG was in 1993, though I have kept in contact with people throughout.

REFERENCES

ARENDT, H. 2002. *Denktagebuch*, vol. 1: *1950-1973*; vol. 2: *1973-1975* (eds U. Ludz & I. Nordmann). Munich: Piper Verlag.

BERKOWITZ, R. 2011. Bearing logs on our shoulders: reconciliation, non-reconciliation, and the building of a common world. *Theory & Event* **14**, 1-16.

BRUDHOLM, T. 2008. *Resentment's virtue: Jean Améry and the refusal to forgive*. Philadelphia: Temple University Press.

CARROLL, R. 2021. The Ballymurphy shootings: 36 hours in Belfast that left 10 dead. *Guardian*, 11 May (available online: *https://www.theguardian.com/uk-news/2021/may/11/the-ballymurphy-shootings-36-hours-in-belfast-that-left-10-dead*, accessed 14 March 2022).

CLARKE, K. 2019. *Affective justice: the International Criminal Court and the pan-Africanist pushback*. Durham, N.C.: Duke University Press.

DERRIDA, J. 2001. *On cosmopolitanism and forgiveness* (trans. M. Dooley & M. Hughes). London: Routledge.

DOUGLAS, M. 1966. *Purity and danger*. London: Routledge.

ELTRINGHAM, N. 2019. *Genocide never sleeps: living law at the International Criminal Tribunal for Rwanda*. Cambridge: University Press.

HEIDEGGER, M. 1962 [1927]. *Being and time* (trans. J. Macquarrie). New York: Harper & Row.

JASPERS, K. 1947. *The question of German guilt*. New York: Dial Press.

JOSEPHIDES, L. 2005. Resentment as a sense of self. In *Mixed emotions: anthropological studies of feeling* (eds) K. Milton & M. Svašek, 71-90. Oxford: Berg.

——— 2008. *Melanesian odysseys: negotiating the self, narrative, and modernity*. Oxford: Berghahn Books.

——— 2009. Ethics of forgiveness. In The ethics of apology: A set of commentaries (ed.) N. Mookherjee. *Critique of Anthropology* **29**, 345-66.

KANT, I. 1972 [1785]. *The moral law: Kant's groundwork of the metaphysics of morals* (ed. & trans. H.J. Paton). London: Hutchinson University Library.

——— 2015 [1788]. *Critique of practical reason* (trans. M. Gregor). Cambridge: University Press.

KEANE, W. 2015. *Ethical life: its natural and social histories*. Princeton: University Press.

LAIDLAW, J. 2014. *The subject of virtue*. Cambridge: University Press.

Journal of the Royal Anthropological Institute (N.S.) **28**, 34-49

LAMBEK, M. 1996. The past imperfect: Remembering as moral practice. In *Tense past: cultural essays in trauma and memory* (eds) P. Antze & M. Lambek, 235-54. London: Routledge.

LEVINAS, E. 1969. *Totality and infinity: an essay on exteriority* (trans. A. Lingis). Pittsburgh: Duquesne University Press.

MAUSS, M. 1974 [1925]. *The gift: the form and reason for exchange in archaic societies* (trans. W.D. Halls). London: Routledge & Kegan Paul.

NAVARO-YASHIN, Y. 2009. Affective spaces, melancholic objects: ruination and the production of anthropological knowledge. *Journal of the Royal Anthropological Institute* (N.S.) **15**, 1-18.

RICOEUR, P. 1996. Reflections on a new ethos for Europe. In *Paul Ricoeur: The hermeneutics of action* (ed.) R. Kearney, 3-14. London: Sage.

——— 2004. *Memory, history, forgetting* (trans. K. Blamey & D. Pellauer). Chicago: University Press.

WILLIAMS, B. 2006 [1985]. *Ethics and the limits of philosophy*. London: Routledge.

WILSON, R.A. 2000. Reconciliation and revenge in post-apartheid South Africa: rethinking legal pluralism and human rights. *Current Anthropology* **41**, 75-98.

Face à ses responsabilités: pourquoi il est important de dire qui est responsable

Résumé

Les débats sur la réconciliation, le repentir, le pardon et l'oubli mettent en jeu des éléments politiques et personnels impliquant des investissements et des engagements considérables. L'autrice met ici en regard deux points de vue : l'un insiste sur un pardon inconditionnel, indépendant du repentir ; l'autre examine l'importance de la responsabilité morale pour la formation de la personne. Pour Ricoeur, être tenu responsable est important pour le développement de soi. Pour Derrida, le pardon est un trait qui définit l'être humain et il est avili quand il est considéré comme une forme légale de justice. À partir d'arguments philosophiques et des écrits ethnographiques sur la Papouasie-Nouvelle-Guinée, Chypre et l'Holocauste, le présent article examine la réconciliation et l'irréconciliation comme stratégies pour réaffirmer ou réimaginer un monde commun.

3

Civil war and the non-linearity of time: approaching a Mozambican politics of irreconciliation

BJØRN ENGE BERTELSEN *University of Bergen*

At least 1 million people died during the Mozambican civil war (1976/7-92). Unfolding after gaining independence from Portugal (1975) and alongside experiments with Afro-socialism in the 1980s, the war, despite its brutality, has not been subjected to global templates of reconciliation processes. Thus it comprises a unique case to probe what irreconciliation might mean – both as a political horizon and as an analytical concept. This text juxtaposes ethnographic material from rural, central Mozambique from the late 1990s and early 2000s emphasizing reconciliation with material from the same spaces from the 2010s onwards, where I identify what I term a 'politics of irreconciliation'. I will make three arguments. First, informed by Hannah Arendt, I approach irreconciliation as fundamentally about the rejection of a world of violence in search of a world shared in common. Second, drawing on recent anthropological theorizing about temporal regimes and chronopolitics, I argue for the salience of a non-linear understanding of the politics of irreconciliation to grapple with the fact that civil war violence is understood as dangerously uncontained rather than nominally past. Third, within the context of Mozambique, forgiveness and its other, *irreconciliation*, are not only intimately tied to the temporally past or present; they are also, as I show, produced by a tangible and intense absence of a productive future.

From 1976/7 to 1992, Mozambique was devastated by a civil war that razed the countryside and thoroughly transformed the social and political landscape (Morier-Genoud, Cahen & do Rosário 2018). The war engulfed society, generating an estimated 1 million casualties with a further 5 million of the around 18 million population (in 1975) becoming internal or external refugees (Lubkemann 2008). Heavily simplified, the civil war involved the forces of the liberation movement-turned-political party Frelimo (Frente de Libertação de Moçambique) fighting a guerrilla war of insurrection waged by Renamo (Resistência Nacional de Moçambique).[1] Alongside the civil war, Frelimo spearheaded an Afro-socialist revolution under the charismatic leadership of Mozambican President Samora Machel. Fuelled by the vision of unlocking the potential of a country downtrodden by Portuguese colonial violent rule since the 1500s, Frelimo revolutionized the country's sociopolitical order (Isaacman 1978). Rolling out a

Journal of the Royal Anthropological Institute (N.S.) **28**, 50-64
© 2022 The Authors. *Journal of the Royal Anthropological Institute* published by John Wiley & Sons Ltd on behalf of Royal Anthropological Institute.

This is an open access article under the terms of the Creative Commons Attribution-NonCommercial-NoDerivs License, which permits use and distribution in any medium, provided the original work is properly cited, the use is non-commercial and no modifications or adaptations are made.

political apparatus oriented around a single political party, Frelimo and Machel attacked systems of racial and colonial privilege (including urban segregation) and systems of forced labour. Furthermore, traditional chiefly powers were replaced by a new political structure, including party secretaries and notions of popular justice (Bertelsen 2016).[2]

The debates addressing the dynamics of the civil war and the reverberations of Mozambique's experimentation with socialism are both extensive and heavily influenced by particular forms of scholarly politics.[3] These debates, which I have dealt with elsewhere (see, e.g., Bertelsen 2002; 2016), often revolve around whether the civil war was internally generated (i.e. by a disgruntled populace) or whether it was (solely) the result of destabilizing efforts from Rhodesia, South Africa, and others.[4] However, in the first decade following the General Peace Agreement (GPA) in 1992, it became commonplace to hail Mozambique as having emerged out of the 'chaos of civil war' more successfully than other conflict-ridden countries: for instance, in works comparing it to the Liberian 'basket case' (e.g. Moran & Pitcher 2004). Reflecting similar celebratory rhetoric, Mozambique was also presented as having completed a bottom-up societal healing type of reconciliation process (Honwana 1996) and achieved some form of stable post-war democratic development – the crux of which was the execution of parliamentary and presidential elections in 1994. Capturing the political optimism of the time, this scholarship also fundamentally rested on a conceptual assumption that the violent past that (once) haunted the body politic of Mozambique had been sequestered or forgotten by political discourses, democratic practices, and popular forms of healing.

Engaging with such a vision of almost organic reconciliation and through engaging with the notion of *irreconciliation* suggested in this special issue, I will broach occurrences in Mozambique that unsettle the understanding of this past as temporally behind us. For the aftermath of the civil war has seen recurrent violent uprisings, skirmishes between various armed groups, and spates of lynchings which have made apparent the spectre of past wars, struggles, and politics (de Brito 2017). Starting with fieldwork in 1998 in and around the city of Chimoio in central Mozambique and later extending to also involve Maputo in the mid-2000s, I have mapped how citizens perceived and related to such violent events. Juxtaposing ethnographic material from two decades, in this text I suggest that the violences of the civil war remain *uncontained* by conventional temporal linear delimitation. I will make three arguments.

First, I will outline what a politics of irreconciliation may look like, including its relation to notions of justice, taking the Mozambican case as a starting point. Informed by Hannah Arendt's deliberations on the power of reconciliation and what she calls 'non-reconciliation' – as also detailed by the introduction to this special issue – I will argue that a politics of irreconciliation revolves around an ontological-political rejection of the world in which large-scale genocidal mass violence unfolds (Berkowitz 2011). Put differently, rather than viewing a politics of irreconciliation as a rejection of reconciliation or forgiveness per se, informed by Arendt I approach it as involving a radical non-acceptance of *what is* in search of a common world. This argument is also inspired by Jacques Derrida's (2001) approach to forgiveness. Central to most definitions of reconciliation, Derrida not only points out that forgiveness derives from a specific cosmological system, Judeo-Abrahamic religious thought, but also that it is inherently contradictory. As he writes, 'One cannot, or should not, forgive; there is only forgiveness, if there is any, where there is the unforgivable. That is to say that forgiveness must announce itself as impossibility itself. It can only be possible in doing the impossible' (2001: 32-3). Derrida insists on forgiveness being oriented towards the

Journal of the Royal Anthropological Institute (N.S.) **28**, 50-64
© 2022 The Authors. *Journal of the Royal Anthropological Institute* published by John Wiley & Sons Ltd on behalf of Royal Anthropological Institute.

past, towards memory, towards bringing history into the present in order to transform the so-called perpetrator (so that s/he becomes an Other, i.e. not the person who perpetrated the act for which forgiveness is sought).

Second, drawing on recent anthropological theorizing about temporal regimes and chronopolitics, I will argue for the salience of a non-linear understanding of irreconciliation to grapple with the fact that civil war violence is widely understood as dangerously uncontained rather than nominally past. Elisabeth Kirtsoglou and Bob Simpson suggest the notion of *chronocracy* to depict the deep and complex relations between time and politics, defining this as 'the ways in which governance is shot through with the power to shape the temporalities in which people live out their everyday lives'. Further, they note that chronocracy makes visible how 'inequality and exclusionary practices and the ontological and economic insecurity they engender are not just spatial matters but also have important temporal dimensions' (2020: 3).

Third, such an attention to what has also been called a non-chrononormative approach to temporality (Jen & McMahon 2017) is crucial if we are to grapple with the non-finite nature of events (Deleuze 2004a [1968]) as well as the 'futurelessness' that fuels contemporary politics of irreconciliation. While recognizing the importance of the past in the present and building on the two arguments already mentioned above, in this text I will argue that within the context of Mozambique, forgiveness and its other, *irreconciliation*, is not only intimately tied to the temporally past – which is often assumed in, especially, the reconciliation literature – but it must also be seen as centrally produced by an intense experience of an absence of a (or any) future (see also Goldberg 2021). Understood this way, and as I aim to show, a *politics of irreconciliation* fundamentally revolves around problematic, looped, and twisted forms of temporality that defy the smooth linearity– from violent past to reconciled present – undergirding the ideology of reconciliation.

Civil war and reconciliation (1976/7-2010)

The death in 1986 of Frelimo leader Samora Machel coincided with the country's abandoning of a socialist politics for a Washington consensus-style economic regime – what Christopher Cramer called 'the largest privatisation programme in sub-Saharan Africa in the 1990s' (2007: 266), including corrupt accumulation and rampant asset stripping. Occurring at the end of the Cold War, the civil war came to an end in 1992 with the GPA signed between the Mozambican government (i.e. Frelimo) and Renamo, after more than a year of negotiation (Hume 1994). Crucially, following the GPA and the subsequent general elections in 1994, Mozambique did not pursue anything like an official 'reconciliation-through-truth'-style process. Instead, reconciliation was believed to be best served through the Mozambican state abstaining from both attempting to ascertain war crimes or taking action against alleged perpetrators. This mode of thinking was already apparent in 1989 in the statements of then President of Mozambique, Joaquim Chissano (quoted in Bueno 2019: 431):

> We extended the Amnesty Law and tried to inform followers of the so-called RENAMO that the Amnesty is a necessity. They think that they have not committed any crimes, but we know that rebellion and resorting to violence are crimes that are illegal in the People's Republic of Mozambique, not to mention the atrocities they commit and have committed against the people that are known throughout the world, and the theft of the people's goods. They don't classify this as theft, but the citizens think that it is and only an Amnesty can give them back their dignity without humiliating them and without even placing them in the position of being defeated. A defeated person has to obey

Journal of the Royal Anthropological Institute (N.S.) **28**, 50-64
© 2022 The Authors. *Journal of the Royal Anthropological Institute* published by John Wiley & Sons Ltd on behalf of Royal Anthropological Institute.

everything, and can't have an opinion about anything. But the Amnesty transforms them into normal people and considers them free from guilt, including in relation to the crime of disobedience and the crime of rebellion.

The GPA in Mozambique thus contrasted sharply with what Richard A. Wilson (2003: 369) aptly calls a 'truth-writing project' – central to the TRC process in South Africa – by being premised upon an all-encompassing amnesty and a refusal to detail the nature of past violent events. Importantly, for the first decade after the 1992 GPA, the scholarly analyses on Mozambique overwhelmingly resembled that of official Mozambican discourse. Patricia Hayner's influential work exemplifies this, arguing that 'reconciliation' in Mozambique means, quoting key politicians, 'we will talk, and we may govern together, but we will not bring up the past' (2001: 191; see also Hayes 1998). Furthermore, Hayner pointed out that there were a number of rituals addressing (or redressing) the past that were undertaken beyond the circles of officialdom, the domains of development agencies, the work of the UN, and the elites of both Renamo and Frelimo.

Underlining Hayner's emphasis on post-GPA society-level rituals, in incisive publications Mozambican anthropologist Alcinda Honwana (1996; 2003) details how there were a multitude of cleansing ceremonies involving those afflicted by war and violence. For Honwana and other anthropological observers (e.g. Igreja 2019), this meant that what was addressed ritually post-war was not the reintegration of perpetrators of violence – or anything resembling organic processes of transitional justice. Instead, these practices were directed at *re*-humanizing those *de*-humanized by an intensity of violence that was widely seen by Mozambicans as irreducible to individual human actors.

In the years since 1998, I have undertaken many longer- and shorter-term periods of fieldwork in a rural area that I call 'Honde' about two hours' walk from Chimoio, central Mozambique. Especially until 2010, fieldwork was often carried out with people in Honde – a zone in which the exceedingly brutal civil war had been at its most intense. My research delved into how rural dwellers made sense of their lives following civil war violence that was intensely destructive of social relations, economic livelihoods, and ritual practices, in addition to its traumatic impact (see also Broch-Due & Bertelsen 2016). Reflecting also the thrust of Honwana's argument, in my work I was, especially in the 2000s, concerned with analysing what I saw as distinct non-state-initiated efforts at re-humanizing those affected by the war. Arguing for the reconstitution of meaning as being central to these practices, I mapped what I called 'reconstructive practices', thus both avoiding the notion of 'reconciliation' and emphasizing the semiotic dimension to what I observed in the day-to-day lives of Honde's peasants (see, e.g., Bertelsen 2002). At the time, there were a host of reasons for making such an analysis, such as widespread participation in collective and collaborative daily agricultural activities (e.g. the weeding and harvesting of the staple maize from the *machambas*, the plots of land); frequent social calls between households where parting gifts of seeds, seedlings, or food were always provided to bring home (linking households through substance) and which created, literally, well-trodden paths through the (re-socialized) landscape; and key ritual activities such as rainmaking ceremonies linking the fertility and well-being of Honde with the ancestral plane or rituals integrating into society potentially dangerous spirits of foreign dead soldiers who would otherwise roam the landscape creating havoc.

Journal of the Royal Anthropological Institute (N.S.) **28**, *50-64*
© 2022 The Authors. *Journal of the Royal Anthropological Institute* published by John Wiley & Sons Ltd on behalf of Royal Anthropological Institute.

The province of Manica (INE 1999) was materially impoverished from the era of the civil war until well into the 2000s – and Honde was no exception to this, having a high infant mortality rate, widespread malnutrition, and a lower than national-level average life span (see also Kalofonos 2021). However, there was, as I have tried to hint at above, a sense of concerted attempts – some reflecting religious and cosmological dimensions of what I have called 'the traditional field' (Bertelsen 2016) – at reconstituting a humane world of life following the deadening of meaning that the war brought. Such a *future-oriented* direction of activities was also expressed by a young neighbour of mine, 'Helder', in 2004. During this scorching hot day in November, we had been inspecting banana plants and sugar cane at his *matoro* – the low-lying plots of land close to rivers and rivulets that were key to food provision during the months before the regular rain-fed plots of land yielded maize. Now in the early evening sitting in the dark on low wooden benches in his household and having shared a plate of the staple *sadza* (maize meal porridge) and a relish of sweet potato leaves, Helder explained how he saw the situation in Honde and Mozambique:

> You, Bigorn [Bjørn] you are interested in the war, how it was, how it is now. I know this, even though I am just a *mwana modoko* [a small boy – he was around 20 at the time]. Listen, you know that the war was bad around here. Bad, bad, bad! My uncle living over there [nodding his head westward] was beheaded with a machete and his head put on a stake. All the houses here – ALL! – were burnt down [pointing in all directions]. So, who did this, you may ask? Well, we did it all. I know the man who killed my uncle. I greet him. I talk to him. I can drink with him. It was the war that killed. Not people. Because during the war people were animals. Now we are not. And we should forget about when we were animals. It was no good.

Besides being an extremely powerful narrative, Helder's account resembled many others during this period of fieldwork: they often revolved around the animalization of war, the need to eclipse violent pasts, and the rich prospects for a future now that the war had ended. The analyses that Honwana, I, and others made in what I here will label *the era of reconciliation* (until 2010) were, thus, undoubtedly informed by empirically observable processes and tangible sentiments – many of which were based on similar outlooks that Helder and many others expressed. Thus, despite setting out to critique simplified, politicized notions of reconciliation, typically these analyses, including my own (Bertelsen 2002), were inadvertently affected by what the excellent reconciliation scholar Richard A. Wilson has shown: that there was an industry of reconciliation processes that was globally uniform, also affecting scholarship. As Wilson writes:

> Whether in Latin America or South Africa or elsewhere, political and religious elites used a remarkable similar language of reconciliation, and their discourse was characterized by the following features: the construction of a new notion of the national self and psyche, the use of organic models of nation, the use of metaphors of illness and health and the creation of formulations of the common good which exclude retribution and encourage forgiveness (2003: 370).

Problems with this global template of reconciliation extend also to the politics of forgiveness and consent (Simpson 2017). As Jacques Derrida notes, 'The "globalization" of forgiveness resembles an immense scene of confession in progress, thus a virtually Christian convulsion-conversion-confession, a process of Christianisation which has no more need for the Christian church' (2001: 31). Derrida's notion of the Christian cosmology underlying the industry of reconciliation in the 1980s and 1990s resonates with academic and political discourses in Mozambique at the time. However, more recently, quite a few studies have challenged these notions of Mozambique achieving post-war reconciliation and being a country governed by sociopolitical forms of stability

Journal of the Royal Anthropological Institute (N.S.) **28**, *50-64*
© 2022 The Authors. *Journal of the Royal Anthropological Institute* published by John Wiley & Sons Ltd on behalf of Royal Anthropological Institute.

(Khan, Meneses & Bertelsen 2019; Monjane & Conrado 2021; Muchemwa & Harris 2019). In the following, I draw on these critiques as well as return to Helder and Honde to describe a situation in which vernacular forms of reconciliation have been replaced by a politics of irreconciliation. Crucially, such revisiting is also informed by the emergence of tangible yet opaque forms of warfare, political violence, and unrest.

Irreconciliation and the problem of time (2010-21)

On 31 October 2019, long-standing rumours of international war in Mozambique were in a sense confirmed in, of all places, *The Moscow Times* (Sauer 2019):

> Seven Russian Wagner Group mercenaries have been killed in two separate shooting incidents involving Islamic State-linked insurgents in Mozambique's northern Cabo Delgado province this month, two Mozambique army sources told The Moscow Times. In a previously unreported attack that took place on Oct. 10 in Cabo Delgado's Macomia district, two Russian Wagner soldiers were shot dead after their group was ambushed by Islamist militant insurgents, a soldier with the Mozambique Defense Armed Forces (FADM) who witnessed the incident told The Moscow Times (Sauer 2019).

A report about this attack was a rare insight into the slow, opaque, and globally linked form of warfare that unfolds in Mozambique and which has been reported since the early 2010s. For, after a period of simmering tension, on 5 October 2017, an armed group of young men occupied the town of Mocímboa da Praia in Cabo Delgado, ransacking buildings, looting shops, and stealing weapons from police posts, before retreating into the bush (Morier-Genoud 2020). This was the first major attack attributed to a group that locally is dubbed al-Shabaab. The group has no identifiable link to either the Somali Jihadists or IS/Daesh, as has been alleged in some mainstream media, and despite IS/Daesh claiming responsibility in its social media outlets (Hanlon 2021). Instead, the group seems to have been formed around a local breakaway Islamic sect comprising young Mozambican men (Morier-Genoud 2020).

Arguably, the opaque violence in northern Mozambique comprises a very modern form of warfare. First, a key dimension fuelling the support for the war, also by local inhabitants, is the construction of a major gas plant in the province – a process that has been ongoing for many years, but which has, similar to such capitalist enclaves of extraction elsewhere (e.g. Appel 2019), not created any significant local development. Second, it is a war in which the Wagner Group is not the only private military group involved: eclipsing the Mozambican armed forces in tactical prowess, for instance, the South African Dyck Advisory Group has been operative for years – again, obfuscating simple visions of a war comprising merely civilians, state forces, and insurgents. Third, and crucially, the war is integral to a political economy of images of enemies – here entailing that the Mozambican government actively labels insurgents as Islamic terrorists, serving to deflect attention from local grievances and illicit accumulation.

The war in the north relates directly to a politics of irreconciliation in the sense that, in all its violence and opacity, it appears to be without end. For, in relation to Cabo Delgado, there is no sign of talks, and the whole prospect of peace, as in the ceasing of violence as the willed outcome of a settlement, seems to belong to an abandoned era of politics. War is, therefore, constituted as unending and its intensity also challenges the gospel of prosperous gas futures that the Total gas developments in Cabo Delgado were meant to realize (see also Lesutis 2022). This temporality of perpetual war is compounded in the everyday for Mozambicans as reports are very scattered and – as with the civil war of the past – conventional notions of veracity, in the sense of basic facts about events, are virtually non-existent. Thus, even more significant than what has

© 2022 The Authors. *Journal of the Royal Anthropological Institute* published by John Wiley & Sons Ltd on behalf of Royal Anthropological Institute.

been called 'the fluidification of warfare' – a term coined by Alessandro Zagato (2018) for Mexico – is the fact that the consecutive waves of rumours, reports, and hearsay reverberate significantly with previous periods of war and unrest. Let me provide an empirical example.

In 2017, a man I have known since my first fieldwork in 1998 – when he was still a child in rural Honde – went to work at an illegal logging operation run by Chinese operators in Sofala province, central Mozambique. While the pay was dismal and the workers camped in the bush, the money was very welcome. One afternoon, several cars with tinted windows pulled up to the roadside where the workers were loading tree trunks onto trucks and started shooting indiscriminately at them, killing several. My friend, let us call him 'Ernesto', ended up being shot in the shoulder and the leg but survived by crawling into hiding. For Ernesto, this event confirmed the perpetual nature of war, and how, as he told me, 'the big ones are still fighting over money, territory, us [meaning the people]':

> My friend, the war is never over. The time of Samora [Machel] is never over. It does not matter who does it. The Chinese are the same as the Party [Frelimo]. We are never now [*nunca estamos agora*]. Suffering always just accumulates without exit [*sem saída*].

Ernesto's conflation of the protracted experience of violence emanating from Frelimo with the Chinese reveals an understanding of a form of accumulation that is temporally unbound by pastness or presentness. His notion of a twisted and contorted timeline was in no way unique: during the many conversations I had with long-standing interlocutors, past, present, and future seemed intermeshed – a phenomenon *not* common in what I above called the era of reconciliation. Arguably, in contexts such as Mozambique, this kind of reverberation is not fully explained by analysing it as people remembering *past* violence when confronted with *present* forms of violence: that is, understanding violence to be inscribed by a form of temporal boundedness or pastness.[5] Instead, violent attacks while working, or reports about dead Russians, bring into being sociopolitical worlds of warfare and upheaval that are not yet finished, not yet contained, and point to a particular form of politics of irreconciliation.

This shift became abundantly clear in 2019 when I again visited my (now middle-aged) interlocutor and friend Helder. In contrast to 2004, Helder had moved to live most of the time in one of the populous *bairros* (poor, urban areas) in Chimoio, having abandoned full-time farming for small-time trading in the informal economy. He still had his plots of land (*machamba* and *matoro*) in Honde, however, and regularly tended to these. When we met, he had just returned from the Malawi border north of Chimoio, a journey which took him through Sofala, a province in which Renamo has remained strong (Wiegink 2020). As in 2004, Helder and I shared a meal together, but this one was outside a stall in a local market in his Chimoio *bairro*. Digging into the plates of *sadza* and goat meat relish while sharing a bottle of Manica beer, we talked about the state of the country's economy and politics. Since I met him the first time, he had gradually grown much more critical not only of politicians – whom he, like many, regarded as thoroughly corrupt – but also of the prospects for peace and the future. He was particularly concerned with the operation of groups of armed men (allegedly belonging to a faction of Renamo) that were commonly believed to have been orchestrating waves of attacks since the early 2010s in central Mozambique (see Pearce 2020). Taking the last sip of his beer and looking across the makeshift stalls, he told me:

Journal of the Royal Anthropological Institute (N.S.) **28**, 50-64
© 2022 The Authors. *Journal of the Royal Anthropological Institute* published by John Wiley & Sons Ltd on behalf of Royal Anthropological Institute.

Helder: Bigorn, look at this. Look! Do you remember how things were when you were here twenty years ago? It is the same now. The same kind of shit! The stalls [at the market] … there is no change. They have the same bad products, now from China. When the war with Renamo [the civil war] ended, we thought it would all be good – that violence was over, that the future would come, that the past was past. Do you remember I also told you? Well, we see now that the war … it never went away.

Bjørn: But the war is over, yes? Renamo is now in parliament, there are elections …

Helder: [*Interrupts*] Ah, the parliament! Who are they? They [the Renamo deputies] in Maputo are just eating from the same plate as Frelimo. Like me and you now! [*Laughing*] … But what is important is this: the war will always be there, like the real Renamo in the bush in Sofala. We may try to forget, try to forgive, but we do not move forward. It is like a bus that is stuck in the mud with wheels spinning. There is no future, no development. What is here, is violence from the [civil] war that continues, that comes back again and again. Like a bad spirit you cannot shake for generations. We are spinning, spinning. But it this spinning we need to kill [*matar*]! It is what they [the state] want! To attack spinning is why some people do war, others participate in strikes [riots], others loot.

Resonating with Ghassan Hage's (2015) notion of 'stuckness' to describe a precarious, profound, and existential sense of immobility, as well as some recent work in anthropology on the 'ebbing away of futures' in contexts which are suffused with conflict and grief (Jefferson & Segal 2019), both Helder and Ernesto underline not only the 'un-pastness' of war and violence but also its continuity as futures are politically eclipsed. Such horizons of continuous, muddled war and violence were indicated also by other long-term interlocutors – including those who seasonally join the sporadic fighting and looting undertaken by armed Renamo men in Sofala province. Crucially, this shift from an era of reconciliation to one of irreconciliation is characterized by an unstable, non-linear form of the temporal. How can we, as anthropologists, approach reoccurrences of violence – a world spinning, to use Helder's term – that one would, conventionally, have thought past?

Irreconciliation, time, and justice: repurposing uncontained violence

What is living, present, conscious, here, is only so because there's an infinity of little deaths, little accidents, little breaks, little cuts in the sound track, as William Burroughs would say, in the sound track and the visual track of what's lived. And I think that's very interesting for the analysis of the social, the city, politics. Our vision is that of a montage, a montage of temporalities which are the product not only of the powers that be, but of the technologies that organize time.

Paul Virilio in Virilio & Lotringer, *Pure war: twenty-five years later* (2008 [1983]: 48)

As Diane M. Nelson (2009) has eloquently shown for the case of Guatemala, accessing the central dynamics animating the so-called 'post-war' terrain situation is exceedingly complex. This is even more so in a context like Guatemala, where, she holds, most people were, to some extent, complicit in or contributed to violence. A similar argument has been made by Carolyn Nordstrom (1997) in her evocative analysis of the Mozambican civil war. There she suggests, like Nelson later did for Guatemala, that the maelstrom of war obfuscates researchers' search for singular truths as to who were perpetrators, victims, and onlookers. Such war-induced opacity, Nordstrom argues, is integral to a Mozambican notion of violence – one that bypasses universally assumed victim/perpetrator distinctions, as well as complexifying understandings of the temporality of violence and war. Similar to Nordstrom and Nelson, in recent decades, scholars have also demonstrated the importance of popular forms of historicity and documented how globally varied formations of memory or unruly forms of pastness impinge on the present.[6] Even though many works commonly challenge state-centric or other hegemonic forms of discourse – for instance, in critiques of post-conflict narratives being integral to politicized national-level reconciliation processes – they often neither fundamentally undo a tripartite division of past, present, and future, nor upset the temporal linearity inherent in such a division (but see Santos 2021).

Arguably, the transition from an era of reconciliation to that of a politics of irreconciliation in Mozambique, as I have demonstrated above, necessitates a revisiting of some critical approaches to time: for instance, Deleuze's post-structuralist analysis of the event (Deleuze 2004b [1969]). For Deleuze (2004a [1968]), the event harbours anti-hierarchical or egalitarian potential, at least if this is taken to mean something which shifts circumstances, ruptures orders, and, as an effect, collapses chronological time – what he called *kairos*. Later, these approaches to *kairos* and events were developed into the pair of *actual* events (tangible, recorded in a linear perspective) and *virtual* events (potential, not yet realized), both constituting the real. Thus, the event has a double temporal location: first, in historical time (*chronos*) and, second, in another temporal dimension of perpetuity (*aion*) – a doubleness underscoring the event's openness and potential to evade the powers of scripting and territorialization. Seen in this way, the event evades accounts along the veins of space (local, national, and global – macropolitical, micropolitical) or historical time (*longue durée* or short-term). However, as we saw above in the transition from the era of reconciliation to the muddled contemporary politics of irreconciliation, the temporality of the civil war itself seems to have been unmoored from *chronos*, for, as much as the *chronos/aion* division offers more sophisticated analytical tools to grapple with past-present relations, the conceptual pair is still future-oriented and, perhaps, inherent in a wider modernist vision of futurity as a taken-for-granted part of the horizon of political time. This is, at least, the case with the notion of reconciliation, which allocates to the present the task of dealing with the past in order to secure a future body politic.

Such critical discussions about futurelessness as a figuration of (political) time are not, of course, solely the domain of irreconciliation or event studies. Building on Frantz Fanon, Achille Mbembe's (2017) critique of both capitalism and racism in an age of the Anthropocene (see also Bertelsen 2021) analyses a thoroughly fragmented subject which Mbembe recognizes as becoming globally common. Centrally, his notion of the 'becoming black of the world' seems to indicate the cancelling of the future in a world that is blackened, as it were, by the violence of Anthropocenic politics. Similarly, David Scott (2014) has explored the domain of Grenada to rethink the temporal scope of postcolonial politics. Concretely looking at the trajectory of the short-lived Grenada revolution (1979-83), he critically interrogates a familiar script in representing many so-called postcolonial contexts: first, a colonial era of repression; then, a time of liberation; then, the institution of a dream of a unified postcolonial society with national sovereignty and a 'cultural-political consensus'; and, finally, collapse – a template trajectory quite similar to conventional portrayals of Mozambican history (Newitt 1995). However, rather than seeing this script as the only possible way in which to conceive of politics, Scott invites us to think about the '*propensities* and *limits* of political action itself, political action in time: in *failure* and ruin as much as success' (2014: 36, original emphasis). Furthermore, he draws on Hannah Arendt to suggest that '[t]ragedy is the price of freedom [and that] the threat of tragedy casts a permanent shadow over political action' (Scott 2014: 62-3). In sum, Scott invites us to leave the essentially modernist vision of time and ask: how can we understand politics without a future?

Journal of the Royal Anthropological Institute (N.S.) **28**, *50-64*
© 2022 The Authors. *Journal of the Royal Anthropological Institute* published by John Wiley & Sons Ltd on behalf of Royal Anthropological Institute.

In the ethnographically identifiable shifts above, both Helder and Ernesto express significant visions about the perennial nature of war, the domination of a single political regime (Frelimo), and the unboundedness of violent temporalities – expressed in the recent war in the north. In order to make sense of this particular chronocratic (Kirtsoglou & Simpson 2020) configuration in Mozambique, the relations between *chronos* and *aion* (despite its future orientation) and the calls to fundamentally rethink the nature of the political subject, by Deleuze, Mbembe, and Scott, respectively, are all helpful. At one level, the current violence in Mozambique, naturally, reflects the failure of reconciliation in a technical sense, including failed integration of Renamo fighters into the military and the configuration of the one-party state (Bueno 2019; Jentzsch 2022; Wiegink 2019). At a more fundamental level, however, while identifying such dimensions is key, I believe the ethnographic material indicates the impossibility of even *thinking* forms of reconciliation without a future. This means that the violence that sometimes emerges and sometimes is painfully present is, essentially, *uncontained* given the collapse of any tangible project of socioeconomic development or permanent peace. Thus, as identifiable in the expressions of Helder and Ernesto, the politics of irreconciliation become integral to the horizon of sociopolitical worlds, constituting, again drawing on Kirtsoglou and Simpson (2020: 6), a chronocracy encompassing 'our "everyday" and [which] structures our ordinary experiences to the point that our common time thickens and becomes saturated with its effects and our labour to mitigate them'.

Given such an understanding of a futureless chronocracy operating in the (nominally) post-civil war, the politics of irreconciliation may here be understood as the temporal figuration where the duration of an event – its intensity – can be expected to be resolved neither by futurity in the form of revolution, peace, and reconciliation, nor by economic development. I therefore ask: can we think of irreconciliation as the temporal figure of the cancelling of the future – the end not of history (in fact, rather the *un-ending* of history) but of linearity in the modernist sense of projecting an improved form of what comes after; what we sometimes call the future?

Conclusion

First, as the cases from Honde and Chimoio show, while the future is not on the horizon, the sense of an intensification of times (in the plural) impinges on Helder's and Ernesto's present. To me, this suggests the emergence of a body politic in which the very possibility of the future as either emancipation or the cordoning off and neutering of the violences originating in events of the past – or both – is rendered meaningless. Such a state form will obviate any notion of reconciliation as a national project and instead generate alternative actions and orientations – also temporal – that may undermine the stability of the sociopolitical order. This reading would also be in line with recent analyses of Mozambican politics where, for instance, Jason Sumich argues that the 'gradual decoupling of any sort of political project of transformation from this sense of revolutionary temporality, a soon-to-be-realized future totally different from the present, has seriously undermined the moral basis of Frelimo's rule' (2021: 595). Thus, building on the analysis of a politics of irreconciliation undertaken here, one may argue for Mozambique that the chronocratic regime is dependent on a semiotically fixed and futureless political ontology (Sumich & Bertelsen 2021).

Second, if we use the notion of irreconciliation to think through notions of justice, development, and war in Mozambique, we end up with a paradoxical figure. At the macro level of the state and inherent in the world of what we used to call development, we see an active cultivation of an end to the future – not least in notions such as resilience or climate change – for the vast majority of the population. At the level of people like Ernesto and Helder, we see an increasing creative engagement with *aion* in situated contexts, such as uprisings or other forms of mobilization. What this volatile context means for notions or instantiations of justice that are not derived from the hands of the people or the death-bringing practices of state forces – or Russian mercenaries in the service of local or transnational elites – is difficult to disentangle. However, I think we have a lot to gain from approaches that move beyond notions of chronological time. For, as we have seen, as the very stuff of time integral to notions of reconciliation, *linearity* is problematic to relate in a context where uncontained and violent temporalities eclipse its very principle. Put differently, it seems like the current chronocracy is one that we need to challenge given a context in which violence continues to emanate from events we normally allocate to the past that threatens to destabilize the sociopolitcal order, and where people like Ernesto and Helder experience temporality itself as inherently violent and non-linear. Thus, while violent events of the past remain uncontained, undercutting the notion of pastness that is inherent in reconciliation, the current politics of irreconciliation does not *necessarily* mean stasis or political stagnancy; it is, as Mookherjee outlines in the introduction to this special issue, a form of rejection of a world that holds such acts, calling for a new order by dismissing the current state of affairs.

Third, while retaining support from certain segments of academic work in Mozambique, including my own, the notion of 'reconciliation' seems to be heavily out of fashion in anthropology and, increasingly, in grey literature also. While we know that, for better or worse, the waxing and waning of terms is a natural feature of academic conceptual ecosystems, I think the waning of the reconciliation concept, also beyond the context of Mozambique, reflects an additional feature: the increasing lack of references to reconciliation mirrors a world order where war has become omni-*present* in the sense of cancelling both the past and the prospects of (a post-war) future. This means, as Allen Feldman notes, that '[w]e are living the time of wartime as a largely unwitnessable time out of time, as a fall out of conventional time that fractures any polemological idea of progress and political achievement' (2019: 175). War, then, in its current configuration of spatiotemporal perpetuity, omnipresence, and unwitnessability, seems to co-produce the rise of a politics of irreconciliation not only as a chronocratic regime but also as a modality to engage with, to resist, and to strive for, in Arendt's sense: 'Non-reconciliation, the act of judging the wrongs of the past to be incompatible with a common world and thereby calling forth a new common world, is one of the very highest political examples of politics action' (Berkowitz 2011: 13; see also Marongwe, Duris & Mawere 2019). As I have tried to illustrate with the case of Mozambique, the shift from an era of civil war and reconciliation to one dominated by a politics of irreconciliation within an increasingly violent context is instructive as it outlines how futurelessness is both key to a temporal regime and identified as that which must be engaged with.

Acknowledgements

Through spanning more than two decades, research for this essay has, naturally, occurred with the support of a range of institutions, including the Meltzer Foundation, the University of Bergen, the European Research Council, and the Norwegian Research

Council. Its publication is supported by the Norwegian Research Council project 'God, Grievance, and Greed? Understanding Northern Mozambique's New Islamic War' (grant no. 316070) led by Liazzat Bonate. I have presented various incarnations of this essay in a number of contexts and have benefited immensely from generous and critical feedback at Emory University (Atlanta, Georgia), HUMA – Institute for Humanities in Africa (Cape Town), the Instituto de Estudos Sociais e Económicos (IESE) (Maputo), the National Chiao Tung University (Taipei), University of Tromsø (Tromsø) and, last but not least, the panel 'The Time of Justice: Explorations through the Debates of Irreconciliation' at the American Anthropological Association's 2019 annual conference (Vancouver). I have also learnt tremendously from receiving comments from Anne K. Bang, Liazzat Bonate, Ralph Borland, Michel Cahen, Sérgio Chichava, Allen Chung, João Feijó, Salvador Forquilha, Divine Fuh, Stig Jarle Hansen, Paolo Israel, Corinna Jentzsch, Bruce Kapferer, Peter Little, Eric Morier-Genoud, Aslak Orre, Helge Rønning, Carmeliza Rosário, and Nikkie Wiegink. In addition to the anonymous reviewers of the *JRAI*, I would also particularly like to thank Nayanika Mookherjee for her dedication, intellectual drive, and support.

NOTES

[1] The author acknowledges that the existence of several other armed forces fundamentally problematizes the Renamo-Frelimo/Mozambican government distinction, including the rebellion in Zambézia Province pre-dating the establishment of Renamo (Morier-Genoud *et al.* 2018) and the so-called traditional army of Naparama (Jentzsch 2017, 2022). While recognizing these complications, I will nonetheless here deal with the Renamo-Frelimo/Mozambican government distinction as these remained the sole parties integral to the peace process and are also those that continue to inform the political and historical horizons of my interlocutors (but see Sumich & Bertelsen 2021).

[2] For some treatments, see Nielsen (2017); Obarrio (2014); Sumich (2018).

[3] See, for example, the fierce debate following Christian Geffray's (1990) controversial analysis of the civil war with incisive interventions from Chichava (2013); Florêncio (2002); O'Laughlin (1992).

[4] Differing positions in this long-standing debate include Alexander (1997); Cahen (2002); Coelho (1998); Dinerman (2006); Hultman (2009); Morier-Genoud *et al.* (2018); Roesch (1992); Vines (1991); Wiegink (2020).

[5] For analyses of trauma in relation to these events, see Broch-Due & Bertelsen (2016); Igreja & Baines (2019).

[6] Antze & Lambek (1996); Feldman (2015); Gilroy (2004); Kwon (2008); Malkki (1995); Mookherjee (2015); Werbner (1998) – all exemplify seminal interventions into this field.

REFERENCES

ALEXANDER, J. 1997. The local state in post-war Mozambique: political practice and ideas about authority. *Africa* **67**, 1-26.

ANTZE, P. & M. LAMBEK (eds) 1996. *Tense past: cultural essays in trauma and memory*. London: Routledge.

APPEL, H. 2019. *The licit life of capitalism: US oil in Equatorial Guinea*. Durham, N.C.: Duke University Press.

BERKOWITZ, R. 2011. Bearing logs on our shoulders: reconciliation, non-reconciliation, and the building of a common world. *Theory & Event* **14**, 1-16.

BERTELSEN, B.E. 2002. 'Till the soil – but do not touch the bones': histories and memories of war and violence in Mozambican re-constructive practices. Cand. Polit. thesis, University of Bergen.

——— 2016. *Violent becomings: state formation, sociality, and power in Mozambique*. New York: Berghahn Books.

——— 2021. A lesser human? Utopic registers of urban reconfiguration in Maputo, Mozambique. *Social Anthropology* **29**, 87-107.

BROCH-DUE, V. & B.E. BERTELSEN (eds) 2016. *Violent reverberations: global modalities of trauma*. New York: Palgrave Macmillan.

BUENO, N. 2019. Reconciliation in Mozambique: was it ever achieved? *Conflict, Security and Development* **19**, 427-52.

CAHEN, M. 2002. *Les bandits: un historien au Mozambique, 1994*. Paris: Centre Culturel Calouste Gulbenkian.

CHICHAVA, S. 2013. 'They can kill us but we won't go to the communal villages!': peasants and the policy of 'Socialisation of the Countryside' in Zambezia. *Kronos: Southern African Histories* **39**, 112-30.

COELHO, J.P.C.B. 1998. *Low-intensity, high impact: the origins and development of the war between Frelimo and Renamo (1976-1992)*. Leeds: University Press.

CRAMER, C. 2007. *Violence in developing countries: war, memory, progress*. Indianapolis: Indiana University Press.

DE BRITO, L. 2017. *Agora eles têm medo de nós! Uma colectânea de textos sobre as revoltas populares em Moçambique (2008-2012)*. Maputo: Instituto de Estudos Sociais e Económicos (IESE).

DELEUZE, G. 2004a [1968]. *Difference and repetition* (trans. P. Patton). London: Continuum.

——— 2004b [1969]. *The logic of sense* (trans. M. Lester with C. Stivale). London: Continuum.

DERRIDA, J. 2001. *On cosmopolitanism and forgiveness* (trans. M. Dooley & M. Hughes). London: Routledge.

DINERMAN, A. 2006. *Revolution, counter-revolution and revisionism in post-colonial Africa: the case of Mozambique, 1975-1994*. New York: Routledge.

FELDMAN, A. 2015. *Archives of the insensible: of war, photopolitics, and dead memory*. Chicago: University Press.

——— 2019. War under erasure: contretemps, disappearance, anthropophagy, survivance. *Theory & Event* **22**, 175-203.

FLORÊNCIO, F. 2002. Christian Geffray e a antropologia da guerra: ainda a propósito de *La cause des armes au Mozambique*. *Revista Etnográfica* **VI**, 347-64.

GEFFRAY, C. 1990. *La cause des armes au Mozambique: anthropologie d'une guerre civile*. Paris: Karthala.

GILROY, P. 2004. *After empire: melancholia or convivial culture?* Abingdon, Oxon: Routledge.

GOLDBERG, D.T. 2021. *Dread: facing futureless futures*. Cambridge: Polity.

HAGE, G. 2015. *Alter-politics: critical anthropology and the radical imagination*. Melbourne: University Publishing.

HANLON, J. 2021. A more complex reality in Cabo Delgado. *New Frame*, 24 March (available online: *https://www.newframe.com/the-lie-of-islamist-terrorists-in-cabo-delgado/*, accessed 16 March 2022).

HAYES, G. 1998. We suffer our memories: thinking about the past, healing, and reconciliation. *American Imago* **55**, 29-50.

HAYNER, P.B. 2001. *Unspeakable truths: confronting state terror and atrocity*. New York: Routledge.

HONWANA, A.M. 1996. Spiritual agency and self-renewal in southern Mozambique. Ph.D. thesis, SOAS.

——— 2003. Undying past: spirit possession and the memory of war in southern Mozambique. In *Magic and modernity: interfaces of revelation and concealment* (eds) B. Meyer & P. Pels, 60-80. Stanford: University Press.

HULTMAN, L. 2009. The power to hurt in civil war: the strategic aim of RENAMO violence. *Journal of Southern African Studies* **35**, 821-34.

HUME, C. 1994. *Ending Mozambique's war: the role of mediation and good offices*. Washington, D.C.: Institute of Peace Press.

IGREJA, V. 2019. Negotiating relationships in transition: war, famine, and embodied accountability in Mozambique. *Comparative Studies in Society and History* **61**, 774-804.

——— & E. BAINES 2019. Social trauma and recovery. In *A companion to the anthropology of Africa* (eds) R.R. Grinker, S.C. Lubkemann, C.B. Steiner & E. Gonçalves, 249-70. Oxford: Wiley.

INE 1999. *II recenseamento geral da população e habitação 1997. Indicadores sócio-demográficos: província de Manica*. Maputo: INE.

ISAACMAN, A.F. 1978. *A luta continua: creating a new society in Mozambique*. Binghampton, N.Y.: Fernand Braudel Center for the Study of Economies, Historical Systems, and Civilizations, State University of New York at Binghampton.

JEFFERSON, A.M. & L.B. SEGAL 2019. The confines of time – on the ebbing away of futures in Sierra Leone and Palestine. *Ethnos* **84**, 96-112.

JEN, J.T. & J. MCMAHON 2017. Timely politics: a political theory of messianic, evangelical, and queer temporalities. *Theory & Event* **20**, 923-49.

JENTZSCH, C. 2017. Auxiliary armed forces and innovations in security governance in Mozambique's civil war. *Civil Wars* **19**, 325-47.

——— 2022. *Violent resistance: militia formation and the civil war in Mozambique*. Cambridge: University Press.

KALOFONOS, I. 2021. *All I eat is medicine: going hungry in Mozambique's AIDS economy*. Berkeley: University of California Press.

KHAN, S.P., M.P. MENESES & B.E. BERTELSEN (eds) 2019. *Mozambique on the move: challenges and reflections*. Leiden: Brill.

KIRTSOGLOU, E. & B. SIMPSON 2020. Introduction: The time of anthropology: studies of contemporary chronopolitics and chronocracy. In *The time of anthropology: studies of contemporary chronopolitics* (eds) E. Kirtsoglou & B. Simpson, 1-30. New York: Routledge.

KWON, H. 2008. *Ghosts of war in Vietnam*. Cambridge: University Press.

LESUTIS, G. 2022. *The politics of precarity: spaces of extractivism, violence, and suffering*. London: Routledge.

LUBKEMANN, S.C. 2008. Involuntary immobility: on a theoretical invisibility in forced migration studies. *Journal of Refugee Studies* **21**, 454-75.

MALKKI, L. 1995. *Purity and exile: violence, memory, and national cosmology among Hutu refugees in Tanzania*. Chicago: University Press.

MARONGWE, N., F.P.T. DURIS & M. MAWERE (eds) 2019. *Violence, peace and everyday modes of justice and healing in post-colonial Africa*. Mankon, Cameroon: Langaa RPCIG.

MBEMBE, A. 2017. *Critique of Black reason* (trans. L. Dubois). Durham, N.C.: Duke University Press.

MONJANE, B. & R. CONRADO (eds) 2021. *Aporias de Moçambique pós-colonial: estado, sociedade e capital*. Cantley, Canada: Daraja Press.

MOOKHERJEE, N. 2015. *The spectral wound: sexual violence, public memories and the Bangladesh war of 1971*. Durham, N.C.: Duke University Press.

MORAN, M.H. & M.A. PITCHER 2004. The 'basket case' and the 'poster child': explaining the end of civil conflicts in Liberia and Mozambique. *Third World Quarterly* **25**, 501-19.

MORIER-GENOUD, E. 2020. The jihadi insurgency in Mozambique: origins, nature and beginning. *Journal of Eastern African Studies* **14**, 396-412.

———, M. CAHEN & D.M. DO ROSÁRIO (eds) 2018. *The war within: new perspectives on the civil war in Mozambique, 1976-1992*. London: James Currey.

MUCHEMWA, C. & G.T. HARRIS 2019. Mozambique's post-war success story: is it time to revisit the narrative? *Democracy and Security* **15**, 25-48.

NELSON, D.M. 2009. *Reckoning: the ends of war in Guatemala*. Durham, N.C.: Duke University Press.

NEWITT, M.D.D. 1995. *A history of Mozambique*. London: Hurst.

NIELSEN, M. 2017. Ideological twinning: socialist aesthetics and political meetings in Maputo, Mozambique. *Journal of the Royal Anthropological Institute* (N.S.) **23**: **S1**, 139-53.

NORDSTROM, C. 1997. *A different kind of war story*. Philadelphia: University of Pennsylvania Press.

OBARRIO, J. 2014. *The spirit of the laws in Mozambique*. Chicago: University Press.

O'LAUGHLIN, B. 1992. A base social da guerra em Moçambique: análise de 'A causa das armas em Moçambique, Antropologia de uma guerra civil', de C. Geffray. *Estudos Moçambicanos* **10**, 107-42.

PEARCE, J. 2020. History, legitimacy, and Renamo's return to arms in central Mozambique. *Africa* **90**, 774-95.

ROESCH, O. 1992. Renamo and the peasantry in southern Mozambique: a view from Gaza province. *Canadian Journal of African Studies* **26**, 462-84.

SAUER, P. 2019. 7 Kremlin-linked mercenaries killed in Mozambique in October – military sources. *The Moscow Times*, 31 October (available online: *https://www.themoscowtimes.com/2019/10/31/7-kremlin-linked-mercenaries-killed-in-mozambique-in-october-sources-a67996*, accessed 16 March 2022).

SANTOS, A.M.S. 2021. 'It's not my story to tell': ownership and the politics of history in Mocímboa da Praia, Mozambique. *Journal of the Royal Anthropological Institute* (N.S.) **27**, 672-90.

SCOTT, D. 2014. *Omens of adversity: tragedy, time, memory, justice*. Durham, N.C.: Duke University Press.

SIMPSON, A. 2017. The ruse of consent and the anatomy of 'refusal': cases from indigenous North America and Australia. *Postcolonial Studies* **20**, 18-33.

SUMICH, J. 2018. *The middle class in Mozambique: the state and the politics of transformation in Southern Africa*. Cambridge: University Press.

——— 2021. 'Just another African country': socialism, capitalism and temporality in Mozambique. *Third World Quarterly* **42**, 582-98.

——— & B.E. BERTELSEN 2021. Just out of reach: imminence, meaning, and political ontology in Mozambique. *Current Anthropology* **62**: **3**. doi: *https://www.journals.uchicago.edu/doi/10.1086/714268*.

VINES, A. 1991. *Renamo: terrorism in Mozambique*. London: James Currey.

VIRILIO, P. & S. LOTRINGER 2008 [1983]. *Pure war: twenty-five years later* (trans. M. Polizzotti). Los Angeles: Semiotext(e).

WERBNER, R.P. 1998. *Memory and the postcolony: African anthropology and the critique of power*. Oxford: Zed Books.

Journal of the Royal Anthropological Institute (N.S.) **28**, 50-64

Wiegink, N. 2019. The good, the bad, and the awkward: the making of war veterans in postindependence Mozambique. *Conflict and Society: Advances in Research* **5**, 150-67.

——— 2020. *Former guerrillas in Mozambique*. Philadelphia: University of Pennsylvania Press.

Wilson, R.A. 2003. Anthropological studies of national reconciliation processes. *Anthropological Theory* **3**, 367-87.

Zagato, A. 2018. State and warfare in Mexico: the case of Ayotzinapa. *Social Analysis* **62**, 55-75.

Guerre civile et non-linéarité du temps : une approche d'une politique de l'irréconciliation au Mozambique

Résumé

La guerre civile au Mozambique (1976/77-1992) a fait au moins un million de morts. Consécutif à l'indépendance du Portugal (1975) et parallèle aux expériences d'afro-socialisme des années 1980, ce conflit brutal n'a pas pourtant été suivi de processus généraux de réconciliation. Il constitue donc un cas unique d'étude de l'irréconciliation, comme horizon politique autant que comme concept analytique. Le présent article juxtapose des matériaux ethnographiques recueillis dans les régions rurales du centre du Mozambique entre la fin des années 1990 et le début des années 2000, qui met l'accent sur la réconciliation, et postérieurs à 2010 provenant de la même région, à partir desquels l'auteur identifie ce qu'il appelle une « politique de l'irréconciliation ». Il avance trois arguments: premièrement, suivant Hannah Arendt, il voit dans l'irréconciliation le rejet d'un monde de violence et la recherche d'un monde partagé ensemble. Deuxièmement, sur la base de récentes théories anthropologiques sur les régimes temporels et la chronopolitique, il défend une compréhension non linéaire de la politique de l'irréconciliation, admettant que les gens perçoivent la violence de la guerre civile comme quelque chose de dangereusement débridé ne relevant pas nécessairement du passé. Troisièmement, dans le contexte du Mozambique, l'oubli et son revers, *l'irréconciliation*, ne sont pas seulement intimement liés au passé et au présent mais sont aussi produits, comme le montre l'article, par l'absence tangible et pesante d'un futur constructif.

4

'I was celebrating the justice that the victims got': exploring irreconciliation among Bangladeshi human rights activists in London

JACCO VISSER *Aarhus University*

This essay investigates transnational human rights activist networks seeking justice for war crimes committed during the Bangladesh War of 1971, especially in light of the International Crimes Tribunal in Dhaka, Bangladesh. Focusing on activists in London, it demonstrates the need to engage with transitional justice initiatives discursively and ethnographically in order to avoid losing sight of the ways in which uses of human rights concepts can veil power dimensions through universalist legalistic abstractions. The essay explores engagements with atrocities of the war by mapping the travel and uses of human rights tropes to articulate claims of justice. It showcases how in addressing the violence of the Bangladesh War, victor justice and punishment are emphasized while futures are imagined in which enemies no longer exist. In the examples, a language of justice is employed to call for prosecution, but justice is reframed so that it is equated with the impossibility of reconciling people on opposing sides during the war.

In academic work on reconciliation and transitional justice, forgiveness is often adopted as an undisputed necessity to address past conflict (Brudholm & Rosoux 2009), while such work is often informed by the conviction that future peace and reconciliation depend on ways of 'coming to terms' with past atrocities. This 'coming to terms' is in turn expected to be achieved through truth commissions and inquiries, which form the 'fixed repertoire of reconciliatory remembrance and are key instruments in managing the transition between a divisive past and new forms of co-existence' (Rigney 2012: 252). However, 'coming to terms' with past violence and atrocities, forgiveness, and 'new forms of co-existence' in the reconciliation paradigm through truth commissions, tribunals, and inquiries does not necessarily correspond to the varying ways societies address conflict.

As I will illustrate in this essay for the case of Bangladesh, drawing on debates on apologies, forgiveness, and injustices (Brudholm & Rosoux 2009; Crapanzano 2020; Derrida 2001; Reich 2006; Thompson 2010), the awareness that an injustice cannot

Journal of the Royal Anthropological Institute (N.S.) **28**, *65-78*
© 2022 The Authors. *Journal of the Royal Anthropological Institute* published by John Wiley & Sons Ltd on behalf of Royal Anthropological Institute.

be rectified or compensated permeates ways of addressing atrocities of the Bangladesh War. Instead of a focus on forgiveness and dialogue, emphasis is placed on the situation after atrocity and the fact that this new situation cannot be reversed to its pre-conflict state. The concern with irreconciliation in this essay is not so much focused on the shortcomings of the reconciliation paradigm, but more on what happens if there is no scope for engagement in reconciliation and different ways of addressing past atrocities. In my research on the ways in which the violence of the Bangladesh War of 1971 is addressed in London in light of increasingly authoritarian politics in Bangladesh (see Visser 2019; 2020), the framework of reconciliation and transitional justice was unable to address contestations over the war. Instead, the reconciliation paradigm stood in tense relation with how politicians and human rights activists, on the one hand, relied on the human rights language central to transitional justice while, on the other hand, rejecting reconciliation and coexistence between people who stood on opposing sides during the war. In the activist initiatives in this essay, there is a tendency to employ language and practices of irreconciliation to not come to terms with the past, and to settle scores once and for all.

I introduce the case and elaborate on the central argument of this essay through an example from the establishment and proceedings of the International Crimes Tribunal (ICT), a tribunal established in Dhaka, Bangladesh, in 2009 to bring to court war criminals from the Bangladesh War. In response to the first convictions of the tribunal in early 2013, the Shahbagh protests – named after the busy Dhaka intersection where they began – erupted, which had the broad aim of addressing the ongoing influence of so-called collaborators from the war in Bangladeshi society. In one of its most high-profile cases, Abdul Quader Mollah, a senior politician from the Jamaat-e-Islami party, was sentenced to life imprisonment for crimes against humanity and war crimes. Because of historical trajectories since the end of the war and the ongoing influence of those siding with the Pakistani army in Bangladeshi society, this verdict was met with mass protests by people who feared that if the government changed hands, the defendant could be set free. To prevent this from happening, protesters successfully demanded the death penalty for Mollah, and he was eventually executed on 12 December 2013. Despite mass support for the Shahbagh protests, the movement was highly controversial for many, both in Bangladesh and in its diaspora, illustrating an ideological divide between an increasing proportion of conservative Muslims in a country where among the Muslim population many practise local and animistic interpretations in their following of Islam. However, positions in this broad divide are varied, complex, at times contradictory, and constantly changing. Illustrating this in the context of the Shahbagh protests, there was a strong reaction against them in the form of a large counter-demonstration and an ongoing political campaign by Hefazat-ul-Islam, a conservative Islamic movement. The main demand of this campaign was a stronger emphasis on religion in Bangladeshi politics and a ban on what it branded as anti-Islamic activities at the Shahbagh protests. Revealing the complexities of the relationships, the ruling party, the Awami League, which set up the ICT and was largely supportive of the protests, had in previous years engaged in a strategic relationship with Hefazat-ul-Islam.

Several solidarity events were organized in London in support of the Shahbagh protests in Bangladesh. These carried important weight, illustrating not only transnational solidarity but also 'international' support, with activists in London pressuring local MPs, media networks, and international human rights organizations, as part of the transnational 'circulatory matrix' (Kennedy 2014) within which human

Journal of the Royal Anthropological Institute (N.S.) **28**, 65-78
© 2022 The Authors. *Journal of the Royal Anthropological Institute* published by John Wiley & Sons Ltd on behalf of Royal Anthropological Institute.

rights work takes place. One of the organizers of the Shahbagh solidarity protests in London, Mala (a pseudonym), explained the need for the death penalty and her reaction to the execution in the following way:

> On the day they executed Quader Mollah, I was thinking, am I cherishing the death of Quader Mollah? No. I was celebrating the justice that the victims got. I never had anything to do with politics, I don't want to kill him, but I don't want anything less punishment for Quader Mollah than that what is in my law. I find it very unfair when people say why are you people demanding capital punishment? If the life sentence was maximum, I would have been happy that he got life sentence, but it is not maximum (Interview with Mala, 24 September 2017).

As Mala's explanation illustrates, activists' demands for the death penalty were made by relying on articulations of justice and human rights, framed as being part of a struggle over the Bangladeshi nation, in which, as Mookherjee (2015) has illustrated, the war is perceived as ongoing. This continuation of struggle is a result of the impunity for those committing atrocities during the Bangladesh War in the decades following. Mala explains that even if the maximum punishment is received by perpetrators for the atrocities they committed, this punishment itself does not undo the earlier violence and thus does not open up the possibility of reconciliatory dialogue. The call for the death penalty here should not be conflated with irreconciliation, which does not necessarily need to involve retribution. However, the example points to the impossibility of fully reconciling past injustices, as any apology or acknowledgement necessarily falls 'short of what is called for by the nature of the injustice' (Thompson 2010: 266). This is not to say that there is no value in acknowledgement at all: acknowledgement can provide important openings for structural adjustments to address political and economic inequalities in the present as a result of atrocities. This resonates with a hope invested in human rights as a framework and its potential for making the international community pay attention. There is, however, a growing realization of the pitfalls of the framework and a sense of disillusionment in terms of what it has delivered so far.

During the Shahbagh protests, and in Mala's explanation of why she participated, law is presented as a natural concept and conflated with justice. To understand these invocations of law as justice, there is a need to account both for the historical and ethnographic trajectory of the idea of law as justice, and for the feelings of injustice and anger based on 'unresolved histories of unacknowledged genocides' (Mookherjee 2020; see also Mookherjee's introduction to this volume). The uses of justice among activists linked to the maximum punishment found in law present justice as reckoning and not as an undoing of earlier injustice. Instead of an emphasis on forgiveness, it presents divergent, irreconcilable futures, one with the existence of collaborators, the other without. The reference to the law by activists tends to veil emotions and power dynamics behind what is constituted as law in a Bangladeshi context, where the independence of the judiciary is questionable at best. Rather, as I will illustrate through the case of Bangladesh, the relevance of the legal hegemony of international human rights discourses needs to be recognized, while being contextualized in their particular invocations (see also Nader 2002). Uses of law as natural in the Shahbagh protests, as existing in and of itself, further veil how the war is personal for many people because these calls for justice as reckoning are presented as separate from the personal impact the war had and continues to have. Mala's anger, and that of many who feel that injustices rooted in the violence of Bangladesh War continue in the present, is further explored in the remainder of this essay by investigating claims of justice as irreconciliation by human rights activists.

In what follows, I draw on anthropological debates on law and transitional justice initiatives (Asare 2018; Nader 1991; 2002; Thompson 2010; Wilson 2003) and scholarship on reconciliation and human rights in memory studies (Kennedy 2014; Rigney 2012) to explore recent calls from London for justice as irreconciliation in Bangladesh. Paradoxically, these calls are partly a result of an emphasis on reconciliation in transitional justice initiatives in the early 1990s. I discuss two examples of Bangladeshi human rights activism in London that seek to address war crimes and crimes against humanity during the war. The first example is the People's Court protests that took place in Bangladesh in 1992, and human rights reports published around them, which I discuss with activists participating in the protests now living in London. The second example consists of recent human rights initiatives that took place in light of the establishment of the ICT in Bangladesh. Here, I analyse a human rights report from the Sreeramshi Welfare Organization in London, sent to government officials in Bangladesh, while also taking a closer look at activism around the so-called Shahbagh solidarity protests in London.

Throughout these examples, the focus is primarily on London because the city is an important place from which to mobilize both support for, and opposition against, the ICT. Discourses originating from London have, for example, posed a direct challenge to dominant discourses in Bangladesh around the war (Zeitlyn 2014), particularly in the context of an increasingly authoritarian political system in Bangladesh, which has reduced the space for oppositional politics in the country (Feldman 2015; Ruud 2018; Ruud & Islam 2016). However, the Bangladeshi diaspora in London is conflicted over the Bangladesh War (Alexander 2013; Glynn 2006). In recent years, London has been fertile ground for the oppositional politics of the Bangladesh Nationalist Party (BNP). This party's more conservative social orientation is more popular in London than the Awami League, but the Jamaat-e-Islami has considerable support in the city too, where its emphasis on a Muslim identity resonates especially among youngsters. This became clear at the Shahbagh solidarity protest in London in 2013, which was outnumbered by the counter-protests immediately organized by the Jamaat-e-Islami. As such, the Shahbagh organizers, and associated initiatives discussed in the remainder of this essay, are minority voices in London. This essay focuses on this minority of transnational human rights activists involved in the Shahbagh protests who attempt to influence the state and governance in Bangladesh, especially in light of the ICT and the issue of war criminals. It does not address the broader Bangladeshi diaspora and the diverse reconciliatory and irreconciliatory opinions and attitudes.[1]

The central role of London in contestations over the war is further illustrated by the sentencing by the ICT of UK resident Chowdhury Mueen Uddin. Mueen Uddin was sentenced to death in absentia in 2013 for killing eighteen people at Dhaka University during the Bangladesh War. The case has been an ongoing point of contestation in and between both countries, with the United Kingdom refusing to deport Mueen Uddin, who holds British citizenship, because of the death penalty. In July 2020, Mueen Uddin started a libel case against UK Home Secretary Priti Patel after he was portrayed as responsible for serious criminal violence, including crimes against humanity during the Bangladesh War of 1971, in a report of the Commission for Countering Extremism. In response, the Nirmul Committee, an organization set up to identify and bring to court collaborators from the Bangladesh War, berated the UK government for not extraditing

Journal of the Royal Anthropological Institute (N.S.) **28**, *65-78*
© 2022 The Authors. *Journal of the Royal Anthropological Institute* published by John Wiley & Sons Ltd on behalf of Royal Anthropological Institute.

Mueen Uddin to Bangladesh. The organization released a statement pointing out that 'there is no alternative to justice and punishment for the perpetrators of genocide, if the world is to be freed from heinous crimes against humanity'. It further demanded that '[t]o maintain communal harmony, rule of law ... and to build a terror-free society and state, Chowdhury Mueen Uddin . . . should be sent back to Bangladesh for execution immediately' (*Daily Star* 2020). The case illustrates both the importance of London in contestations over the Bangladesh War and the ways in which the irreconciliation that characterizes these contestations depends on peculiar interpretations and expectations of the rule of law, justice, and punishment.

In light of these ongoing developments, I focus on the role of London as a site where a renegotiation of Bangladesh's national past takes place, as well as a site where human rights activism can be employed by Bangladeshi human rights activists, while being an important place where those accused of war crimes reside and are politically active. I do so within the largely unexplored context of diasporas more broadly as increasingly critical sites of national memory (Alexander 2013: 595). In addition, London is an important site for the Bangladeshi government to strengthen its legitimacy by claiming international support, despite human rights activists' multiple and at times conflicting positions in relation to the government and its policies. Before unpacking these dynamics further, I first provide a brief background to the Bangladesh War and how the atrocities of the conflict were addressed until the turn of the century.

Accountability, irreconciliation, and the Bangladesh War: 1971-99

Between the Partition of British India in 1947 and the Bangladesh War in 1971, Pakistan consisted of two territories: East Pakistan (what is now Bangladesh) and West Pakistan (what is now Pakistan). This new Pakistan was envisaged as a homeland for Muslims, while ignoring the social, cultural, linguistic, political, and economic differences between both territories (Van Schendel 2009). The Bangladesh War broke out in 1971 after the population of East Pakistan voted overwhelmingly for the Bengali Nationalists of the Awami League in Pakistan's general elections held on 7 December 1970. Refusing to give up power after protracted negotiations, the Pakistani army, supported by local collaborators, eventually launched a military crackdown in March 1971. Following nine months of war, during which large-scale atrocities were committed, many of which are associated with collaborators, India entered the conflict after Pakistan attacked its western border. Once the Indian army interfered in/supported (contextually read) East Pakistan, the war ended within two weeks.

After the Bangladesh War ended on 16 December 1971, attempts to address the atrocities of the conflict did not fare well. The need to assist Pakistan's allies (notably the United States) led to the repatriation of the 195 Pakistani prisoners held in India. Consequently, criminal responsibility for the war became 'entrenched in global politics and post-war diplomacy' (Sen 2012: 37). Because of the limitations when it came to addressing crimes committed by the Pakistani army, initiatives to address war crimes focused on acts committed by residents of East Pakistan. To this end, the Collaborators Act was passed in January 1972 to try people who had sided with the Pakistani army, opposed the Bengali nationalist forces, or committed other criminal acts. However, a national amnesty granted by Prime Minister Sheikh Mujibur Rahman on 30 November 1973 led to the release of the majority of prisoners who were not accused of war crimes.

Rahman's assassination on 15 August 1975 by officers of the Bangladeshi army dealt a major blow to efforts to try war criminals. The death of Rahman marked the beginning

Journal of the Royal Anthropological Institute (N.S.) **28**, 65-78
© 2022 The Authors. *Journal of the Royal Anthropological Institute* published by John Wiley & Sons Ltd on behalf of Royal Anthropological Institute.

of fifteen years of military rule in Bangladesh. During this period, the Collaborators Act was repealed, military victory was emphasized over civilian contributions, and collaborators who had left the country to flee prosecution, many of whom settled in the United Kingdom, but also in the United States, Canada, and elsewhere, were invited back to Bangladesh and received full citizenship rights (Mookherjee 2015: 37). Critically, the Jamaat-e-Islami, a political organization supporting the Pakistani army during the war, and which is associated with multiple wartime atrocities, was reinstated as a legitimate political party (Chopra 2015: 212).

It took until 1991 before democratic elections took place in Bangladesh. After multi-party democracy was established, narratives about the past shifted accordingly. The return of democracy was initially accompanied by the rehabilitation and re-establishment of collaborators in Bangladeshi society, because the BNP, which won the 1991 elections, formed an alliance with the Jamaat-e-Islami. In 1992, in response to this development, the Nirmul Committee was set up with the aim of identifying and bringing to court collaborators from the Bangladesh War and contesting the influence of the Jamaat in politics. This committee was headed by prominent public figures more or less associated with a left-leaning civil society. To achieve their objectives, the Nirmul Committee organized a public mock court called the *Gono Adalat* (People's Court). Illustrating the migration of human rights initiatives, the chairperson of the Nirmul Committee, Shahriar Kabir, told me in London that these courts were modelled after the Russell tribunals held in Stockholm in the 1960s by Bertrand Russell and Jean-Paul Sartre to bring to light and condemn human rights violations of the US army in Vietnam.

Those organizing the People's Court were largely aligned with the Awami League at the time of the initial protests, partly because of the rivalry between the Awami League and the BNP, which sought to repress the movement. The Awami League integrated some of the movement's language and framing of the issue into its own political programme, but in an act of political opportunism it formed an alliance with the Jamaat-e-Islami in 1995 to call for new elections. In doing so, it drew on international human rights language, for example by using phrases like 'bringing war criminals to justice'. It also laid the groundwork for, and was important in envisioning, a tribunal to bring war criminals to court, although it would take close to two decades before such a tribunal was set up.

Liberal, left-leaning civil society networks played an increasingly pivotal role in seeking to bring to attention the atrocities in the early 1990s. An example of this is a human rights commission called the Peoples' Inquiry Commission in Bangladesh, which was set up during the first anniversary of the People's Court gatherings on 26 March 1993, with the aim of investigating the roles of eight collaborators in war crimes. In the years after the People's Court gatherings, several reports were drawn up by the commission to pressure the Bangladeshi government to prosecute war criminals. These reports inform later calls for investigations into war crimes, which I discuss in the next section. This example clarifies how initiatives from the People's Court influenced later human rights activism and state initiatives, while the court itself was shaped by earlier political developments in Bangladesh as well as increasingly ubiquitous Holocaust discourses from the 1980s onwards.

In March 1994, one year after being established, the commission published an overview of its findings titled *Report on the findings of the People's Inquiry Commission on the activities of the war criminals and the collaborators*. The report was a starting

Journal of the Royal Anthropological Institute (N.S.) **28**, 65-78
© 2022 The Authors. *Journal of the Royal Anthropological Institute* published by John Wiley & Sons Ltd on behalf of Royal Anthropological Institute.

point for later investigations of war crimes, both in documenting human rights violations and in establishing a tradition of civil society initiatives researching atrocities in Bangladesh. The People's Court movement, which was supportive of the newly established democracy in Bangladesh in the early 1990s, was involved in protests against the military dictatorship in the country prior to the democratic elections in 1991. Sufia Kamal, a celebrated poet, an activist in the nationalist movement, and a prominent civil society leader after the Bangladesh War, writes in the report:

> The historic war crime trials of Nuremberg and Tokyo form the basis for all international laws regarding trials of war criminals. After that, various covenants, declarations, and human rights documents of the United Nations have laid stress on the need to ensure trial of war crimes and crimes against humanity ... In order to safeguard the independence and sovereignty of Bangladesh, it is necessary to bring these killers, collaborators and war criminals to justice. Today, Bangladesh has a democratically elected government in power. The government and all opposition political parties are talking about establishing democracy in the country. The Commission believes that it would not be possible to establish democracy, rule of law or human rights, by avoiding the trial of those who participated directly or indirectly in the Pakistan army's campaign of genocide, rape, arson, looting etc. (Imam & Kamal 1994: 27).

The comparison between the Bangladesh War and the Nuremberg and Tokyo trials is made to demonstrate the need for prosecution within the frame of international human rights, including the submission to the narrative structures of an increasingly hegemonic international human rights discourse during the 1990s (Wilson 2003). These changes took place in the light of concentrations of power and a new world order in which the Americanization of laws was near universal (Nader 2002: 3) and discourses of transitional justice were increasingly influential. In the Bangladesh case, rather than providing the formation of a transnational memory culture that has the potential to become a foundation for a global human rights politics, as Levy and Sznaider (2006) envisaged, the Holocaust is imposed as a benchmark (Mookherjee 2011) in the context of the post-Cold War world order. This further requires crimes against humanity to be framed within liberal humanitarian discourses, as illustrated by the direct line drawn from the Nuremberg and Tokyo trials and the United Nations guidelines on crimes against humanity to the democratization of Bangladesh. The reference to human rights allows activists to make claims to national institutions in aligning their call for justice with democracy and international law. What is at stake here is a dynamic very similar to the transnational nationalism described by Kapralsky (2014), in which nation-building is centred on the mobilization of a collective experience of suffering and victimhood, which is fundamentally transnational in its borrowing from Holocaust discourses. This process is informed by transnational activism that facilitates the travel of these discourses while being rearticulated in the light of nation-building efforts. In the following section, I demonstrate how the People's Court movement and the Inquiry Commission were connected to London and how these connections illustrate the 'circulatory matrix' of human rights reports.

Since the 1990s, the People's Court initiatives and related organizations, such as the Nirmul Committee, have been connected to London through the transnational political networks that were mobilized around the Bangladesh War. In London, I interviewed Ansar Ahmed Ullah, an activist involved in the committee from London. He has been active for several decades in trying to identify suspected war criminals from the Bangladesh War now living in London and has been trying to get them extradited to Bangladesh. He has also been a vocal supporter of the tribunal, while being part of a

Journal of the Royal Anthropological Institute (N.S.) **28**, 65-78
© 2022 The Authors. *Journal of the Royal Anthropological Institute* published by John Wiley & Sons Ltd on behalf of Royal Anthropological Institute.

transnational left-leaning civil society associated, despite sometimes being at odds, with the Awami League and the Bangladesh government. He takes a strong position against the influence of war criminals in Bangladesh and the United Kingdom when speaking about bringing them to trial. He explained the initial campaign in Bangladesh in the early 1990s, the People's Court movement, by pointing to the essential role of Jahanara Imam, who led the movement in the early 1990s. Ansar discusses Imam's well-known diary *Of blood and fire*, before turning to campaigns from London organized around the same time.

> We continued to work and campaign to raise awareness and to seek support from London for the trial in the international domain: the UN, European Union, British MPs – many of them morally and politically supported what we were asking them for. Obviously, nobody is going to say no to justice. That is what we asked them for. We asked that because major crimes were committed and people are responsible, they should stand for what they did. (Interview with Ansar Ahmed Ullah, 18 September 2017).

As indicated above, earlier opportunities for reconciliation through legal means and sociopolitical initiatives were missed in Bangladesh. As a result, historical injustices continue to stand in the way of a shared future between people who were on different sides of the war, and their descendants who continue to be ideologically divided, especially over the role of religion and the nation-state. In current attempts to address atrocities, justice as punishment through legal frameworks is put forward as the only possibility, which remarkably gains credibility in an international arena of human rights activism. In this context, justice almost becomes an empty referent, as demonstrated by Ansar, who explained that 'Obviously, nobody is going to say no to justice'. However, this justice is envisaged not as a path forward to reconciling both sides, but as a means of eliminating war criminals altogether by asking for the death penalty. These calls were made during the 1990s when there was an increasing awareness that several former collaborators with the Pakistani army suspected of committing war crimes during the war were living in London, which sparked investigations into the possibilities of prosecuting them.

Because of obstacles to investigating war crimes in Bangladesh, UK-based human rights activists David Bergman and Gita Sahgal investigated war crimes committed during the Bangladesh War for Britain's Channel 4 and broadcast a documentary titled *The War Crimes File* in 1995. The film led to renewed calls for the prosecution and extradition of alleged war criminals who were living in London, while the men featured in it successfully subjected it to a libel charge. As was common during the 1990s, *The War Crimes File* narrated the atrocities of the Bangladesh War drawing on Holocaust remembrance, referring to atrocities as 'Gestapo-like raids' and 'a Nazi-like pogrom'. Despite the fact that several of the accused were living in the country at the time the documentary aired, the impact of the film was limited in the United Kingdom and did not go much beyond raising interest among human rights activists and leading them to formulate renewed calls for prosecution of the accused. This lack of awareness of the Bangladesh War in public discourses in the United Kingdom (as elsewhere outside South Asia) illustrates the geographical and racial hierarchies of conflict and commemoration, and raises questions about when a conflict becomes relevant. To raise awareness in the United Kingdom, activists, often unsuccessfully, attempt to compare the atrocities of the Bangladesh War with the Holocaust to make them more relatable.

Journal of the Royal Anthropological Institute (N.S.) **28**, 65-78
© 2022 The Authors. *Journal of the Royal Anthropological Institute* published by John Wiley & Sons Ltd on behalf of Royal Anthropological Institute.

Despite its limited success in raising interest in the United Kingdom, *The War Crimes File* had a bigger impact in Bangladesh and fuelled calls to bring alleged war criminals to court. This impact needs to be placed in the light of developments since the end of the Cold War, which saw the reinstatement of a fragile democracy in Bangladesh in the early 1990s. Around the same time, civil society movements in Bangladesh, inspired by activism for trials and tribunals in a range of countries under the new hegemony of an international human rights discourse specific to the post-Cold War years (Meister 2011; Moyn 2017), sparked investigations into crimes committed during the war. Together, the examples of the Nirmul Committee and *The War Crimes File* illustrate how initiatives addressed the violence of the Bangladesh War from London, while providing a key background to the ICT and initiatives undertaken in London since.

The International Crimes Tribunal

In 2008, the Awami League won the national elections in Bangladesh by a two-thirds majority, partly because of an election promise to establish a tribunal for alleged war criminals from the Bangladesh War, and it has been in power ever since. Shortly after the election, the ICT was established. The ICT employs international human rights concepts, such as crimes against humanity and war crimes, but diverts from international legal standards in defining these legal concepts, relying on a curious mix of domestic and international law. While at first sight it appears to comply with the standards of international law in its reliance on terminology such as 'crimes under international law', 'crimes against humanity', and 'war crimes', upon closer inspection the tribunal abandons the internationally recognized definitions for these terms, while not adhering to international human rights procedures and practices, relying on domestic law instead.

At the ICT, all defendants are political rivals of the Awami League government, mainly members of the Jamaat-e-Islami and the BNP. Some of those who fought on the side of the Bengali nationalists have been exempted from investigations of war crimes, partly as a result of Prime Minster Hasina's pledge in the Awami League 2008 election manifesto that the tribunal would restore 'the dignity and status of the freedom fighter … the greatest sons of the nation' (Robertson 2015: 12-13). This led to accusations of 'victor's justice' against the now commonly held belief in international law that those fighting for a winning side cannot be exempt from prosecution for that reason. Further doubts were raised over the proceedings when *The Economist* (2013) revealed that judges from the ICT has been in contact with members of the government about cases. The application of the death penalty has further fuelled criticism from human rights organizations and foreign governments.

The ICT thus seems to resonate with Wilson's observation that truth commissions and tribunals are set up to institutionalize history writing. While drawing on the ideological power of truth finding, they seek to instil moral values to construct a new vision of the nation subject to state morality and elite interests (Wilson 2003: 369). This hints at a broader flaw in contemporary models of these tribunals, exacerbated by the difficult political circumstances in Bangladesh, in that 'transparency of communication and clarity in reception are presumed; the unevenness of social field and their saturation with power are not' (Ross 2003: 327). As such, the tribunal functions as a 'transformative ritual' (Trouillot 2011: 174), central to the transformation of Bangladesh, changing the relationship to historical acts of violence by providing a more narrow, unidirectional narrative of the war through the institutionalization of victor's justice.

These contestations over the tribunal, in line with Robben's (2012) observations in Argentina, illustrate how tribunals can make reconciliation seem further away. What such discourses of reconciliation do not capture in their emphasis on building bridges between former enemies are nation-states' needs to redress past unresolved injustices, which can supersede the need to reconcile with the past. As a result, the ICT sought accountability and retributive justice, which included punishment and the death penalty for politically established collaborators.

Regardless of my critical engagement with the tribunal and discourses of reconciliation, I do not deny the need for a tribunal to address the violence that occurred during the Bangladesh War. However, I am sceptical about government interference and the decontextualized, floating uses of human rights terminology in its proceedings. Critique of the tribunal is uncomfortable because, for some, any criticism of the proceedings is taken as indicating solidarity with those on trial or those convicted. This development has been accompanied by the reduced independence of the judicial system and increasingly limited space for public debate, which has led to the increased use of antagonistic binary articulations of victims/perpetrators and liberators/collaborators. The final section of this paper essay unpacks tendencies towards irreconciliation in a human rights initiative that seeks to address the violence of the Bangladesh War from London.

The Sreeramshi Welfare Association

In the context of the hegemonic role of an international human rights regime since the 1990s, tribunals have been employed for nation building, especially in relation to establishing 'absolute truths' and constructing a shared vision of the nation (Asare 2018; Wilson 2003). An initiative in London influenced by human rights activism in the 1990s is a report on war crimes written by an organization called the Sreeramshi Welfare Association UK. The association is run by London-based expatriates from the village of Sreeramshi in Bangladesh's northeastern province of Sylhet. On 31 August 1971, the Pakistani army, assisted by local collaborators, rounded up and executed villagers in Sreereamshi who were suspected of aiding the Bangladesh nationalist movement. Forty years later, in 2011, the Sreeramshi Welfare Association published a report describing the war crimes committed. The report was handed in person to the High Commissioner to the United Kingdom for Bangladesh in London and sent to several government officials in Bangladesh while being directed to Shafique Ahmed, the then Minister for Law, Justice, and Parliamentary Affairs of Bangladesh, with the objective of bringing to court perpetrators of war crimes committed in Sreereamshi. The report urges the minister to start investigations against local collaborators and members of the Pakistani army who committed war crimes in the village. The signatories also ask the government to identify local collaborators so that 'exemplary punishment' can be inflicted on them through the ICT. They further request any information about members of the Pakistani army involved in the atrocities to be referred by the government to the International War Crimes Tribunal in the Hague in the Netherlands, because the Pakistani government does not recognize the ICT in Bangladesh.

The report is part of a broad range of activities that the association undertakes. According to the association, there are around 2,000 expatriates from the village living in the United Kingdom, while the village's population in Bangladesh numbers around

Journal of the Royal Anthropological Institute (N.S.) **28**, 65-78
© 2022 The Authors. *Journal of the Royal Anthropological Institute* published by John Wiley & Sons Ltd on behalf of Royal Anthropological Institute.

6,000 people. The UK association engages in the administration of the village, including social, political, and economic functions, as part of wider transnational networks between Sylhet and London that are shaped by kinship structures (see also Gardner 1993; 2008). It further organizes an annual commemoration and prayer ceremony for the victims of the massacre that took place in the village during the Bangladesh War, which is held in the Brick Lane Mosque in the London borough of Tower Hamlets. The 'Londoni' network gives the village access to the Bangladesh government that is uncommon for other comparable villages in the country. The signatories use this access to ask the government to identify local collaborators so that they can be prosecuted through the ICT. Written in English, the report states that:

> The objective of this submission is to bring the war criminals to justice on the following grounds; a) that it is a moral and ethical imperative on us as a nation to punish these war criminals for their heinous and inhuman crimes, b) that it is an obligation for us as a nation to establish what they did was wrong and c) it is also imperative on us as a nation to set a precedent so any nation at war never again dares to commit such heinous and brutal atrocities against civilians and transgress the civilized code of honour and conduct (Miah & Ali 2011: 6).

The use of international human rights language in the memorandum serves to highlight the obligation of the nation to be 'good', while setting an internationally recognized precedent by using the terms 'war criminals' and 'justice' and the trope 'never again'. These terms serve to appeal to the 'moral and ethical imperative' of the nation to make a claim of justice as punishment, allowing activists to make claims to national institutions. This process is informed by transnational activism that facilitates the travel of these discourses while being rearticulated in the light of nation-building efforts. The state has an important role in framing specific initiatives, which point to recent changes in hierarchies in which an authoritarian political system has cemented the narrow framing of national articulations.

Human rights reports, such as the report above, are important sites for the transnational circulation of human rights violations and tend to draw on international human rights discourses that facilitate their acceptance in the public sphere (see Kennedy 2014). However, when primarily directed at national governments, the selective use of human rights language in such reports can serve to reinforce nationalist claims and lead to competitive, absolutist rhetoric. This necessitates accounting for how such human rights reports are also shaped by national discourses around violent pasts, which are in turn influenced by legal and political frameworks that need to be understood in the light of their discursive trajectories.

For this example, the use of international human rights language in the memorandum serves to highlight the obligation of the nation to be 'good', while setting an internationally recognized precedent through the decontextualized use of the Holocaust trope of 'never again'. The use of 'never again' is central to understanding references made to other violent events in the remainder of the memorandum, as well as the objectives set out in the above. In the Bangladeshi context, 'never again' is a primary example of a genocidal cosmopolitanism, described by Mookherjee as 'a process which describes genocides through the evocation of various local, national and global tropes' (2011: S80) at 'innumerable junctions of Bangladesh's fractured historical and political trajectory' (2011: S87). It allows the initiators to engage in a conversation through the aesthetics of 'never again' while teasing out the 'implications for the Bangladeshi nation' (2011: S73). The trope serves to appeal to the 'moral and ethical imperative' of the nation

Journal of the Royal Anthropological Institute (N.S.) **28**, 65-78

of Bangladesh, which the memorandum refers to, and to make a claim for justice for the nation. At the same time, the memorandum invokes the Holocaust as 'a zero-sum game of competition with memory over other histories' (Rothberg 2009: 9), by narrating the war as exceeding all other acts of genocidal violence that have taken place in the world.

> It should be commented upon that the atrocities committed by the Pakistani Army exceeded even the brutalities committed in My Lai (Vietnam) by the USA, Illa [sic] (Iraq) by the USA, Shrevernitza [sic] (Bosnia) by the Serbs and the crimes committed by Adolf Hitler during the Second World War (Miah & Ali 2011: 6).

The common uses of genocidal cosmopolitan tropes in the Bangladeshi context, articulated while making demands on the Bangladeshi state, further provide new insights into the ways in which activists, by drawing on tropes associated with transnational justice, close off more reconciliatory engagements with the national past. By emphasizing that the atrocities of the Bangladesh War are the worst atrocities ever, the report places the events outside the possibility of a dialogue over the war, and sketches the future of the nation as irreconcilable. By demanding an absolute victory, a situation in which scores have been settled and unwanted aspects of the nation are removed, the nation is cleansed. Combined, the emphasis on the punishment of war criminals and the incomparability of the crimes displayed in the report of the Sreeramshi Welfare Association illustrate how the nation, in a future state rid of the 'inhumanity' and the wrongs committed by the losing side in the war, is reclaimed as pure and moral.

Conclusion

Through a discussion of transnational human rights activism around the ICT in Dhaka, I have demonstrated how efforts to address the violence of the Bangladesh War from London are best understood through a lens of irreconciliation. Although framed as part of human rights discourses commonly associated with broader aims of reconciliation, the activities of Bangladeshi human rights activists end up promoting irreconciliation. It is important to take seriously these reconciliatory sentiments, both because they occupy such a prominent place in the Bangladesh context, and because these responses help demonstrate a wider range of reactions of people to past atrocities. These ways of addressing atrocity are not captured in many transitional justice initiatives as they do not fulfil the demand of forgiveness (Brudholm & Rosoux 2009). The activists involved in the initiatives do not see the scope for such forgiveness as an essential precondition for addressing the problem of wrongdoing (Arendt 1998 [1958]) as they do not see a possibility of coming to terms with the past. These past injustices are, by definition, irreconcilable as no act can undo the initial injustice (see Thompson 2010). In the Bangladesh case, the silence on the atrocities committed by so-called collaborators in the Bangladesh War has prevented the acknowledgement of past wrongs, and so perhaps made the inability to seek justice for these acts more pronounced than elsewhere. These persisting inequalities as a result of past atrocities, and ways to reverse them through justice as reckoning, permeate the different examples in this essay. Addressing the violence of the Bangladesh War takes the form of victor's justice and punishment, emphasizing futures in which enemies no longer exist. In these initiatives, the abstract language of human rights calls for the prosecution in terms of justice, but reframes justice so that it comes to be equated with an impossibility to reconcile people on opposing sides during the war.

Journal of the Royal Anthropological Institute (N.S.) **28**, 65-78
© 2022 The Authors. *Journal of the Royal Anthropological Institute* published by John Wiley & Sons Ltd on behalf of Royal Anthropological Institute.

Acknowledgements

I am grateful to Nayanika Mookherjee for her helpful feedback on earlier versions of this essay, and for organizing a panel to develop this special issue on irreconciliation at the American Anthropological Association in Vancouver in November 2019. I also want to express my thanks to two anonymous peer reviewers for their constructive comments. Finally, I am indebted to all those in London who helped me gain an insight into the limitations of reconciling the atrocities of the Bangladesh War.

NOTE

[1] There are members of the UK diaspora who want to reconcile. However, this reconciliation does not seem to entail reconciliation about the Bangladesh War but rather a majority of the diaspora identifying with Islam as a key marker of identity which provides ways of everyday reconciliation. Such everyday acts of reconciliation in the United Kingdom, which often exist across communities around the axis of minoritarian identities, are beyond the remit of this essay. The focus in this essay, instead, is specifically on the Bangladesh War and a group of human rights activists seeking to influence politics and governance in Bangladesh in relation to how the war is addressed.

REFERENCES

ALEXANDER, C. 2013. Contested memories: the Shahid Minar and the struggle for diasporic space, *Ethnic and Racial Studies* **36**, 590-610.

ARENDT, H. 1998 [1958]. *The human condition* (Second edition). Chicago: University Press.

ASARE, A. 2018. *Truth without reconciliation: a human rights history of Ghana*. Philadelphia: University of Pennsylvania Press.

BRUDHOLM, T. & V. ROSOUX 2009. The unforgiving: reflections on the resistance to forgiveness after atrocity. *Law and Contemporary Problems* **72**, 33-50.

CHOPRA, S. 2015. The International Crimes Tribunal in Bangladesh: silencing fair comment. *Journal of Genocide Research* **17**, 211-20.

CRAPANZANO, V. 2020. The contortions of forgiveness: betrayal, abandonment and narrative entrapment among the Harkis. In *The interview: an ethnographic approach* (ed.) J. Skinner, 195-210. London: Routledge.

DAILY STAR 2020. War Criminal Mueen in UK: Nirmul Committee slams 'audacious' lawsuit, hails Patel. 21 July (available online: *https://www.thedailystar.net/city/news/war-criminal-mueen-uk-nirmul-committee-slams-audacious-lawsuit-hails-patel-1933605*, accessed 18 March 2022).

DERRIDA, J. 2001. *On cosmopolitanism and forgiveness* (trans. M. Dooley & M. Hughes). London: Routledge.

ECONOMIST 2013. Another kind of crime. 23 March (available online: *http://www.economist.com/news/leaders/21573990-bangladeshs-war-crimes-tribunal-sullying-its-judicial-and-political-systems-another-kind?zid=306&ah=1b164dbd43b0cb27ba0d4c3b12a5e227*, accessed 18 March 2022).

FELDMAN, S. 2015. Bangladesh in 2014: illusive democracy. *Asian Survey* **55**, 67-74.

GARDNER, K. 1993. Desh-Bidesh: Sylheti images of home and away. *Man* (N.S.) **28**, 1-15.

——— 2008. Keeping connected: security, place, and social capital in a 'Londoni' village in Sylhet. *Journal of the Royal Anthropological Institute* (N.S.) **14**, 477-95.

GLYNN, S. 2006. The spirit of '71: how the Bangladeshi War of Independence has haunted Tower Hamlets. *Socialist History Journal* **29**, 56-75.

IMAM, J. & S. KAMAL 1994. *Report on the findings of the People's Inquiry Commission on the activities of the war criminals and the collaborators*. Dhaka: Ekattorer Ghatak Dala Nirmul Committee.

KAPRALSKY, S. 2014. Memory, identity, and Roma transnational nationalism. In *Transnational memory: circulation, articulation, scales* (eds) C. De Cesari & A. Rigney, 195-217. Berlin: de Gruyter.

KENNEDY, R. 2014. Moving testimony: human rights, Palestinian memory, and the transnational public sphere. In *Transnational memory: circulation, articulation, scales* (eds) C. De Cesari & A. Rigney, 51-78. Berlin: de Gruyter.

LEVY, D. & N. SZNAIDER 2006. *The Holocaust and memory in the global age*. Philadelphia: Temple University Press.

MEISTER, R. 2011. *After evil*. New York: Columbia University Press.

MIAH, A.L. & A. ALI 2011. A memorandum to Barrister Shafique Ahmed, Minister for Law, Justice and Parliamentary Affairs, the People's Republic of Bangladesh. Unpublished document.

MOOKHERJEE, N. 2011. 'Never again': aesthetics of 'genocidal' cosmopolitanism and the Bangladesh Liberation War Museum. *Journal of the Royal Anthropological Institute* **17**: S1, S71-91.

———— 2015. *The spectral wound: sexual violence, public memories, and the Bangladesh War of 1971*. Durham, N.C.: Duke University Press.

———— 2020. Affective Justice Symposium: law's emotional (im)possibilities. *Opinio Juris*, 26 May (available online: *https://opiniojuris.org/2020/05/26/affective-justice-symposium-laws-emotional-impossibilities/*, accessed 18 March 2022).

Moyn, S. 2017. *Human rights and the uses of history*. London: Verso.

Nader, L. 1991. *Harmony ideology: justice and control in a Zapotec mountain village*. Stanford: University Press.

———— 2002. *The life of the law: anthropological projects*. Berkeley: University of California Press.

Reich, W. 2006. Unwelcome narratives: listening to suppressed themes in American Holocaust testimonies. *Poetics Today* **27**, 463-72.

Rigney, A. 2012. Reconciliation and remembering: (how) does it work? *Memory Studies* **5**, 251-8.

Robben, A. 2012. From dirty war to genocide: Argentina's resistance to national reconciliation. *Memory Studies* **5**, 305-15.

Robertson, G. 2015. *Report on the International Crimes Tribunal of Bangladesh*. Sarajevo: International Forum for Democracy and Human Rights.

Ross, F. 2003. On having voice and being heard. *Anthropological Theory* **3**, 325-41.

Rothberg, M. 2009. *Multidirectional memory: remembering the Holocaust in the age of decolonization*. Stanford: University Press.

Ruud, A. 2018. The Osman Dynasty: the making and unmaking of a political family. *Studies in Indian Politics* **6**, 209-24.

———— & M. Islam 2016. Political dynasty formation in Bangladesh. *South Asia: Journal of South Asian Studies* **39**, 401-14.

Sen, J. 2012. The trial of errors in Bangladesh: the International Crimes (Tribunals) Act and the 1971 War Crimes Act. *Harvard Asia Quarterly* **14**: **3**, 33-43.

Thompson, J. 2010. Is apology a sorry affair? Derrida and the moral force of the impossible. *The Philosophical Forum* **41**, 259-74.

Trouillot, M. 2011. Abortive rituals: historical apologies in the global era. *Interventions: International Journal of Postcolonial Studies* **2**, 171-86.

Van Schendel, W. 2009. *A history of Bangladesh*. Cambridge: University Press.

Visser, J. 2019. Bangladesh's 'Father of the Nation' and the transnational politics of memory: connecting cross-scale iterations of Sheikh Mujibur Rahman. *International Journal of Politics, Culture and Society* **32**, 163-79.

———— 2020. 'May you live with us forever Father!': Rethinking state and kinship among Bangladeshi long-distance nationalists in London. *Contributions to Indian Sociology* **54**, 259-79.

Wilson, R. 2003. Anthropological studies of national reconciliation processes. *Anthropological Theory* **3**, 367-87.

Zeitlyn, B. 2014. Watching the International Crimes Tribunal from London. *South Asia Multidisciplinary Academic Journal* **9**, 1-18.

« Je célébrais la justice qu'ont reçu les victimes » : explorer l'irréconciliation parmi les activistes des droits humains bangladais à Londres

Résumé

Le présent essai se penche sur les réseaux transnationaux d'activistes des droits humains réclamant justice pour les crimes de guerre commis pendant la Guerre du Bangladesh de 1971, en particulier à la lumière des auditions du Tribunal pénal international de Dacca au Bangladesh. Centré sur des activistes à Londres, il démontre la nécessité d'approcher les initiatives de justice transitionnelle du point de vue discursif et ethnographique, afin de ne pas perdre de vue les manières dont l'utilisation des concepts de droits humains peuvent masquer les dimensions de pouvoir sous des abstractions légalistes et universalistes. L'article explore l'approche des atrocités de la guerre par la cartographie des voyages et des usages des tropes des droits humains servant à formuler les revendications de justice. Il montre comment, en examinant la violence de la guerre au Bangladesh, la justice et le châtiment par les vainqueurs sont mis en lumière, tandis que l'on imagine des futurs dans lesquels les ennemis n'existent plus. Dans les exemples, le langage de la justice est employé pour appeler à poursuivre les coupables mais la justice est recadrée pour l'ajuster à l'impossibilité de réconcilier ceux qui se sont affrontés pendant la guerre.

Journal of the Royal Anthropological Institute (N.S.) **28**, 65-78

5

Perpetration, impunity, and irreconciliation in Canada's Truth and Reconciliation Commission on Indian Residential Schools

RONALD NIEZEN *McGill University*

The influence of institutional mandates on knowledge can be seen particularly clearly in the preferences and absences of truth and reconciliation commission (TRC) proceedings. A recent trend in TRCs involves a shift away from the exercise of judicial powers and the quest for justice and towards more concern with affirming the experience of victims or 'Survivors'. Canada's TRC on Indian Residential Schools illustrates the consequences of the shift towards victim-centrism, which left gaps in knowledge – particularly about perpetrators – that was conveyed to the commission and produced conditions of impunity for those responsible for mass harm. This impunity coalesced into irreconciliation as the commission gave voice to people who had been forgotten, marginalized, and given little chance in life, while leaving out of the picture those who had actually stolen their lives and dignity.

Wilton Littlechild, addressing a rapt audience at a side event of the 2016 meeting of the United Nations Permanent Forum on Indigenous Issues, carried the authority of someone who had served as commissioner for Canada's Truth and Reconciliation Commission (TRC) on Indian Residential Schools and who himself was a residential school Survivor (spelled with a capital 'S' in the commission documents). Just a few months previously, the commission had completed its hearings and submitted its report, with ninety-four wide-ranging 'Calls to Action', the culmination of its ambitions for social reform.[1] Littlechild began by describing the work of the commission from its first meeting in Winnipeg in 2010 to the submission of its final report in Ottawa in December 2015, with an emphasis on the experience of Survivors and their families. Explaining how the commissioners approached the 'sacred trust' of their work for the commission, Littlechild pointed to a basic premise on which all of its hearings were based: 'We thought we should get guidance from the Survivors themselves'. Based on this guidance, the commission set itself the task of hearing from and supporting the Survivors, while recognizing how difficult it was for them to give expression to painful memories. The documents, transcripts, and audio and video recordings provided by those who gave statements were to be housed in the National Centre for Truth and

Reconciliation hosted by the University of Manitoba. Based on that essential starting point, the rest would follow. 'We take that truth', Littlechild said, 'and try to shape reconciliation'. With these words, he received a standing ovation.[2]

I begin this essay with Littlechild's address at the Permanent Forum because it introduces the conditions that led Canada's TRC in a direction that does not at all correspond to the usual meanings of the term 'reconciliation'. The commission became much more than a source of audience approval or receptacle of knowledge; it brought the categories of *survivor* and *perpetrator* sharply into focus and made the status of 'residential school Survivor' a positive source of identity.

An important quality of Canada's TRC, perhaps *the* defining feature in comparison with other commissions, is the fact that there was no change of regime at its origin. It was not formed in the aftermath of war or revolution followed by constitutional renewal. Its origins were in a flood of lawsuits against the churches and the government responsible for the schools. This means that Littlechild's goal of 'shaping reconciliation' was in one sense foreclosed from the beginning. Similar to the post-atrocity situation in Bangladesh discussed by Visser elsewhere in this issue, there was no pre-conflict state to be returned to, no rectification of injustice or form of compensation capable of redressing the mass harm in question. In Canada, this was quite simply because the harm, in different forms, was ongoing.

When the commission completed its work and submitted its six-volume final report in 2015, it had gathered statements over a period of five years from some 6,750 people in 1,355 hours of recording.[3] These statements provide a harrowing picture of the schools, including stories of emotional, physical, and sexual abuse. Approximately 150,000 Indigenous students had been housed – or incarcerated, since students were often prevented from returning home during holidays or receiving visits from family members – in 139 federally funded (but church-operated) Indian residential schools in Canada.[4] At least 4,118 students died while incarcerated in the schools, a figure arrived at through the ongoing work of a National Residential School Student Death Register.[5] The schools were in existence for over a century, with the last school finally closing in 1996. Some 80,000 of these students are alive today.[6]

This sketch of the conditions of mass harm resulting from the Indian residential school system brings into relief the problem of what to do in the aftermath of atrocity. The pathway followed by Canada's TRC corresponds fairly closely to what some see as a wider shift in the direction taken by truth commissions, which are now generally less concerned with the exercise of judicial powers and the quest for justice and more concerned with affirming the experience of victims or 'Survivors'.

Truth commissions began with a regional focus in Latin America and with a tendency towards judicial inquiry, investigating crimes of the state, identifying the institutions and individuals responsible, and issuing recommendations oriented towards facilitating transitions from impunity and abuse to democracy (Hayner 2011; James 2017). The South African TRC of the 1990s offered a different model, with 'reconciliation' as the key ingredient that influentially reshaped the idea of the truth commission. A significant literature has emerged that points to the values of the South African TRC as having been taken up in a wider, almost global shift towards 'victim-centrism'. Nneoma Nwogu (2010), for example, in a study of truth commissions that aspire to overcome the harms of ethnicity-based violence in Africa, finds a tendency for the categories of 'victim' and 'perpetrator' to be essentialized and for commissions to shy away from exploration of the complex motivations behind violent actions. Adam

Kolchanscki puts such local observations to the test in a global comparison of forty-four truth commissions that took place between 1974 and 2015. Among the trends he identifies are those towards multifaceted mandates that emphasize performative public truth telling and away from support for human rights-based prosecutions (Kolchanski 2020: 127).

Canada's TRC was similarly victim-centric. Its mandate and educational, publicity-oriented goals combined to produce the reification of Survivor experience, with a focus on sexual abuse, trauma, and crises of cultural loss, along with the reinvigoration of Indigenous cultural traditions. Yet, as I will show here, the ennoblement and restoration of Survivor identity within a limited bandwidth of experience obscured the complete range of the consequences of – and responsibility for – violence and suffering.

When we consider what those who survived mass atrocity *actually* say, or want to say, it becomes clear that truth commissions are often conduits of very limited ranges of ideas, which, in turn, obscure the nature and consequences of harm. It is only when they speak away from the templates and exclusions of formal efforts towards truth telling that the varied forms of their views and experiences come to light.

In this essay, I want to show how a narrow range of testimony oriented towards affirmation of victim experience may well accomplish many goals of restoring dignity and shaping public opinon, but at the same time it limits the ability of the commission and the nation as a whole to grapple with *perpetration*. This limitation can be seen at three levels of involvement with mass harm that correspond to three kinds of perpetrators, each of which invites a different form of intervention: (1) *criminal perpetrators*, those who as individuals committed crimes within the wider context of mass harm; (2) perpetrators-by-association or accomplices, those whom the TRC identifies as *participants* in the institutions and actions of mass harm without themselves being directly implicated in any crime; and (3) members of the wider *public* as the ultimate source of support of the policies that resulted in mass harm, which introduces questions of collective responsibility and guilt.

The TRC's focus on victim affirmation as a pathway to healing and reconciliation avoided the narrow conceptions of harm and procedural quagmires that tend to result from legal procedure; but in producing a mandate removed of all judicial authority, it bypassed the opportunity to inquire meaningfully into the origins and motivations of perpetration in its varied forms, including through recommending prosecution or even identifying those responsible for the worst harm. The conditions of victim-centrism with which Canada's TRC conducted its work invite us to reflect on Nayanika Mookherjee's conception of irreconciliation as a 'vigilance against impunity', which she presents in the introduction to this issue. Irreconciliation took root in blanket conditions of impunity as the commission gave voice to Survivors, whose traumatic experience of the schools often coincided with ongoing conditions of precarity and loss of dignity.

The method in the mandate

I want to clothe my discussion of Survivor narratives, perpetration, and impunity with insights drawn from an ethnographic study of Canada's TRC. To go beyond the flood of public statements put out by the commission, I engaged in what might be called 'institutional ethnography' or 'event ethnography', or, better, a combination of both. Together with a team of research assistants (numbering between one and five in each event), I took part in all seven of the Commission's National Events (in

Winnipeg, Halifax, Inuvik, Saskatoon, Vancouver – which I followed through the TRC's livestream on the internet – Montreal, and Edmonton), as well as a regional event (Victoria), two community events (Iqaluit and Ottawa), and the closing ceremonies (Ottawa). My assistants and I recorded and transcribed many of the official speeches and hundreds of the statements made at these events. I also went further afield by staying for three days in the residence for retired Oblate priests in Albertville and four days in the parish headquarters in Iqaluit. In these places of retreat, I took an informal, non-directive approach to hearing the priests' views of the ongoing commission. I also interviewed sixteen Oblate priests and brothers in their residences in Montreal, Albertville (near Edmonton, Alberta), Ottawa, Iqaluit, and Winnipeg, as well as eleven grey sisters in two group interviews in Winnipeg. My assistants and/or I completed a dozen interviews with school Survivors and seven interviews with employees of the commission, including those responsible for 'health support' during the National Events (Niezen 2016: 925). This, at any rate, was the methodological background to my discussion of Canada's TRC in *Truth and indignation* (2017).

My research did not end with the submission of the commission's six-volume report in December 2015. I attended the 2016 Session of the UN Permanent Forum on Indigenous Issues, at which there was considerable attention given to Canada's change of government (with representatives of a newly sworn-in government of Justin Trudeau attending), including the work of the just-completed TRC. As a member of McGill University's Faculty of Law, I also participated in the process of implementing the Commission's 'Calls to Action' that related to Indigenous participation in higher education and in bringing Indigenous legal traditions to the Faculty. What I was not able to accomplish in terms of an uninterrupted study of the commission, I tried to make up for by long-term engagement with the subject matter.

None of this attention to the variety of events and the aftermath of the commission, however, would have resulted in worthwhile observations if I had not also paid attention to a document that was not part of the visible spectrum of ethnographic observation: the TRC's mandate.[7] While notions of the personal encounter at the heart of ethnographic inquiry might lead one to be averse to wading through the content of legal documents, it is in the commission's terms of reference that we find the essence of what it does and the limits of what it cannot do.

Canada's TRC was established in 2008 as one outcome of the 2007 Indian Residential Schools Settlement Agreement, which resulted from thousands of individual and class action lawsuits against the government and churches by former students. This agreement was far-reaching and multidimensional. It included several years of funding for the Aboriginal Healing Foundation (which dealt largely with the mental health impacts of residential schools), and a compensation package that was to exceed C$3 billion (equivalent to US$2.3 billion today), at the time the largest judicial settlement in Canadian history.

Compensation was divided between a Common Experience Payment (CEP) for all those who could document their attendance at a recognized Indian residential school and an Independent Assessment Process (IAP), which established a system of out-of-court hearings and financial compensation for those who experienced harm in the schools. The settlement agreement also brought into being the TRC and a National Centre for Truth and Reconciliation where the information the commission gathered would be kept.

While many TRCs are 'victim-centric', Canada's commission was noteworthy in terms of the extent to which its mandate excluded judicial powers.[8] It could not hold formal hearings or act as a public inquiry, and it had no subpoena powers to compel unwilling witnesses to give testimony. This left it with solely voluntary participants: those who wanted to tell their stories. They were not referred to as 'witnesses' in the judicial sense, were not cross-examined or subjected to any factual substantiation, and, what is more, they were not allowed to reveal the identity of anyone they remembered as being an un-prosecuted perpetrator of a crime.

This non-judicial mandate also meant that those federal officials who established or implemented the residential school policy were under no obligation to offer statements. The federal government kept the events of the TRC at arm's length, with ministers or deputy ministers giving mostly non-committal statements supporting the activities of the commission. The churches sent high-level representatives to acknowledge responsibility, deliver eloquent apologies, and offer 'gestures of reconciliation' such as DVDs providing information about church-sponsored healing initiatives.

The strictly voluntary nature of testimony to a commission that had no judicial powers was not straightforwardly imposed by the government and the churches in efforts to limit the criminal liability and public exposure of 'naming names' in the commission's hearings. Rosemary Nagy's (2014) detailed and nuanced account of the Settlement Agreement negotiations shows a complex variety of actors and interests at the table. These included, initially, a tense difference of approach between the Assembly of First Nations (AFN), which sought mechanisms of judicial accountability inspired by the International Center for Transitional Justice (ICTJ) (also present at the table), and the government of Canada, which pressed for (and ultimately achieved) a 'victim-centred' commission lacking judicial powers. A strange-bedfellows alignment in favour of victim affirmation came from Christian representatives, who emphasized the need for spiritual elements of reconciliation, and Survivor organizations, which placed emphasis on restorative justice, healing, and reconciliation. In pursuit of these values, the South African model (minus its subpoena powers and conditional amnesty for perpetrators who gave testimony) loomed large.[9] For Kathleen Mahoney, representing the AFN at the negotiating table, a considered view of the harmful consequences of litigation was ultimately paramount. She considered the experience of the Irish Truth Commission, which, in trying to investigate industrial schools using subpoena powers, became so paralysed with litigation that it was disbanded (Mahoney 2014: 7). This experience inclined her towards the view that 'healing and community-building remedies are antithetical to the adversarial, torts-based system that lawyers are used to as products of the Anglo-American legal system' (2014: 7).

The result of these negotiations was therefore a complex alignment of interests. The weak mandate of the Canadian commission spared the government from a wider, more dramatic public exposure of the crimes of the state. For their part, Survivors were encouraged to create an affirmative process for themselves, protected from possible encounters with unrepentant perpetrators, along with their denials, justifications, and distorted visions of history. The commission was purposefully defanged from the outset, with the goals of healing emphasized over the discomforts of facing, confronting, and hearing the words of those who fitted within (or were consigned to) the category of perpetrators.

Journal of the Royal Anthropological Institute (N.S.) **28**, 79-94
© Royal Anthropological Institute 2022.

Survivor-centrism

Unlike, say, the aftermath of a civil war or of apartheid in South Africa, where the abuses of the state were widely known and experienced, Canada's commission assumed from the outset that most non-Indigenous Canadians did not know anything about residential schools. Thus, it took on the task of public education and of reforming the dominant historical narrative of the country.

To an unusual degree among truth commissions, it faced the challenge of persuasion, of convincing public audiences that the reality depicted in the trials and negotiations leading up to the Settlement Agreement had a historical dimension that called for reform of the dominant narrative of the state. The focus of the commission's efforts up to and including its closing ceremonies and the public unveiling of its six-volume final report in December 2015 involved outreach to conventional media outlets, local newspapers, journals, and televised news outlets that covered each of the National Events, as well as the use of the TRC's webpage, sponsored videos, Facebook page, and Twitter feed. As the TRC moved towards the completion of its mandate, this aspect of its work developed into a veritable campaign to convey information about the history of residential schools and the work of the commission.

How might the TRC have channelled narrated experience into basic, complementary essentialisms, while excluding the representation of unwelcome countervailing meaning? What are the processes that make it possible for some forms of experiences – and not others – to become, in a relatively short period, an essential, normal, natural, meaningful aspect of the self, in company with others – and in narrative performance before others?

In the Commissioners' Sharing Panels, usually held in conference centres with as many as 1,000 people in attendance, participants spoke into a microphone with quavering voices, often pausing for breath – receiving comfort from a friend or family member – sometimes hiding their trembling hands under the table, their images recorded and cast onto two giant screens behind them. The emotions of those who made statements were contagious. Mental health providers were available to offer comfort to those most openly expressing sympathetic grief. The commission also brought together Survivors in more intimate 'sharing circles' – groups free of stigma in which those who experienced the harm of the schools could safely recount their stories. They told stories dominated by themes of separation, confusion, loss, and abuse.

Affirmation in commission hearings occurred in part through what I refer to elsewhere as 'templates' (Niezen 2016; 2017). The TRC's templates were clearly recognizable in the opening speeches and early stages of the Commissioner's Sharing Panels, in which the organizers acted to 'set the tone', or, more instrumentally, try to establish thematic and behavioural patterns. On each of the opening days of the National Events in Inuvik and Halifax, for example, the commission screened 'highlight reels' of the most poignant statements of abuse, loss, and loneliness, and invited Survivors who were experienced in giving testimony to be the first to present public statements. The screening encouraged other former students to push past whatever inhibitions they might have had about publicly disclosing traumatic experiences and made it possible for survivors of abuse to speak. The films emphasized the themes of loss and suffering, both within the schools and in adult lives broken by the experience, the heightened emotion of grief (but within certain bounds of self-control and composure), and, in a closing narrative, a positive story of healing and rediscovery of that cultural heritage once slated for destruction through the schools.

Journal of the Royal Anthropological Institute (N.S.) **28**, 79-94
© Royal Anthropological Institute 2022.

These films were similar in thematic content and structure to material later posted on the TRC website, the main difference being the wider scope of the online video, which was able to draw from several National Events. In these films, the commission was able to select out many hours of video from community hearings those moments that resonated, that deftly captured not only what the speaker was trying to say, but also, more significantly, what the commission itself was trying to convey.

In the Commissioner's Sharing Panels, this kind of security and guidance for those on the list of speakers was also provided by preliminary, vetted, rehearsed testimony from individuals with experience in witnessing. This first set of witnesses at several of the National Events had been placed on the agenda and introduced by one of the commissioners, it would appear, not only because they tended to be confident in front of large audiences, but also because they had previously touched on themes emphasized by the commission. Effective stories have the capacity to shape the narrations and audience responses that follow, acting 'to set the tone' for the experience of bearing witness (Niezen 2017: 20).

These symbolic and storied expressions of school experience, whether intentionally or not, acted to establish narrative themes and encourage witnesses to publicly present their painful memories; and in the process they gave shape to emotional expression, opinion, and understandings of the history of institutional practice, ultimately to be made manifest in new categories and criteria of distress and belonging.

This affirmation of experience extended to what remained 'unsayable', the topics and opinions that tended to be absent or approached with caution. The things not being said tended to be the stories that did not evoke strong emotion. Former students tended not to come forward to publicly narrate ordinary experience in residential schools, the more commonplace, quotidian indignities of excessive discipline and the shared, yet deeply individual, loneliness of removal from families. It remained possible for them to make private statements, recorded or unrecorded; but they saw the stage as the wrong place for 'inconsequential' accounts of loneliness, drudgery, or petty indignities in their school experience. Those who thought of themselves as having suffered only minimally or not at all also believed they had little or nothing to say.

Impunity and irreconciliation

Others who had little or nothing to say to the commission were federal officials and former employees. In keeping with protocol, there were ministers or deputy ministers at the opening sessions of the Commissioner's Sharing Panels who usually said something supportive about the commission's work and then left to catch a plane.[10] But we never heard from the government people who ran the schools, the administrators, the inspectors, the school councillors, or people who filled other roles. There wasn't even a category for them in the form that had to be filled out before getting on the speakers' list. I found this puzzling, especially given that in 2005 the Supreme Court, in *Blackwater v. Plint*, attributed 75 per cent of the responsibility for the schools (and an equal proportion of their harm) to the federal government. Why, under these circumstances, was the government not a *constant* presence in the commission's activities?

In Canada's TRC, the idea of 'reconciliation' was fraught from the beginning. Survivors had to contend with the fact that, even though the schools had closed a little more than a decade previously, the regime that had brought about the school policy had never been replaced. There was no revolution or war that had toppled an illegitimate government and brought about demands for an inquiry into its past abuses.

Even though the last of the residential schools had closed in the mid-1990s, the system of governance, including many of the ideas that inspired the schools in their origins, were still very much present in their lives. To reconcile with a dominant society in these circumstances would mean accepting conditions that were the ultimate sources of their oppression.

One solution the commissioners found to address this problem of inherent irreconciliation at the national level was to look for reconciliation within families or communities. At each of the National Events, the commissioners hosted meetings oriented towards intra-family reconciliation, mostly among those who had been harmed by the intergenerational impacts of the schools. For Morley Googoo, addressing a gathering of the Outreach Residential School Atlantic Committee, the solution to the challenge of reconciliation was similarly to be found within: 'We have to reconcile among ourselves'.[11] This view was consistent with a consensus in this meeting of Survivors, to the effect that 'Reconciliation starts at home', and 'We've always had knowledge about how to reconcile', at least in the sense of restoring peace among those in conflict in the community.[12]

In the truth sharing of commission hearings, this understanding of reconciliation sometimes extended into transgressive political statements emphasizing the state's reconciliatory obligations. At the Saskatchewan National Event in June 2012, for example, residential school Survivor Myrna Whiteduck challenged Aboriginal Affairs Minister John Duncan, who had spoken before her, urging him to withdraw Canada's appeal against a human rights complaint on differential funding for First Nations child welfare (Nagy 2012: 65). She framed her intervention with the idea that 'reconciliation means reparation'.[13] And in Montreal in April 2013, Alvin Tolley was among those for whom hope lay in international criminal law: 'To have a true reconciliation we are asking justice from the International [Criminal] Court to resolve Canada's genocide'.[14] With a mandate and events that emphasized permissive truth sharing from Survivors, the idea of reconciliation, like other key terms that guided the commission, was obliquely challenged through impromptu expressions of ideas, impressions, stories, and experiences.

The commission events were sites at which conceptions of perpetration were assumed and occasionally contested, but almost always in the absence of those categorized as perpetrators. The testimonial practices of the commission reflected conditions of impunity for those responsible for mass harm that began with exclusion of judicial powers and extended into *knowledge* of perpetration. The commission and its participants worked within these conditions of absence at three levels: *criminal perpetrators*, *participants*, and the *public*.

Criminal perpetrators

The silence from and about perpetrators was consistent with the commission's sharply limited judicial powers (as I discussed above). Survivors did not always accept this limitation; and consistent with almost any effort to restrict the accepted range of human expression, they found ways around it. Sylvester Green, recalling his statement about the Edmonton Residential School to one of the Survivor Committee's Sharing Panels in a YouTube video, offers an example: 'I said, this is all bullshit. Here's the names of the people that abused me, three white assholes that abused me in Edmonton. [*Gives the names.*] These bastards, they are the ones that abused me when I was a little kid'. In his use of social media to express indignation, Green is refusing the legally circumscribed templates of the commission and engaging in doxing as the only form of justice left available to him.

The full extent of these conditions of impunity became more evident after the commission had completed its work. As a part of the tasks set out in the Indian Residential School Settlement Agreement (IRSSA), the government contracted seventeen private investigation firms to locate those people who were accused of physically and sexually abusing students in federal Indian residential schools. These investigations eventually resulted in a list of 5,315 alleged abusers, including both employees and students in the schools. On the surface, the list may seem to have offered a solid foundation for the kind of justice that many school Survivors (like Sylvester Green, cited above) were hoping would be an outcome of the Settlement Agreement. The purpose of identifying these individuals, however, was *not* to investigate the accusations with a view to possibly pressing criminal charges, but to invite them to participate in IAP hearings in which their names had been mentioned in testimony. These IAP hearings were being held in parallel to the TRC events, to determine compensation for residential school Survivors who claimed to have been harmed while resident in a school.[15] Investigators were responsible merely for locating the accused, not inquiring into the accusations against them. Only 708 alleged abusers of the 5,315 located by investigators agreed to participate in the IAP hearings (Troian 2016). With no power to compel evidence, the commission was left with scant information about the perpetrators and their motives, or about the institutions that harboured them. Such perspectives remained largely confined to what could be gleaned from documents, unembellished by the emotion and immediacy of public testimony.

Aside from questions of impunity and (in)justice, why is it important to *understand* the perpetrators of mass atrocity? Why in particular delve into the motives of those who were violent towards children, paedophiles in particular? The absence of perpetrators from the work of the commission facilitated the construction of labels that foreclosed further inquiry into the living, breathing, offending individuals behind them. When someone is labelled a paedophile, all interest in them becomes itself a transgression. If we are actually committed to preventing a form of violence from happening again, wouldn't it behove us to better know what happened, including from the perspective of the offenders who committed the greatest harm? If one seeks meaningful affirmation of victims, one has to understand those who harmed them. Preventing repetition of mass harm begins with knowledge of the individuals responsible for it and their motivations at its origin.

Participants

A broader category of perpetrator includes those who participated in the harm without incurring criminal liability. This is another of the blind spots of victim-centric truth commissions more generally. What are the views and experiences of those who accepted the institutional premises of mass harm and even went so far as to make them a foundation of their values and life commitments? And how might their understanding of their role in the harm have changed through the influence of truth telling?

The churches did send high-level representatives who acknowledged responsibility, delivered eloquent apologies, and offered 'gestures of reconciliation'. But again, what about the people who ran the schools? I addressed this question, in part, outside the events of the commission, in conversation with the priests and brothers of the Missionary Oblates of Mary Immaculate and the grey sisters, the nuns, all of whom had some role in running the schools. The Oblates in Canada were once responsible for 60 per cent of the country's residential schools. They operate in three Oblate provinces that represent diverse ministries. Yet all those with whom I spoke conveyed broadly similar deflections and rejections of the TRC and its testimonies. Far from feeling reconciled with the Survivors, those who were collectively viewed as alleged 'perpetrators' were indignant and felt that they were themselves the victims of an injustice. They were never forced to confront the contrary opinions and experiences of those who were harmed by them, nor, with few exceptions, were they interested in doing so.[16] As I sat through these interviews, I couldn't help recalling the horrors I had heard from statements gathered by the commission and was struck by the interviewees' obliviousness to or denial of Survivors' experiences.

They uniformly rejected the accusations levelled at them. 'I never heard of the, [what] they call, the physical abuse and sexual abuse. I never heard of that', said one priest. 'I heard that years after I left there, when they started to sue me'. This priest was accused through the IAP; he was neither brought under criminal charges nor exonerated. One priest, proudly recalling the military drills given to students in the Fort Qu'Appelle Indian Residential School in Saskatchewan, exclaimed, 'We gave them personalities!' The drills were to him character-forming in the sense that the students did not have characters before being subjected to them. The values of assimilation in their statements were undiminished and unapologetic: 'They keep their culture with language', said another priest. '[We] give them the tools to survive in this new society where they're dominated by Europeans or whites … You need new skills. Integration'.

It was not only the ordinary clergy who remained largely out of the picture. Through the commission's regime of 'truth telling', the federal government remained largely an abstraction, a source of policy, funding, and administration, an occasional irritant in the form of brief appearances by ministers or their representatives, but not a subject of far-reaching inquiry. The federal government's presence and participation at the TRC meetings was, for the most part, formal and formulaic, this despite the fact that the government was primarily responsible for the residential school policy, the schools' funding, and, ultimately, providing oversight of the operation of the schools themselves.

The commissioners did not draw attention to this absence. Through its mandate, the commission both navigated and reinforced conditions of impunity. And even when the absence of officialdom was noted by Survivors, as very occasionally happened, the focus of the hearings soon returned to the churches as the most immediate, remembered source of their suffering. Those with experience administering and operating the schools, whether under the auspices of the federal government or the churches, rarely showed any interest in sharing their stories, and the commission had no leverage to compel or induce them to do so.

That is to say, there were yawning gaps in the narratives presented to and reported by the commission. Corresponding to these gaps, there were no 'history wars', no clashes between competing interpretations of the past, in either the commission's proceedings or the public reception of them. The priests, brothers, and nuns with whom I spoke simmered in anger in their retirement residences.

Many, if not most, Survivors, meanwhile, were perfectly happy to not hear from them. As one former student remarked to me in objecting to my reporting on interviews with clergy in a talk at McGill's Faculty of Law, 'The churches have had the dominant discourse for more than 100 years. Now it's our turn'. The experiences of Survivors were narrated in conditions of (in Audra Simpson's terms) a *refusal* to reconcile, in the sense of 'having their stories told for them' (2016: 328). Out of this mutual condition of refusal, there were no (or precious few) direct confrontations between those who held contrary views, not to mention anything resembling an official reckoning for the crimes (and criminals) of the state.

Publics

It is worth reiterating that Canada's TRC was not, strictly speaking, a 'transitional justice' initiative, at least not in the sense that it occurred in the aftermath of a war or revolution in which the actions of a criminal regime were discredited. If we combine this observation with the fact that perpetrators and other direct participants in the schools were largely absent from the work of the commission, the question of collective guilt then comes into prominence. To what extent were ordinary members of the public who supported residential school policy from a perspective of ignorance and prejudice ultimately responsible for things like the separation of families and loss of language that followed from the implementation of the school policy? If, as found in *Blackwater v. Plint*, the government of Canada was vicariously responsible for the harms that occurred in the schools, should not some of that responsibility also be attributed to the electorate that supported the government and its policies? Implicit behind the concept of cultural genocide that guided the commission (particularly in its final report) is the idea of genocide *tout court*, of a dominant culture, a settler society that through deeply held norms and values deems itself superior and condones the elimination of Indigenous cultures that it considers inferior.[17] How can we pinpoint responsibility for this ultimate source of mass harm if not by giving perpetration a collective dimension?

The question of German guilt for the Holocaust has produced some reflections that continue to be more broadly relevant to the challenge of collective guilt. To some, the prosecution of war criminals after the Second World War was incomplete. There remained the question of assigning (or self-assigning) some form of collective guilt to those who hold (or are seen to hold) responsibility for mass crime. Karl Jaspers identified this phenomenon in the immediate aftermath of the Second World War in a series of lectures on German guilt, with the Nuremberg Trials as a reference point: 'The citizen feels the treatment of his leaders as his own, even if they are criminals. In their persons the people are also condemned' (2001 [1947]: 46). Hannah Arendt, building on Jaspers' argument, points to the impunity that follows from a too-ready acceptance of collective responsibility for mass crime. 'The cry "We are all guilty" that at first hearing sounded so very noble and tempting has actually only served to exculpate to a considerable degree those who actually were guilty. Where all are guilty, nobody is' (Arendt 1987: 43).

This resonant, slogan-like idea, 'where all are guilty, nobody is', goes to the heart of Arendt's use of the term *non-reconciliation*, recast in Nayanika Mookherjee's introduction to this issue as *irreconciliation*. Collective guilt for mass crime was to her chimerical, an impossibility, because it invited no realistic response. Neither forgiveness nor justice is possible in response to acts that cannot be forgiven and for which no punishment is possible. This leaves non-reconciliation, rejection of the imperfect world and the pursuit of rebuilding the world anew.

There is a sense in which Canada's TRC unwittingly acted on this insight, through its efforts towards consciousness-raising and rebuilding public policy and politics at the foundation of ongoing injustice in Indigenous peoples' lives. Its events focused attention on 'truth sharing': that is to say, on encouraging, cultivating, and publicizing Survivor narratives as a way to shape opinion, and that effort, in turn, it saw as a way to recast the settler-Indigenous relationship.

However, media representations of the commission events, as Matt James says, 'show the almost total failure of mainstream discussions to grasp anything of the core reality that would prove so central to the TRC report: that residential schooling was part of a deliberate scheme of cultural genocide that aimed to further an agenda of land and sovereignty dispossession' (2017: 367). Rather, the reporting on themes of reconciliation tended overwhelmingly to be 'quietistic rather than substantive', expressing the commission's goals in 'affective terms of listening, learning, and goodwill' (James 2017: 365). Rosemary Nagy and Emily Gillespie, in an overview of media coverage during the TRC hearings, find that even when the commission began to bring substantive issues of sovereignty and dispossession more centrally into its events, the mainstream media 'exiled the broader colonial project to the periphery' (2015: 36). For example, panels in the Montreal National Event organized by the local Kanien'kehaka people that were oriented to issues of land rights, treaties, and gender equality were not considered newsworthy. 'Instead, reporting was primarily framed around survivor testimony and stories of individual abuse, forgiveness, and healing' (Nagy & Gillespie 2015: 8). The hollow media representations of public education tended to emphasize truth telling as therapy (see Niezen 2020). Witnessing, as part of the therapeutic paradigm of public confession, was seen as sufficient unto itself as a pathway towards reconciliation, as in the prevalent idea that 'Survivors, in speaking their truth, release settlers from their ignorance' (Nagy & Gillespie 2015: 38). This deafness to substantive issues of concern of the Survivors represents another, more general form of impunity, one in which the populace untimately responsible for conditions of harm and irreconciliation acted on the TRC's work through quietistic listening and expressions of regret and goodwill.

Against the limitations of public persuasion, there was a corresponding trespass by the commission, manifest in the ninety-four recommendations or 'Calls to Action' of its final report. These go well beyond the limited scope of its mandate, beyond even the prevalent themes of the commission's Suvivor-affirming events, and represent an effort to leverage policy to address the wide-ranging consequences of a long-term colonial relationship. Each of these 'Calls to Action' identifies a specific problem area of Indigenous peoples' relationship with the dominant society and governments and proposes basic outlines of policy engagement.[18]

There are already signs of the limits of the commission's 'Calls to Action' that highlight the inherent contradictions in seeking justice for Indigenous peoples in the context of a national economy based on natural resource extraction. Within months of closing the book on Canada's TRC (in November 2016), Prime Minister Trudeau approved the Kinder Morgan Trans Mountain pipeline expansion project, building on an existing 1,150-km pipeline from Edmonton to the Pacific coast, much of it through territories claimed by Indigenous peoples. It also rankles with many that there are some 480 outstanding Indigenous land claims in various stages of negotiation, adjudication, or review in Canada, many of them involving resource-rich territories.[19] The contours of the reception of the 'Calls to Action' are not dissimilar from the disjunctures between ready acceptance of goodwill and resistance to substance in the public's consumption of Survivor testimony. Simple notions of equity and access to services have always been easier for non-Indigenous publics in settler societies to accept than more fundamental and far-reaching claims of sovereignty and rights to land and resources.

Journal of the Royal Anthropological Institute (N.S.) **28**, 79-94
© Royal Anthropological Institute 2022.

'While I have the microphone'

Human actors will predictably go off any kind of tracks carefully laid for them. In keeping with this truism, the templates with which the commission ran its Sharing Panels were occasionally disrupted by Survivors who had their own things to say. They sometimes acted in opposition to the commission's testimonial preferences by adding complexity to the victim/perpetrator dichotomy. By conforming to and then trespassing beyond the proffered templates of truth telling, they offered alternative visions of injustice and impunity. In these 'while I have the microphone' moments, they often rejected the boundary that separated their remembrances of the schools from other, personally felt wrongs. The subjects preferred by Survivors and their audiences extended well beyond the mandate of the commission, to include a variety of ongoing forms of state-sponsored exclusion, dispossession, racism, and assaults to the pride of (and sometimes originating from) the community to which one belongs. This involved transgressing beyond commonly held notions of individual criminal perpetration in the schools to include the very kinds of prejudice, non-recognition, and indignity that go a long way towards explaining the schools' origins.

Publicly remembering the abuses of childhood led speakers almost seamlessly into accounts of political usurpation, unresolved treaty claims, the indignities of criminal prosecution, the apprehension and fostering of their children by provincial child protection agencies, the experience of ostracism in reserve communities, even the quality and price of the food available at the commission's event – any active, irritating, burning cause of indignation had the potential to find its way into witnesses' narrations.

The failings of the criminal justice system were especially often discussed by Survivors. Under circumstances in which 3 per cent of the adult Canadian population is Indigenous, while comprising 26 per cent of prison, Survivors often presented stories of arrest and incarceration, with rankling senses of injustice as an emotional backdrop.[20] Consistent with this theme, the TRC on Indian Residential Schools was soon followed by a similarly structured commission of inquiry into Missing and Murdered Indigenous Women, which pointed to inherent inequities and racism built into policing and criminal justice.

These 'moments' point to wider conditions of injustice and impunity that lay in the background of the work of the commission. A similar point is made by Paulette Regan, whose work with Indigenous communities in northern British Columbia leads her to take a strong stance on ongoing conditions of oppression: 'To those who argue that former IRS [Indian residential school] students should just get over it and move on, I say that asking victims to bury a traumatic past for the "greater good" of achieving reconciliation does not address the root of the problem – colonialism' (2010: 4).

Conclusions

The public orientations of truth commissions are shaped in important, but largely unrecognized, ways by the laws that bring those commissions into being, the powers they possess, and the approach they take to the 'victims' or 'survivors' of the abuse of states. The influence of the law can be seen in the preferences and absences of commission proceedings; these include the templates that shape survivor testimony and conditions of moral affirmation and insecurity that influence the presence or absence of those who give testimony and how their statements are presented and received.

Canada's TRC on Indian Residential Schools began with a mandate that prevented any kind of judicial reckoning for those responsible for abuse in the schools. The result was one of the more survivor-centric truth commissions in recent years. This victim-centric approach, which since the 1990s has become dominant in representations of atrocity and traumatic history, makes it difficult to fully understand the views and experiences of those who designed, implemented, and operated the instruments of harm. The goal of Survivor affirmation was accompanied by efforts to elicit the testimony of those who were the most traumatized and durably harmed by their school experience – and persuasive in their narration of it. Those who experienced abuse in the schools and shame in their adult lives had need of the restoration of their dignity. The commission's encouragement of Survivors included processes by which disparate experiences were shaped into a common historical narrative and idiom of personal experience.

The templates and exclusions of the commission, however, produced significant gaps in understanding and coming to terms with perpetration. Its mandate was designed not only to affirm and re-dignify the experience of Survivors, but also to establish conditions of impunity for those responsible for the harm of the schools. The limitations imposed on the commission go some way towards explaining the impossibility of reconciliation and, in Audra Simpson's (2017) terms, the *refusal* of Indigenous peoples to reconcile.

In this essay, I have approached perpetration and impunity broadly, to include those who committed crimes, those who participated in the harm, and the wider publics that supported the politics at the origin of the harm. Each area of perpetration and impunity was associated with its own form of refusal. The prohibition on 'naming names' and recommending perpetrators for prosecution was sometimes refused by those who had expected the commission to have greater judicial authority and to name and prosecute those who had harmed them. The relative absence of priests, brothers, and nuns from commission events resulted from a double refusal: that of many Survivors to willingly include them as 'truth tellers' and their own tendencies to refuse the legitimacy of the commission and the Survivors' experiences of crime and abuse on which it cast light. Government officials, too, were all but absent from the work of the commission. Finally, the media and their publics engaged in a refusal to go beyond the comfortable platitudes of goodwill and truth telling as therapy, or of what Nayanika Mookherjee in the introduction to this issue refers to as a '"window-dressed", symbolic performance of redress'. For its part, the commission transcended the limits of its original terms of reference with a surprise ending: the ninety-four 'Calls to Action', which refused the 'listening' orientation of its mandate and early hearings by wading deeply into the political.

The consequences of impunity are not limited to criminal justice but extend to the *knowledge* we have of perpetrators. This lack of knowledge, in turn, has consequences for redress and the prevention of harm. The commission was able to offer school Survivors respect, reverence, affirmation, healing rituals, and gift bags, but it was not able to bring wrongdoing individuals into the picture, to hear their part of the story, possibly to hear their expressions of regret; it was unable to overcome obfuscation, non-co-operation, and denial from responsible institutions and individuals. With attention focused on the pain, struggle, and redemption that characterized a particular kind of Survivor experience, the responsibility for atrocity escaped from view; and our knowledge of the perpetrators, their motives, and the institutions that harboured them was left obscured. The commission gave voice to people who had been forgotten, marginalized, and given little chance in life, while leaving out of the picture those who had actually stolen their lives and dignity.

Journal of the Royal Anthropological Institute (N.S.) **28**, 79-94
© Royal Anthropological Institute 2022.

Acknowledgements

The research for this essay was funded through an SSHRC Insight Grant, a Canada Research Chair in the Anthropology of Law, and the Katharine A. Pearson Chair in Civil Society and Public Policy. I am grateful to all those who spoke with me and in some cases invited me into their homes and lives, Survivors and clergy alike.

NOTES

[1] *https://web.archive.org/web/20200506065356/http://trc.ca/assets/pdf/Calls_to_Action_English2.pdf* (accessed 22 March 2022).

[2] Jody Wilson-Raybould (2016), as the (then) newly appointed Justice Minister in Justin Trudeau's government, expressed a different ambition for reconciliation in her address to the plenary of this same meeting: 'Beyond the necessary truth telling and healing, reconciliation requires laws to change and policies to be rewritten'.

[3] *https://ecampusontario.pressbooks.pub/indigstudies/chapter/truth-and-reconciliation-commission-of-canada/* (accessed 22 March 2022).

[4] Truth and Reconciliation Commission of Canada, *https://nctr.ca/about/* (accessed 22 March 2022).

[5] National Center for Truth and Reconciliation, University of Manitoba, *https://memorial.nctr.ca/?page_id=570* (accessed 22 March 2022).

[6] The figures of 86,000 and 80,000 for the number of living survivors were in wide use during the years when the TRC held its events, from 2010 to 2015. This figure has not since been updated, despite the decease of many Survivors.

[7] See the Indian Residential Schools Settlement Agreement, 2016, *http://www.residentialschoolsettlement.ca/irs%20settlement%20agreement-%20english.pdf* (accessed 22 March 2022).

[8] Mark Freeman (2006) identifies four main criteria of the investigative and reporting powers of truth commissions: (1) subpoena power, (2) search and seizure power, (3) the ability to organize public hearings, and (4) the power to attribute individual responsibility (i.e. to 'name names'). Of these, Canada's TRC only had authority to organize hearings.

[9] Phil Fontaine, former Grand Chief of the AFN and a participant in the negotiations of the Settlement Agreement as a representative of the survivors, expressed this view to me in a question-and-answer period after I had presented my work. In his account of the negotiations over the mandate of the TRC, he emphasized the needs of the survivors for affirmation and, in his brief remarks, did not mention the AFN's initial vision of an accountability process. Faculty of Law, University of Toronto, 9 February 2016.

[10] Article 10(A)(k) of Schedule N of the Settlement Agreement states that National Events of the Commission '*should*' include the participation of high-ranking government and church officials as a 'common component'. Since, based on this language, their presence at TRC National Events was not a formal requirement, I refer to it here as a matter of protocol.

[11] Chief Morley Googoo, statement to the Outreach Residential School Atlantic Committee, meeting under the auspices of the Atlantic Policy Congress of First Nations Chiefs Secretariat, Glooscap Heritage Centre, Millbrook, Nova Scotia, 6 March 2012.

[12] Interview with Andrea Colfer, Millbrook, Nova Scotia, 7 March 2012.

[13] Myrna Whiteduck, Commissioner's Sharing Panel, TRC Saskatoon National Event, 22 June 2012.

[14] Alvin Tolley, Commissioner's Sharing Panel, TRC Montreal National Event, 26 April 2013.

[15] With 89 per cent of the IAP claims processed, the government of Canada has disbursed C$3.233 billion in 26,707 hearings, with an average of C$91,466.40 per claim. See *http://www.iap-pei.ca/stats-eng.php* (accessed 22 March 2022).

[16] The most significant exception to this absence of opinon from clergy was a statement from Brother Cavanaugh in the National Event in Halifax, which I discuss in some detail in *Truth and indignation* (Niezen 2017).

[17] David Bruce MacDonald, in *The sleeping giant awakens* (2019), offers sustained attention to the notion of cultural genocide adopted by Canada's TRC.

[18] This essay, however, is not the place for a wide-ranging assessment of the extent to which the 'Calls to Action' have been acknowledged and acted on.

[19] Government of Canada, Specific Claims, *https://www.rcaanc-cirnac.gc.ca/eng/1100100030291/1539617582343* (accessed 24 March 2022).

[20] Department of Justice, 'Spotlight on *Gladue*: challenges, experiences, and possibilities in Canada's criminal justice system', *https://www.justice.gc.ca/eng/rp-pr/jr/gladue/p2.html* (accessed 22 March 2022).

REFERENCES

ARENDT, H. 1987. Collective responsibility. In *Amor mundi: explorations in the faith and thought of Hannah Arendt* (ed.) J.W. Bernauer, S.J., 43-50. Boston: Martinus Nijhoff.

FREEMAN, M. 2006. *Truth commissions and procedural fairness.* Cambridge: University Press.

HAYNER, P. 2011. *Unspeakable truths: transitional justice and the challenge of truth commissions.* New York: Routledge.

JAMES, M. 2017. Changing the subject: the TRC, its National Events, and the displacement of substantive reconciliation in Canadian media representations. *Journal of Canadian Studies* **51**, 362-97.

JASPERS, K. 2001 [1947]. *The question of German guilt* (trans. E.B. Ashton). New York: Fordham University Press.

KOLCHANSKI, A. 2020. Mandating truth: patterns and trends in truth commission design. *Human Rights Review* **21**, 113-37.

MACDONALD, D.B. 2019. *The sleeping giant awakens: genocide, Indian residential schools, and the challenge of conciliation.* Toronto: University Press.

MAHONEY, K. 2014. The settlement process: a personal reflection. *University of Toronto Law Journal* **64**, 1-16.

NAGY, R. 2012. The scope and bounds of transitional justice and the Canadian Truth and Reconciliation Commission. *The International Journal of Transitional Justice* **7**, 52-73.

———— 2014. The Truth and Reconciliation Commission of Canada: genesis and design. *Canadian Journal of Law and Society* **29**, 199-217.

———— & E. GILLESPIE 2015. Representing reconciliation: a news frame analysis of print media coverage of Indian residential schools. *Transitional Justice Review* **1:3**, 3-40.

NIEZEN, R. 2016. Templates and exclusions: victim centrism in Canada's Truth and Reconciliation Commission on Indian Residential Schools. *Journal of the Royal Anthropological Institute* (N.S.) **22**, 920-38.

———— 2017. *Truth and indignation: Canada's Truth and Reconciliation Commission on Indian Residential Schools* (Second edition). Toronto: University Press.

———— 2020. Human rights as therapy: the healing paradigms of transitional justice. In *The subject of human rights* (eds) D. Celermajer & A. Lefebvre, 153-71. Stanford: University Press.

NWOGU, N. 2010. When and why it started: deconstructing victim-centered truth commissions in the context of ethnicity-based conflict. *International Journal of Transitional Justice* **4**, 275-89.

REGAN, P. 2010. *Unsettling the settler within: Indian residential schools, truth telling, and reconciliation in Canada.* Vancouver: UBC Press.

SIMPSON, A. 2016. Consent's revenge. *Cultural Anthropology* **31**, 326-33.

———— 2017. The ruse of consent and the anatomy of 'refusal': cases from indigenous North America and Australia. *Postcolonial Studies* **20**, 18-33.

TROIAN, M. 2016. Indian residential schools: 5,300 alleged abusers located by Ottawa. CBC News, 2 February (available online: *https://www.cbc.ca/news/indigenous/residential-school-alleged-abusers-iap-1.3422770*, accessed 22 March 2022).

WILSON-RAYBOULD, J. 2016. Justice Minister Jody Wilson-Raybould's Opening Address at UN Permanent Forum on Indigenous Issues. *Northern Public Affairs*, 9 May (available online: *http://cendoc.docip.org/collect/cendocdo/index/assoc/HASH82cd/de4e9c7a.dir/PF16Jody000p.pdf#search=%22Jody%20WILSON-RAYBOULD%22*, accessed 25 March 2022).

Violation, impunité et irréconciliation dans la commission Vérité et réconciliation du Canada sur les pensionnats indiens

Résumé

L'influence exercée sur le savoir par les mandats conférés à des institutions apparaît de façon particulièrement claire dans les préférences et les lacunes des actes de la Commission de vérité et réconciliation (CVR). Ces commissions ont tendance, depuis peu, à s'écarter de l'exercice des pouvoirs judiciaires et de la quête de justice pour porter davantage la parole des victimes ou des « survivants ». La CVR canadienne sur les pensionnats indiens illustre les conséquences de ce déplacement vers un victimocentrisme qui laisse des lacunes dans les connaissances apportées à la commission, notamment à propos des auteurs des faits, contribuant ainsi à l'impunité des responsables de souffrances de masse. Cette impunité s'est cristallisée en irréconciliation lorsque la commission a donné la parole à des personnes oubliées et marginalisées depuis longtemps, défavorisées au cours de leur vie, tout en laissant hors champ ceux qui leur avaient, de fait, volé leur vie et leur dignité.

Journal of the Royal Anthropological Institute (N.S.) **28**, *79-94*

6

Irreconciliation, reciprocity, and social change (Afterword 1)

RICHARD ASHBY WILSON *University of Connecticut*

Anthropological critiques of reconciliation

Reconciliation, understood in a thin sense as mere coexistence and in a thick sense as fulsome forgiveness, is usually motivated by a desire to end an armed conflict, establish a political system that can resolve disputes peacefully, and reintegrate those involved in mass atrocities. Starting in the 1990s, a veritable industry arose to promote restorative justice, reconciliation, and post-conflict peace building, and in the early 2000s the UN Security Council (2004) formally endorsed reconciliation as an indispensable element in the transition away from an era of political violence.

It fell to anthropologists, the social researchers perhaps most intimately familiar with communities affected by political violence, to puncture the growing consensus and identify the many drawbacks in the type of reconciliation pursued by government institutions such as the Truth and Reconciliation Commission (TRC) in South Africa (Ross 2002; Wilson 2001; 2020). Extending Laura Nader's (1990) critique of the 'harmony ideology' of alternative dispute resolution, ethnographers pointed out how institutions of reconciliation were often repurposed as instruments of social control and became coercive in their treatment of communities affected by violence. For instance, far from being a traditional African structure dispensing authentic community reconciliation, *gacaca* courts in Rwanda represented a conduit for the Kagame regime's imposition of party hegemony in the countryside (Doughty 2016; Waldorf 2009). Adam Branch (2014: 608) finds that support for traditional and community justice institutions (or 'ethnojustice') from international donors and the Ugandan state enforced social discipline and patriarchy within Acholi society and ensured impunity for Ugandan state actors.

The language of reconciliation, it is claimed, facilitates an emotional disposition of forgiveness on the part of survivors, promises beneficial psychological consequences by facilitating 'catharsis', and allows the nation to 'work through' a violent past

Journal of the Royal Anthropological Institute (N.S.) **28**, *95-102*
© Royal Anthropological Institute 2022.

(Minow 1998; Tutu 1999). Yet anthropologists found that these calls for reconciliation from national leaders demand a great deal from survivors and they subordinate the complex individual process of grieving and healing to the needs and timeline of the state (Hamber & Wilson 2002). Reconciliation discourse often engages in a sequestration of survivors' experiences and silences the desire for retribution or legal remedy.[1]

Further, the harmony ideology inherent in the concept of reconciliation often degrades the quality of the epistemological inquiry, as Ronald Niezen demonstrates in his essay in this volume on Canada's Truth and Reconciliation Commission on Indian Residential Schools. The limited legal mandate of the Canadian TRC and its inability to subpoena witnesses to testify guaranteed that there was no meaningful participation by government officials or sexual offenders in the co-construction of a new collective narrative on the past. That there was no face-to-face encounter between priests and nuns and their former students had obvious implications for the kind of knowledge the commission produced. Further, the prohibition on naming offenders extinguished the possibility that the commission could advance a programme of legal remedy or moral accountability.[2]

The erasure of legal accountability (including criminal prosecution and civil liability) is a generalized feature of TRCs. In virtually all instances, including in Argentina, Chile, El Salvador, East Timor, Guatemala, South Africa, and Uruguay, national and international TRCs authorized amnesty and abjured any legal accountability for high-ranking intellectual authors of the violence. We can justifiably conclude that the discourse and institutions of reconciliation are designed to elide the mass crimes of the past and leave impunity uncontested in the putatively democratic and post-conflict present.

The anthropological critique of reconciliation as a feature of post-conflict governance subverted the conventional view that the political transition was actually democratic and peaceful after all. Ethnographers have documented acts of irreconciliation that repudiate national narratives of reconciliation and noted the inadequacy of the institutions designed to address the patent anger, frustration, and desire for revenge in affected communities (Godoy 2006). This volume makes a vital contribution to the transitional justice literature by coining the umbrella term 'irreconciliation' to encompass a range of emotional dispositions and practices that defy political leaders' exhortations to reconcile. As the authors amply illustrate, irreconciliation takes many forms and runs the gamut from a passive refusal to participate in collective reconciliation programmes, to public declarations of the names of perpetrators (Niezen, this volume), to calls for the death penalty in the name of human rights (Visser, this volume). Bjørn Enge Bertelsen's study of popular justice in Mozambique is a particularly poignant reminder of how settings deemed to be 'post-conflict' by the international community may still be afflicted by private or collective acts of revenge and violent retaliation, including outbreaks of lynchings and armed confrontations between historically opposed groups.

We see in Nayanika Mookherjee's and Jacco Visser's essays an illustration of anthropology's essential role in contextualizing debates about reconciliation and irreconciliation and connecting them to the literature on human rights. There is clearly a need to evaluate these rarified abstractions in the complex social scenarios in which they are reframed, operationalized, and often abused.[3] Visser's account of the campaign of London-based activists in favour of the International Crimes Tribunal in Dhaka explains how the concept of 'human rights accountability' can be transformed from

Journal of the Royal Anthropological Institute (N.S.) **28**, 95-102
© Royal Anthropological Institute 2022.

reparations or criminal sanctions into a lethal form of political vengeance that actually violates human rights norms of due process and cruel and inhuman treatment. In this volume, the act of contextualizing reconciliation also implies a concern with the temporal aspects of reconciliation. Each conception of reconciliation contains within it a theory of time and temporal periodization. For instance, Mookherjee directs our attention to the chronological language in reconciliation projects of 'confronting the past', 'achieving closure', and 'moving forward'. Bertelsen develops a critique of the linear assumptions about time that are implicit in reconciliation discourse and documents how violent retribution is motivated by a sense that ordinary Mozambicans do not have a future. In Visser's analysis, London-based activists campaigning for the death penalty recognize that no apologies or forgiveness can take Bangladesh back to its pre-conflict state. Each of these essays offers an insight into the limitations of the temporal dimensions of projects of both reconciliation and retribution, and the adverse consequences for survivors that this implies.

Irreconciliation, reciprocity, and accountability

The unique contribution of this volume lies in the positive and even normative case it makes for irreconciliation as a widespread and necessary element of transitions from mass violence. After two decades of anthropological critique, it is not enough to count the ways in which reconciliation is flawed and inadequate to the needs of the population; what is needed is an affirmative argument that identifies the potential benefits of irreconciliation. As Mookherjee proposes in her introduction, it is first necessary to acknowledge that irreconciliation is not dysfunctional and does not simply represent an absence of reconciliation and a commitment to sociality. Irreconciliation is a feature of social relationships that regularly arises in settings of mass violence and may lead to positive outcomes as well as harm and injury. The state of irreconciliation is, to recall Durkheim, an irreducible social fact in itself with independently generated consequences for social behaviour.

What might an affirmative case for irreconciliation look like? We could further develop the insight that irreconciliation is inherently social rather than asocial by examining anthropological concepts of reciprocity, exchange, and retaliation. Anthropologists have long maintained that reciprocity is the basis for society. Reciprocity takes two forms: positive reciprocity, understood as exchange that may include the circulation of people and symbolic and material goods; and negative reciprocity, understood as retribution for violating the rules of positive reciprocity, for instance by cheating, lying, or freeloading (Davis 1992; Fehr & Gächter 2002). Co-operation is therefore profoundly associated with retaliation for norm violation, and both expressions of reciprocity are widely observed attributes of human sociality (Axelrod 1984). Much as the advocates of reconciliation wish to dismiss it as an unwelcome aberration, irreconciliation is fundamentally social, functional, and relational in both its intentionality and its consequences.

In this volume, Lisette Josephides develops a compelling theoretical justification for irreconciliation based upon conceptions of accountability (understood in the broad sense), moral responsibility, and, intriguingly, an anthropological notion of reciprocity. She begins by rejecting Jacques Derrida's (2001) famous thesis that a defining aspect of being human is to forgive the unforgivable purely, unconditionally, and irrespective of any apologies or repentance by the offender. This represents a secularization of the Judaeo-Christian approach to forgiveness in a way that is parallel to Jacques Maritain's secularization of the Christian concept of dignity in the 1948 UN Declaration of Human Rights (Coundouriotis 2006). By not requiring an admission of guilt or an acceptance of responsibility, Josephides maintains that Derrida's concept of forgiveness does not show a sufficient concern for the humanity of the guilty person.

Josephides prefers Paul Ricoeur's framing in *Memory, history, forgetting* (2004), which is inspired by Hannah Arendt and conditions forgiveness on accountability[4] and moral responsibility on the part of the offender. Ricoeur draws on Mauss's *The gift* (1974 [1925]) to argue that Derrida's unconditional forgiveness undermines the possibility of mutual recognition and continues the rupture in the rules of reciprocity and exchange. Instead, Ricoeur's framework allows the offender to re-establish reciprocity with the survivor by recognizing the harm, apologizing and accepting moral responsibility for the injury. This makes possible the severance of the agent from the act, the recovery of their humanity, and the possibility of their resocialization. The injured party has the freedom to act as they see fit and may then extend forgiveness if they are so disposed. Because any forgiveness that occurs is premised upon mutual recognition and the acceptance of responsibility by the offender, it is far removed from the mass-produced industry-standard reconciliation promoted by governments and international agencies, which usually requires little or no participation from the architects or material perpetrators of mass atrocities.

A cornerstone of the ethnographic endeavour (and liberal political theory, as it happens) is a resistance to political authorities legislating private thoughts and feelings (or 'conscience') and an acceptance of the full range of human emotions as legitimate and appropriate to the circumstances, including resentment, hatred, and a desire for revenge. Making the case for the political value and significance of anger and bitterness is still an emergent project and here our anthropological conversation could be profitably informed by the arguments of political theorist Sonali Chakravarti in her monograph *Sing the rage: listening to anger after mass violence* (2013). Although she does not use the term 'irreconciliation', Chakravarti speaks to the same themes as this volume: anger and a desire for revenge that defies the programme of reconciliation advocated in South Africa after apartheid, Germany after the Holocaust, and elsewhere.

Chakravarti portrays the anger expressed by South African anti-apartheid activists as a valid response to mass violence and as an appeal for improved socioeconomic opportunities for Africans (2013: 2). She also sees anger as necessary to restoring the bonds of citizenship after mass violence by addressing the destruction of trust by the authoritarian state. 'Listening to anger', she argues, 'ushers in a transformation from victim to citizen' that is necessary for the restoration of political agency of victims (2013: 23). Instead of marginalizing anger, as the South African TRC did, it should be brought into the political sphere, engaged with, listened to, and conjoined to a wide-ranging programme of justice (2013: 4-5). For Chakravarti, anger is an essential driver for redrawing the social contract between citizen and state to establish a new political era that is distinct from the last.

Beyond the reconciliation industry

Chakravarti's *Sing the rage* takes us beyond the standard reconciliation industry view of anger as mere expression, as catharsis with supposed therapeutic benefits, and it connects irreconciliation to a programme of political change. We could build on her arguments further, starting with the observation that the transition from armed conflict or authoritarianism is not a single event. A centuries-old structure of exploitation and violence does not simply evaporate with the signing of a peace accord or the holding of multi-party elections, crucial as these events are.

Calls for reconciliation are often made in the context of the continued oppression of those who suffered the greatest effects of mass violence. As Niezen observes, Indian residential schools have been closed for years, but the system of governance of indigenous communities is still present in the lives of survivors. Similarly, racism against Africans did not die with the end of apartheid in South Africa, and racism against indigenous peoples continues unabated after the end of the armed conflicts in Chile, Peru, and Guatemala (Theidon 2013). In Colombia, the main FARC guerrilla group signed the 2016 peace accord, but the ELN currently fights on, and discontented elements of the FARC have now returned to the armed struggle. Extraordinary levels of violence continue unabated in supposedly 'post-conflict' societies, and in some cases there are higher homicide rates in the post-conflict era than during the armed conflict. For instance, in 1997, there were nearly three times the number of homicides in South Africa than in 1986, the high point of the popular rebellion against apartheid (Wilson 2013: 455).

Undoing centuries of colonialism, structural inequality, and racism is a generational project that requires a massive society-wide political movement for change. Yet transitions from a period of mass violence usually occur in the context of compromise and accommodation between the opposed parties. Especially where there is a military stalemate, peace agreements are elite bargains signed in backrooms that usually encapsulate an agreement on the economic and political model of the transition. For the past several decades, political transitions have embraced neoliberal economics and the wholesale privatization of state functions (Moyn 2018). This has resulted in states that are too feeble to provide basic services or to ensure justice and order, and left behind weak transitional states that are easily captured by powerful actors that include national and multinational corporations. In a materialist analysis, reconciliation is often the propaganda component of an elite bargain that seeks to convince the population not to push for legal accountability and for socioeconomic change that would challenge the terms of the elite agreement. Bertelsen's comment that Mozambicans opposed to reconciliation feel betrayed by the national political elite is intelligible as a way of combining the popular resistance to national reconciliation with a critique of neoliberal state policies. Forgiveness and closure on past violations also implies forgoing the political project to transform the structural conditions that ignited mass violence. Reconciliation compels acceptance of the status quo and with it the preservation of systems of exploitation, corruption, and inequality that caused the mass violence in the first place.

Accountability understood as criminal or civil liability for the main actors in a conflict is a prerequisite of sociopolitical transformation. In contrast, the vast majority of TRCs either have been accompanied by amnesties or, as in South Africa, have themselves granted amnesty to those who have committed mass human rights violations (Wilson 2003). Holding political leaders accountable for orchestrating mass crimes and for presiding over systems of exploitation and corruption is a necessary step in any process of social change, democratization, and establishing a new regime that respects human rights. Tricia Olsen, Leigh Payne, Andrew Reiter, and Eric Wiebelhaus-Brahm (2010) found in their statistical analysis of dozens of TRCs over a thirty-year span that they tend to have a negative impact on human rights, unless they are established in combination with criminal trials. Impunity for the crimes of the past implies an acceptance of immunity for crimes of the present, with deleterious effects on the prospects for democracy, even of the low-grade liberal kind.

These observations go to the heart of the struggle over the meaning and content of human rights and law more generally in the transitional setting. Most social science theories of law conceive of law and rights as a site of contestation between competing interest groups. The legal statutes that are codified in any particular historical moment represent a crystallization of the relative strength of the competing groups at the creation or interpretation of law. The state and its legal apparatus therefore symbolizes the balance of social interests in society, and this is one reason why Marx and Engels wrote in *The German ideology* that the state 'exists only for the sake of private property' (1974 [1846]: 80) when describing the hegemony of the bourgeoisie in mid-nineteenth-century Europe. Marx turned away from reforming the state and its laws as an avenue for social change, but in the modern transitional context, campaigners for democracy and human rights do not have that luxury. It matters what social forces are instantiated in law, and it matters to survivors a great deal that there be official recognition of the harms they suffered and that there exist legal remedies that can provide material reparations and/or criminal accountability. If human rights are to mean anything in the post-conflict setting, then they must advance criminal prosecutions and civil reparations for the main violators of human rights and propel a structural analysis of the conditions that gave rise to widespread political violence.[5] My critique of the South African TRC was that it did neither (Wilson 2001).

Adopting a stance of irreconciliation, repudiating the status quo, and refusing to be mollified by the national discourse on reconciliation is to continue to insist on a programme of social change that addresses deep-seated inequities in society. This is the value of irreconciliation, which can be justified according to both deontological and consequentialist arguments. If the impetus behind irreconciliation gathers wider momentum, irreconciliation can serve as the basis for a political and legal mobilization that pressures governments to implement the socioeconomic rights clauses often present in peace agreements, as in the Colombian peace accord of 2016. We could end by noting that around the world, there are no autonomous grassroots social movements for reconciliation. In Latin America, where the modern movement for reconciliation as an element of transitional justice began, reconciliation is a dead letter. Meanwhile, social movements campaigning on a platform of inconvenient irreconciliation are thriving, and they occasionally receive support from international institutions such as the Office of the United Nations High Commissioner for Human Rights.

On the day of writing, the Inter-American Court of Human Rights reiterated its position to the State of Guatemala that the state cannot impose amnesties, statutes of limitations, or other legal hindrances to criminal prosecution of the four senior military officers who detained, tortured, and sexually assaulted the political activist Emma Molina Theissen and killed her 14-year-old brother Marco in 1981. Legal proceedings that insist on civil liability or criminal accountability for the most powerful actors in society, even four decades after the events occurred, provide ample reason to take irreconciliation seriously, and impel scholars to make a positive case for it as a necessary part of the move away from violence and the structures of inequality that foster it.

NOTES

[1] On the gender aspects of silencing in post-genocide Rwanda, see Buckley-Zistel (2006).

Journal of the Royal Anthropological Institute (N.S.) **28**, 95-102
© Royal Anthropological Institute 2022.

[2] In this essay, I distinguish between legal accountability, which includes both criminal prosecutions and civil claims, and moral accountability, which includes a range of non-legal forms of attributing responsibility for harms. The two may overlap in certain legal and quasi-legal processes.

[3] See also Anders & Zenker (2014) on the contrast between lofty promises and social realities and Shaw & Waldorf (2010) on the need to localize transitional justice.

[4] In defining accountability, Josephides draws from Ricoeur's concept of the development of the self, which presupposes an admission of guilt and an acceptance of personal responsibility.

[5] There is no reason why criminal accountability and structural change are incompatible. Instead, they may work in tandem to challenge elite-controlled institutional structures of racism, misogyny, corruption, and violence, as has occurred in Guatemala and elsewhere (Burt 2019; Wilson 2020).

REFERENCES

ANDERS, G. & O. ZENKER (eds) 2014. *Transition and justice: negotiating the terms of new beginnings*. Special Issue *Development and Change* **45**: 3.

AXELROD, R. 1984. *The evolution of cooperation*. New York: Basic Books.

BRANCH, A. 2014. The violence of peace: ethnojustice in northern Uganda. *Development and Change* **45**, 608-30.

BUCKLEY-ZISTEL, S. 2006. Remembering to forget: chosen amnesia as a strategy for local coexistence in post-genocide Rwanda. *Africa: The Journal of the International African Institute* **76**, 131-50.

BURT, J.-M. 2019. Gender justice in post-conflict Guatemala: the Sepur Zarco sexual violence and sexual slavery trial. *Critical Studies* **4**, 63-96.

CHAKRAVARTI, S. 2013. *Sing the rage: listening to anger after mass violence*. Chicago: University Press.

COUNDOURIOTIS, E. 2006. The dignity of the 'unfittest:' victims' stories in South Africa. *Human Rights Quarterly* **28**, 842-67.

DAVIS, J. 1992. *Exchange*. Minneapolis: University of Minnesota Press.

DERRIDA, J. 2001. *On cosmopolitanism and forgiveness* (trans. M. Dooley & M. Hughes). London: Routledge.

DOUGHTY, K.C. 2016. *Remediation in Rwanda: Grassroots legal forums*. Philadelphia: University of Pennsylvania Press.

FEHR, E. & S. GÄCHTER 2002. Altruistic punishment in humans. *Nature* **415**, 137-40.

GODOY, A.S. 2006. *Popular injustice: violence, community, and law in Latin America*. Stanford: University Press.

HAMBER, B. & R.A. WILSON 2002. Symbolic closure through memory, reparation and revenge in post-conflict societies. *Journal of Human Rights* **1**, 35-53.

MARX, K. & F. ENGELS 1974 [1846]. *The German ideology* (Second edition; ed. C.J. Arthur). London: Lawrence & Wishart.

MAUSS, M. 1974 [1925]. *The gift: the form and reason for exchange in archaic societies* (trans. W.D. Halls). London: Routledge & Kegan Paul.

MINOW, M. 1998. *Between vengeance and forgiveness: facing history after genocide and mass violence*. Boston: Beacon Press.

MOYN, S. 2018. *Not enough: human rights in an unequal world*. Cambridge, Mass.: Harvard University Press.

NADER, L. 1990. *Harmony ideology: justice and control in a Zapotec mountain village*. Stanford: University Press.

OLSEN, T.D., L.A. PAYNE, A.G. REITER & E. WIEBELHAUS-BRAHM 2010. When truth commissions improve human rights. *International Journal of Transitional Justice* **4**, 457-76.

RICOEUR, P. 2004. *Memory, history, forgetting* (trans. K. Blamey & D. Pellauer). Chicago: University Press.

ROSS, F. 2002. *Bearing witness: women and the South African Truth and Reconciliation Commission*. London: Pluto Press.

SHAW, R. & L. WALDORF (with P. Hazan) (eds) 2010. *Localizing transitional justice: interventions and priorities after mass violence*. Stanford: University Press.

THEIDON, K. 2013. *Intimate enemies: violence and reconciliation in Peru*. Philadelphia: University of Pennsylvania Press.

TUTU, D. 1999. *No future without forgiveness*. London: Rider Books.

UN SECURITY COUNCIL 2004. The rule of law and transitional justice in conflict and post-conflict societies. Report of the Secretary General. S/2004/616 (available online: *https://www.un.org/ruleoflaw/blog/document/the-rule-of-law-and-transitional-justice-in-conflict-and-post-conflict-societies-report-of-the-secretary-general/*, accessed 23 March 2022).

WALDORF, L. 2009. Remnants and remains: post-genocide narratives of suffering in Rwanda's *gacaca* courts. In *Humanitarianism and suffering: the mobilization of empathy* (eds) R.A. Wilson & R. D. Brown, 285-305. Cambridge: University Press.

WILSON, R.A. 2001. *The politics of truth and reconciliation in South Africa: legitimizing the post-apartheid state.* Cambridge: University Press.

——— 2003. Anthropology and national reconciliation. *Journal of Anthropological Theory* **3**, 363-83.

——— 2013. A gangster's paradise? Framing crime in sub-Saharan Africa. *Humanity: An International Journal of Human Rights, Humanitarianism and Development* **4**, 449-71.

——— 2020. Justice after atrocity. In *The Oxford handbook on law and anthropology* (eds) M. Foblets, M. Goodale, M. Sapignoli & O. Zenker, 1-19. Oxford: University Press.

7

Irreconciliation as practice: resisting impunity and closure in Argentina

NOA VAISMAN *Aarhus University*

In Argentina, irreconciliation is created through everyday practices of vigilance against closure and collective struggles against impunity. In this essay, I show how over several decades since the fall of the dictatorial regime (1976-83), human rights activists and laypeople have devised ways to keep the past alive while attending to injustices through embodied collective engagements with the country's history and its legacies. By examining large protests, the everyday experiences of impunity, and a filmic exploration of kinship bonds and their entanglement with civilian complicity in the repression, the essay illustrates the ways in which irreconciliation is materialized and enacted as a form of social reconstruction many years after state terrorism.

Within a few hours of the Argentine Supreme Court ruling in the Muiña case on 3 May 2017, Twitter and Facebook were abuzz with messages of rage and disbelief. Old and new slogans appeared almost instantaneously calling 'Never Again' and 'No to 2×1' (i.e. the so-called 2 for 1 law – see below), and human rights activists and politicians alike used every available public channel to express their dismay at the ruling and its possible implications.

Luis Muiña, whose case the Supreme Court deliberated, is a convicted criminal. He was tried for perpetrating horrendous human rights violations, including kidnapping, torture, and assassination, during the last military dictatorship in the country (1976-83). The application of the so-called 2 for 1 law, which stated that after two years in pre-trial detention the time spent in prison before a conviction would count as double time towards the period of imprisonment, was, in effect, a way to set him free. The public outcry against this sentence was immediate and lasting. Exactly one week after the ruling, around half a million people gathered in the Plaza de Mayo in central Buenos Aires to denounce the Court's decision (Pertot 2017). Similar demonstrations were held across the country (Meyer 2017) and abroad (e.g. Spain, France), all making the same claim: '*Señores Jueces: Nunca Más. Ningún Genocida Suelto* [Your Honours: Never Again. No *Genocida* Free]'.[1]

Journal of the Royal Anthropological Institute (N.S.) **28**, *103-117*
© 2022 The Authors. *Journal of the Royal Anthropological Institute* published by John Wiley & Sons Ltd on behalf of Royal Anthropological Institute.

The outcry was not limited to the case or to the fact that the 2×1 law was repealed and no longer in effect at the time of the ruling. Rather, the outrage was against what both the Court and the ruling's numerous critics understood: the 'rehabilitation' of the law meant the possible release of most convicted perpetrators of human rights crimes in the country. In effect, the ruling undermined the tremendous process of justice making that has been taking place in the Argentine Federal Courts since the mid-2000s (Anitua, Álvarez & Gaitán 2014; Figari Layús 2015a; 2018; Vaisman 2020; Vaisman & Barrera 2020; van Roekel 2020). It raised, yet again, the spectre of impunity in the midst of a process known worldwide as a prime example of post-transitional justice (Collins 2010; Sikkink 2008).[2]

Reflecting on the tremendous social response to the Supreme Court decision, and the subsequent political and legal reactions, in this essay I consider the everyday meaning of irreconciliation. The term, as I propose here, refers to the ongoing active practice of vigilance against impunity and to the collective engagement with a living past. In particular, I am interested in interrogating the ways in which irreconciliation implies particular experiences of time, embodiment, memory, and social relations. While in previous works I have argued against the notion of reconciliation, and, more broadly, the possibility of closing the books and consigning the harms committed to the past – as much of the transitional justice literature seems to demand (Elster 2004; Fletcher & Weinstein 2002; Ní Aoláin & Campbell 2005; for a critique, see Gready & Robins 2019; Leebaw 2008; Turner 2013) – in this essay I examine the everyday experiences of the active practice of vigilance against closure and its possible motivation and long-term implications.[3]

On reconciliation and the Argentine case

The term 'reconciliation' is difficult to define and hence has had many different uses in the academic literature on post-conflict reconstruction (Skaar 2012). Broadly, it connotes a form of closure in the face of a difficult past,[4] sometimes as an outcome of silence and a political decision to 'close the books' (Elster 2004); sometimes as a product of apologies, truth-telling initiatives, and reparations; and sometimes as a result of judicial accountability measures that allow a society to face the future collectively (Haber & Wilson 2002). For Priscilla Hayner, '[R]econciliation is often cited as a goal in national peace processes . . . [but] it is rarely clear exactly what is meant by the term' (2011 [2001]: 182). While she sees official accounting about the past as a necessary step in creating the conditions for reconciliation on a national level, on the individual level the picture is far more complicated. Drawing on the work of Veena Das and Arthur Kleinman (2002), Paul Gready (2011: 156) explains that reconciliation requires the repair of social relations, a public narration of silenced voices, and public recognition of the marginalized and excluded. Others studying societies transitioning into liberal democracy offer broader definitions. Renowned law professor Martha Minow defines reconciliation as 'societal healing' that requires some form of forgiveness and truth telling (in Wilson 2003: 372), while legal anthropologist Rosalind Shaw (2005) explains that reconciliation implies, at least in Sierra Leone in the early 2000s, 'social forgetting'. Anthropologist John Borneman, in his analysis of reconciliation in the aftermath of ethnic cleansing, suggests an even broader definition. For him, reconciliation is the 'project of *departure from violence*' (2002: 282, original emphasis) requiring an agreement between warring parties to refrain from repeating the past by 'reconciling the self and the group with the permanence of loss' (2002: 297). While engineering

Journal of the Royal Anthropological Institute (N.S.) **28**, 103-117
© 2022 The Authors. *Journal of the Royal Anthropological Institute* published by John Wiley & Sons Ltd on behalf of Royal Anthropological Institute.

this end goal may take place through truth-telling processes and judicial accountability measures, reconciliation is no more and no less than the facilitation of 'an ongoing recuperation of a loss that is not recoupable' (2002: 302). Borneman's definition thereby encompasses its own impossibility, much in the vein of Derrida's notions of forgiveness or justice (Derrida 1992; 2001; Vaisman 2017; 2021).

In Argentina, the concept has had a volatile history. Reconciliation has been pronounced, refused, and advocated for by Argentine religious leaders, political rivals, surviving victims, and human rights activists (Bonnin 2009; Borrelli & Ochoa 2016; Ranalletti 2010). Today, the term is directly associated with impunity and is rarely used in human rights circles, while making only sparse appearance in political discourse.[5] Drawing on pivotal historical moments where the concept was used, I explore its ecology: that is, the different cultural assumptions and political desires it harbours or coexists with.

One of the term's first legal uses was in the National Pacification Act (law 22,924), which was passed by the Armed Forces shortly before the return to democratic rule in 1983. As part of their attempt at 'self-amnesty', the Armed Forces called for an end to violence, for forgiveness and peace building 'in a gesture of reconciliation' (law quoted in Crenzel 2015: 23; see also Bonnin 2015). While the law was annulled ten days after Raúl Alfonsín, the first democratically elected President, took office, reconciliation was mentioned in some of Alfonsín's public pronouncements throughout his time in power, and was prominent both in pronouncements of the church's leadership and among members of the Armed Forces.

These first years after the fall of the regime were shaped by the creation of a national investigative committee (CONADEP),[6] a major criminal trial of the Juntas' leaders, and monetary reparations for victims and their family members. These initiatives emerged in a tense context where the Armed Forces offered a narrative of heroism in a bid to defend their actions against 'subversion' (Salvi 2015: 40-1), part of the Catholic Church called for healing, peace, and conciliation,[7] and Human Rights Organizations (HROs) established by family members of the disappeared claimed that reconciliation could only be reached once justice was meted out and the truth uncovered (Bonnin 2015).

Soon after, political tensions and threats to democratic stability led to the passing of two laws – Full Stop (1986) and Due Obedience (1987) – which blocked most judicial proceedings and limited their scope.[8] These so-called 'impunity laws' were followed closely by amnesties in 1989 and 1990, in what the second democratically elected President, Carlos Menem, explained as an act of closing the books: '[T]he pardons will put an end to a tragic history. There was a dirty war and there are guilty [persons] on both sides. It is best to forget it' (quoted in Galante 2019: 215). Together, these laws and decrees ushered in a period of silence and widespread impunity (Galante 2019; Jelin 2017).[9]

According to Amnesty International, 'Impunity is an exemption from punishment, which "negates the values of truth and justice and leads to the occurrence of further [human rights] violations"' (quoted in Sanford 2003b: 253-4; see also Sanford 2003a). In the Argentine context, impunity in the first two decades of democracy implied the release of convicted criminals, the foreclosure of legal adjudication for most cases of human rights crimes,[10] and an invocation of 'pacification', oblivion, and conciliation by the political leadership.

In this context, the public confession of Navy Captain Adolfo Scilingo about his participation in the 'death flights' (Verbitsky 2005 [1996])[11] caused shock waves resulting in, on the one hand, the opening of the truth trials (*Juicios por la Verdad*) (Andriotti Romanin 2013; Filippini 2006)[12] and, on the other hand, the emergence of alternative routes to truth, memory, and justice. The latter included, for example, mass mobilization on commemoration days and *escraches* – loud and colourful public interventions – led by H.I.J.O.S.[13] that aimed not only at outing perpetrators but also at unravelling impunity by teaching the population about the past, generating spaces for the reknitting of the social fabric, and creating popular justice from below (Benegas 2011; Rúa 2010; Vaisman 2017). Alongside these, a vibrant memory culture emerged that included official and grassroots initiatives. This consisted of the construction of commemoration sites, such as the Memory Park (Druliolle 2011) and the Space for Memory and Human Rights in the Ex-ESMA (Andermann 2012),[14] as well as literary, theatrical, and filmic representations that reflected on both the period and its aftermath (Blejmar, Mandolessi & Perez 2017; Garibotto 2019). Together with other initiatives,[15] a lively engagement with the dictatorial past and its legacies has consolidated in the country.

These projects and struggles were accompanied by and became symbolically embedded in a set of public slogans, for example: the well-known demand '*Nunca Más*'[16] ('Never Again') and '*ni olvido ni perdón*', a demand publicized by the Mothers of the Plaza de Mayo in 1983 that later morphed into '*no olvidamos, no perdonamos, no nos reconciliamos*' ('we do not forget, do not forgive, do not reconcile') – a slogan appearing in the vast majority of H.I.J.O.S.'s public statements (see also Bonnin 2015: 236). Together these expressed a refusal to forgive and forget, a position that is key to the notion of irreconciliation.

By the early 2000s, the tide on impunity was starting to turn (Balardini 2016) and the social-judicial struggles began to bear fruit. In the *Simón* case of 2001 a first instance court overturned the impunity laws, and in June 2005 the Supreme Court delivered an opinion on the same case recognizing human rights violations committed under the dictatorial rule as 'crimes against humanity' and hence imprescriptible. Along with a new political leadership (Néstor and Cristina Kirchner's administrations, 2003-15) that incorporated many of the HROs' causes into its mainstream agenda[17] and a Supreme Court decision from 2007 that held the presidential pardons unconstitutional,[18] the path to judicial accountability was drawn (Varsky & Balardini 2013). For well over a decade now, trials have been held in local Federal Courts and under the country's regular code of criminal procedure. To date, 3,596 individuals have been investigated, of whom 1,058 individuals have been condemned for crimes against humanity and 165 have been absolved.[19]

These advances in legal accountability have also slowly transformed the social sphere. While certain religious leaders have called on the population to put the past behind it,[20] other voices and themes emerging over the past decade and a half mark a different path: the path of irreconciliation. First, around the trials, supporters of the Armed Forces, particularly family members of perpetrators, founded vocal organizations demanding 'Complete Memory' and questioning judicial accountability measures.[21] Second, themes that were taboo in earlier periods, such as the sexual assaults that took place in the clandestine camps, were discussed openly (Jelin 2012). Third, around the fortieth anniversary of the coup (2016), a dramatic expansion of voices depicting complex and unsettling positions emerged (see Vaisman 2019 for the case of the 'living disappeared'). Among these were the voices of children of perpetrators (see Arenes & Pikielny 2016; Colectivo Historias Desobedientes 2019), some of whom

Journal of the Royal Anthropological Institute (N.S.) **28**, *103-117*
© 2022 The Authors. *Journal of the Royal Anthropological Institute* published by John Wiley & Sons Ltd on behalf of Royal Anthropological Institute.

have been struggling to defend the Armed Forces' actions and historical narrative and others who have testified to the tense existence between affective ties to kin and a critical moral stance towards the dictatorship and its crimes. These narratives allowed for a textual and, in some cases also, embodied dialogue to open up around questions of justice, truth about the past, and unsettled coexistence.

The resistance towards reconciliation has been criticized most recently by a number of established academics in Argentina and abroad. Claudia Hilb, an Argentine sociologist, has argued that the insistence on retributive justice along with the refusal of the generation that had suffered most to take responsibility for their actions (i.e. armed political struggle) has blocked the path to reconciliation (Hilb 2012: 51). Relying on Arendt's writings, she states that reconciliation can only materialize when the collective takes responsibility for 'what had happened that *should not have happened*' (Hilb 2012: 52, original emphasis). By understanding how it had happened, each individual could also repent for his or her part in the events and it is only then that reconciliation is imaginable. She contrasts the Argentine inability to reach reconciliation to what she deems is the successful South African example (Hilb 2011),[22] while the anthropologist Antonius Robben (2012) argues that Argentina resists national reconciliation. According to Robben, tensions surrounding the ongoing trials create further political contestation, while the 'genocide discourse is impeding such objective [i.e. reconciliation interpreted as national coexistence] because guilt has become collectivized and accountability has expanded from the military to civil society. The suspicion of complicity with genocide is now hovering over many people and hardening adversarial positions, recollections and actions' (2012: 306).

While I recognize the social and ideological tensions both authors are depicting, and although I acknowledge that the position I put forth here is indebted to – but is also critical of – the popular narrative of HROs about the past in Argentina, my reading of the historical conditions and their present outcomes is quite different. My contention is not only with the comparison to the South African case or the claim that it is a worthy model to follow,[23] nor is it just with the claim that the use of the term 'genocide' has generated an inability to compromise (see Crenzel 2019; Vaisman 2021). Rather, my argument is that we need to reconsider whether reconciliation is the model to strive for.[24] Instead, I propose that irreconciliation may be a better or more manageable target to work with and towards.

Irreconciliation, as I define it here, is an agentive act of social reconstruction. It demands neither forgiveness nor pardons but rather vigilance and action. It is an active acceptance of ambiguity and contradictions that is founded on a state of full alertness against emerging impunity and possible forgetting. Irreconciliation may not lead to closure but, at least in the Argentine case, it does lead to a heightened sensitivity to collective existence, and a powerful ability to come together. I believe that irreconciliation issues from civic education to act, a refining of attention towards injustices, and a recognition of the ability to respond collectively (see also Vaisman 2020 for a very different case). Irreconciliation is not only a moral stance towards horrendous human rights crimes, as Jean Améry (1980 [1966]: 72) has argued for resentment in a very different context. It is, rather, a broader response to the experience of impunity and an outcome of long-term societal cultivation of vigilance against oblivion and inaction. I expound on these in the sections below while exploring the 'ecology' of the term 'irreconciliation' and its many resonances.

Journal of the Royal Anthropological Institute (N.S.) **28**, *103-117*
© 2022 The Authors. *Journal of the Royal Anthropological Institute* published by John Wiley & Sons Ltd on behalf of Royal Anthropological Institute.

Everyday impunity and a torqued sense of time

In the previous section, I offered a historical overview of the struggles for truth, memory, and justice. Here I want to explore the everyday experiences of impunity and temporality. I am particularly interested in considering the effects of a subtle but lingering acknowledgement that even with the ongoing trials and the public and active support of the political leadership, impunity may never be eradicated. This recognition could give rise to rancour, revenge, and social polarization, but as I show, in Argentina it has led instead to an openness towards the complexity of affective and moral realities and simultaneously to the establishment of vigilance against impunity and proclivity for collective action.

It was early afternoon on a sunny day in the winter of 2017. I was standing on the corner of two bustling streets in the city centre of La Plata, but my thoughts were on the interview I was running late for in Buenos Aires, an hour's bus ride away. Aware of the time, I jumped into the first cab that passed by and asked the driver to take me to the central bus station. I had been waiting for close to three hours to speak to a judge with whom I had set up an interview two weeks earlier, but the trial he was presiding over took longer than expected and during a short interval he came out of the courtroom and suggested that we set up a new time to meet. Sitting in that taxi, I abruptly became aware of the driver's complaints about the traffic. Soon, he noted, a new light rail would open in the city. He explained that plans for it were already in place in 1976, under (Jorge Rafael) Videla's rule, and they had begun to lay the rails down. 'I was in the Armed Forces at the time', he commented. This short addition caught me by surprise. I remember thinking: he seems like a nice old man, how old is he? I looked at his big hands and his long fingers holding the wheel – was this driver involved in the crimes committed during the dictatorial rule (1976-83)? Could these hands have been involved in the assassination of a friend's father in La Plata only two years prior to the coup d'état? Or maybe he was just a conscript doing his obligatory military service at the time? La Plata is a small city where everyone knows everyone. Would a description of his appearance allow friends to identify him and inquire about his past?

Not knowing how to respond to his spontaneous comment, I kept quiet. I was surprised that he felt at ease mentioning his participation in the Armed Forces during that period in Argentina's history and I wondered whether he felt immune in the face of the ongoing investigations and oral trials (including the one that opened a few days earlier in the city). Maybe, I thought to myself, he had already been tried and acquitted? Reflecting on my uneasiness, I realized it stemmed from my inability to know for certain if I was in the presence of a perpetrator of human rights crimes, but also from my quick judgement and somewhat uncritical identification with the position of the many human rights activists who have been my interlocutors for close to two decades. The taxi stopped in front of the bus station and the driver kindly indicated the buses I could take to Buenos Aires. I thanked him and left, never having asked about his past.

The interview I was almost late for took place in an old Buenos Aires establishment, a café with dark red chairs, wooden tables, and mirrors on the walls. My interviewee, a man in his early forties, walked in and, after a quick scan of the empty space, sat down across from me. I had asked to meet so he could tell me about his experiences growing up with the knowledge that he has a sister or a brother whom he has never met and who, if alive, had been, in all likelihood, raised by members of the Armed Forces or their accomplices. There are an estimated 500 individuals who were abducted and appropriated or illegally adopted as babies during the dictatorial rule. Their origins were

Journal of the Royal Anthropological Institute (N.S.) **28**, 103-117
© 2022 The Authors. *Journal of the Royal Anthropological Institute* published by John Wiley & Sons Ltd on behalf of Royal Anthropological Institute.

kept secret and, to this day, many of them are still unaware of their biological identities, real names, and correct dates of birth (Vaisman 2019). Explaining choices he has made throughout his life to engage with the search for his brother or sister, my interlocutor stopped to reflect. He explained that growing up with this knowledge has also meant that every time he crosses the street, goes out for lunch, or sits in a café, the thought crosses his mind that the person next to him or in front of him may be his brother or sister. He described it as a constant awareness, a form of vigilance, because it also means that the person crossing the street with you, standing in line behind you at the bakery, or sitting next to you in a local restaurant could have been involved in the disappearance, torture, and assassination of your parents.

After he recounted his experiences, I told him about my encounter in La Plata. He explained that this was the essence of impunity, the visceral uneasiness that comes with the understanding that the past is lurking everywhere but is never fully transparent and known. The possible existence of a sibling and the missing body of a mother, who is neither alive nor dead but is disappeared, torques the experience of chronological or linear time. Instead, the past is very much alive in the present, not as a memory but as an ongoing experience. This coexistence of past and present erupts in small encounters and gestures, like when crossing the street makes you look twice because the person who accidentally brushed his hand against yours has the same nose or the same eyes as your aunt or grandmother.

Complicity and the long tentacles of past violence

What is the nature of impunity in the everyday of kin relations, and what might its implications be for irreconciliation? In this section, I consider one of the first filmic representations of both the civilian complicity with the dictatorial regime and, more importantly, the complex relationship that some family members of the perpetrators have with their familial legacies.

The documentary film *70 y Pico* came out in 2016, a time marked by political change as the newly elected government, headed by Mauricio Macri (2015-19), began to dismantle many of the initiatives and institutional structures created over previous years to face the past and its legacies (Balardini 2016). Many documentary and fiction films that have come out since the end of the dictatorial rule have dealt with the difficult past and its legacies, particularly the impact of forced disappearances on the lives of the disappeared's children and Argentine society as a whole (Ros 2012), but this one was different. The film is a nuanced exploration of the involvement of Héctor Mario Corbacho, the Dean of the Faculty of Architecture and Urbanism (FAU) (1976-82) and a professor of technical drawing at the ESMA, with the repressive apparatus. Built around intimate conversations recorded on camera between the film's director and his grandfather Corbacho, it explores the political climate and historical events that transpired in the FAU before the dictatorial rule and following the coup d'état. It further draws on archival material and interviews with students and professors in the institution in an attempt to understand Corbacho's role in the disappearance of 130 students and professors during the years of state terrorism.

Civilian complicity during the dictatorship has been a topic of interest in recent years in Argentina (Bohoslavsky & Opgenhaffen 2010). Some cases have reached the courts, raising awareness about the extent of the repression and the long tentacles of violence that were covered up during and after the dictatorship (Dandan & Franzki 2015). Without making direct accusations or fully endorsing the claims made by students and professors that Corbacho provided the lists marking people for abduction and disappearance, the film uncovers the close ties between Corbacho and the director of the ESMA (Zylberman 2020). It shows him on camera explaining that during his regular visits to the ESMA he did not see anyone being tortured, before later adding that he knew people were being tortured in the ESMA's basement and that pregnant women were held captive there.

The film's handling of the case of civilian complicity depicts the magnitude of the culture of violence and repression, exposing the ways in which civilians were important in the functioning of the repressive apparatus. As the director explains: 'My grandfather fulfilled a role like many other civilians that the Dictatorship nurtured so as to be able to commit its massacre. At the minimum, he was functional to this political and repressive project' (Hendler 2016). The film's temporal framing also allows for a re-evaluation of the historical context, including the violence of the guerrilla movements that threatened Corbacho's life. In this way it complicates the narrative of the past, allowing for a more nuanced picture to emerge. It is important to stress that the movie does not support the 'two-demons theory', according to which Argentine society was caught between two warring bands: the armed guerrilla movements and the Armed Forces. Rather, it shows the multi-layered nature of repression, silence, and complicity, including the affective ties between the director and his grandfather, and his inability to reconcile the image of a loving grandfather with that of the civilian accomplice.

The movie generated debate and was shown at a number of commemoration events and public screenings. Its power lies, I believe, in its capacity to expose the futility of the demand to close the books on the past, and, simultaneously, its active desire to explore, understand, and exist with the contradictions and ambiguities that are entangled in affective and kinship bonds and moral positions that repudiate certain actions and behaviours.[25] The movie generates questions and reveals the many dimensions of Argentina's violent history and its legacies without trying to settle between them. This stance towards the living-embodied past is key to irreconciliation. It is also, I believe, a good foundation for collective existence in the aftermath of violence.

Irreconciliation as vigilance and *'poner el cuerpo'* as a public practice

The 10 May 2017 demonstration with which I began this essay was dramatic in magnitude, collective organization, and repercussion. The plaza de Mayo overflowed with people, including members of HROs and other grassroots political and civil associations and individuals with no direct affiliation. Among them was a daughter of a perpetrator who later helped to form the collective Historias Desobedientes, composed of children (mostly daughters) of perpetrators who reject their fathers' acts and desire to collaborate with the judicial process and show their support for the ongoing trials. Everyone in the plaza held in their hand a white handkerchief: the emblematic symbol of the Mothers of the Plaza de Mayo. This symbol was lifted up a number of times throughout the demonstration, gesturing to the unity of the crowd and the collective repudiation of the Supreme Court ruling (Pertot 2017). The demands of the crowd were read aloud by members of the HROs from a stage that overlooked the plaza. They included a vehement rejection of the legal decision and the resulting impunity. The text also highlighted the law's original aim[26] and the fact that the crimes committed during the period of state terrorism do not have a statute of limitation. More significantly, the text offered a vision of post-dictatorship collective life. It stated that those in the plaza, and Argentine society as a whole, 'do not wish to coexist (*convivir*) with the assassins ... nor that future generations would have to'. 'The [Argentine] people . . . do not deserve to be condemned to oblivion.' Even forty-one years after the dictatorial rule, the perpetrators have not offered information about the disappeared, nor have they helped in identifying the 'living disappeared'. This law would result in the liberation of hundreds of *genocidas* 'who will walk the streets along with us [members of the HROs], along with all of you'.[27]

The text highlighted the role that HROs, family members of the disappeared, and surviving disappeared (ex-detained disappeared) have had in struggling for justice and truth, while never taking the law into their own hands: that is, never acting in violent revenge. It clarified that since the Supreme Court verdict, many judges had rejected numerous requests for the release of convicted perpetrators of human rights crimes, and that on that same day, Congress had passed a law that limited the application of the 2×1 law in cases of crimes against humanity. The text ended with a depiction of the path taken by the Argentine people since the return to democratic rule.

> The HROs are not alone like [we were] in earlier ill-fated epochs . . . here is the *pueblo* [the people]. A people more wise, more committed, stronger [and able] to resist those attacks that bring us back to a sinister past and that would like to consolidate as both the present and the future. Because, regrettably, the dictatorship is not a foregone past. The children, grandchildren, and great-grandchildren of the Argentine people will be affected by these new winds of impunity . . . We know that democracy is constructed among all [of us], every day . . . Here we are, in this plaza and in all the plazas in the country raising our voice against oblivion . . . Honourable Justices: Never Again. No *Genocida* Free.

The reading of the text ended with the collective call '30,000 Detained Disappeared, Present! Now and Forever!' and the plaza turned a sea of white as all those present lifted their handkerchiefs to the sky.

The text's refusal to accept impunity in the release of hundreds of convicted perpetrators is essentially a call for irreconciliation. It demands to keep the past alive, not as a form of revenge but as a way to 'set things right' by having the perpetrators pay for their acts. This irreconciliation is not fixed on the past alone. Rather, it looks to the future and to the nature of collective existence that the Argentine people want to create for themselves. This future is envisioned not as a new start, a clean page that has no marks of the past, but as an everyday that involves struggles and ambiguities while actively excluding the perpetrators.[28] Irreconciliation is a result of civic education that develops from the ground up and, over years, brings people together – suffice to mention the thousands who gathered in plazas across the country and abroad against the 2×1 Supreme Court decision. This is an education to 'put oneself on the line' for a cause, as the Argentine term '*poner el cuerpo*' implies. It means to involve oneself fully and with all one's heart and body in a cause, sometimes to the point where physical existence is at stake (Sutton 2007). Finally, irreconciliation is a form of learned vigilance, a practice of being on constant alert that is enacted by member of HROs, social and political activists, and laypeople alike. It demands that one be attentive to the changing winds of politics and justice and respond when they seem to draw new paths towards impunity.[29] The ecology of irreconciliation does not encompass revenge or violence (a point made repeatedly by human rights activists), neither does it aim for healing or closure; instead, it entangles a demand for information (truth) and for institutional (legal) accountability with long-term education for collective action and vigilance against impunity. Moreover, particularly in recent years, it has implied an openness to ambiguity, tensions, and contradictions in individual relations and social worlds (for an example, see Vaisman 2019).

The position of irreconciliation that I have described in this essay resonates with Jean Améry's writing on resentment (1980 [1966]: 62-81). Améry, a survivor of Nazi concentration camps, refused to forgive and forget. Instead, he advocated for, or at least attempted to explain, his resentment.[30] In an intellectually and emotionally complicated text, he lays out his moral position and its sources. While space does not permit me to do justice to this essay, a short quote will offer some insight into how I have tried to understand the Argentine case.

> I hope that my resentment – which is my personal protest against the antimoral natural process of healing that time brings about, and by which I make the genuinely humane and absurd demand that time be turned back – will also perform a historical function . . . This demand is no less absurd and no less moral than the individual demand that irreversible processes be reversed . . . Well then, the problem could be settled by permitting resentment to remain alive in the one camp and, aroused by it, self-mistrust in the other (Améry 1980 [1966]: 77).

In my reading of the Argentine case, the victims and their family members (HROs) have attempted to hold on to their resentment against what Améry calls the natural healing brought about by time. This position demanded, at different points in the country's history, to reverse time and to undo the past, as expressed in such calls as 'bring them back alive' or 'Detained Disappeared Present! Now and Forever!'[31] This demand to undo the crime and to reverse time is, in part, an outcome of the particular nature of the crime of forced disappearance (see Gatti 2014; Vaisman 2020; Buthpitiya and Clarke, this volume). Moreover, closure is foreclosed when the perpetrators of the crime provide no information about the disappeared (and the 'living disappeared') or their remains. Very concretely, with no body to bury or a living individual to entangle in ties of kin and affect, there is no possibility of reaching full closure. The result is a particular form of irreconciliation that does not accept apologies or pardons, and that resists impunity by keeping vigilant and calling out when justice is thwarted.[32] This irreconciliation is an act of defiance. It demands, as Améry writes, that those who are 'in the other' camp – the perpetrators, their family members and supporters – experience some form of self-mistrust. I have read the film *70 y Pico* and other recent developments such as the emergence of the collective Historias Desobedientes in this light. I believe that the Argentine example is particularly powerful because irreconciliation is not limited to the victims or their family members; instead, through many years of struggles and civic education, many Argentines have come to share in acts of irreconciliation.

Conclusion

Social reconstruction in the long aftermath of the dictatorship in Argentina is an act of irreconciliation. It takes place through human rights activism, art and memory work, judicial accountability measures, and the embedding of a human rights culture through education and public and civic acts. Irreconciliation is neither a passive position, nor is it a mere set of feelings that shape an individual's stance towards the world. Rather, it is *an active practice against closure*. Its manifestations are vigilance against impunity, public agitation, and collective (physical) resistance. It does not harbour any attempt or desire to forgive the unforgivable (Derrida 2001); instead, irreconciliation keeps the past alive by allowing people to coexist with contradictions, to inquire into and explore different affective and ethical positions, and to recognize and accept the complexity of social and kin bonds. Importantly, I am not claiming that irreconciliation has enabled all types of discourse to exist, nor that it has accepted all possibilities for revising and revisiting historical events. In fact, there are numerous positions and inquiries that have been

Journal of the Royal Anthropological Institute (N.S.) **28**, 103-117
© 2022 The Authors. *Journal of the Royal Anthropological Institute* published by John Wiley & Sons Ltd on behalf of Royal Anthropological Institute.

closed off over the years, but with time, it seems to me, irreconciliation has ushered in more openness to affective ambivalence while maintaining and strengthening alertness towards impunity and injustice. Thus far, it has proven the strength of Argentine democracy in the face of very difficult economic and political crises. And, I believe, it has proven to be a noteworthy example of post-dictatorship social revival.

Acknowledgements

This text is a product of extended research and engagement with the sociopolitical upheavals in Argentina and was developed through fieldwork and ongoing discussions with friends and colleagues there. I would like to thank Leticia Barrera for her intellectual generosity and close readings of much of my work, and for her friendship over many years. Thank you to Camilla Meijide and Karina Manoli who have helped with my investigations in Argentina. A heartfelt thank you to Nayanika Mookherjee for insightful conversations and attentive reading of this text as well as other parts of my work. I would also like to acknowledge an Aarhus University Research Foundation (AUFF) grant (AUFF-E-2016-FLS-&-4HD) and an Arts and Humanities Research Council grant (AH/M006115/1) that have supported my research over the past few years.

NOTES

[1] The term *genocida* is used in Argentina to describe those who perpetrated human rights crimes during the dictatorial rule. While there is extensive controversy over whether the crimes committed during this period constitute genocide in its international legal definition, the term is commonly used in public discourse (see Feierstein 2006).

[2] In Argentina the term 'transitional justice' (TJ) is rarely used by laypersons and professional alike. As Figari Layús (2015*b*) demonstrates, this is in part because the trials are not considered a temporary or extraordinary measure – unlike the way judicial proceedings are conceptualized within the TJ framework – but instead are held in regular courts under the ordinary criminal code and with no clear end date.

[3] The article is based on research conducted in Buenos Aires, Argentina, over the last decade. Data were collected through ethnographic fieldwork and textual and visual analysis.

[4] Audra Simpson's definition of reconciliation as a 'political language game and largely state-driven performance art that attempts to move elements of history forward in order to "move on" from the past, to transition out of one period of history into another, better one' (2017: 23-4), is particularly insightful.

[5] As far as I could trace, President Alberto Fernández (2019-present) has yet to mention the word in his numerous statements about the past and the ongoing trials. He has, however, had to clarify his statement about the Armed Forces' 'turning the page', by which he had meant that today there are no active members of the Armed Forces who participated in state terrorism. See *https://www.pagina12.com.ar/249346-alberto-fernandez-aclaro-su-frase-sobre-las-fuerzas-armadas* (accessed 28 March 2022).

[6] National Commission on the Disappearance of Persons (Comisión Nacional Sobre la Desaparición de Personas).

[7] Fabris (2013) and Bonnin (2015) offer a detailed discussion of positions held within the church vis-à-vis judicial accountability, truth, and reconciliation. They both complicate Mignone's (1986) early typology to show a heterogeneity of voices existing between two extremes: national reconciliation through mercy, love, and oblivion; and reconciliation as a utopian reality that cannot materialize without repentance, information (truth), and justice. Varied positions along the continuum were intertwined with political developments and used by social actors for different ends (Fabris 2013).

[8] The Full Stop Law established a period after which it would not be possible to file criminal charges for human rights violations, while the Due Obedience Law established that lower-ranking officers were not punishable because they were following orders. The laws led to the closing or freezing of hundreds of investigations (Filippini 2011).

[9] As Figari Layús notes, what may seem like a uniform chronological narrative is in fact a 'simultaneous co-existence and tensions of legal and de-facto impunity, minimal accountability and implementation of some reparations laws' (2015*b*: 14 fn. 5)

[10] The impunity laws did not cover cases of robbery, seizure of private property, fraud, and child theft.

[11] During these flights, naked and forcibly sedated disappeared people were thrown alive into the River Plate.

[12] These are 'judicial proceedings aimed at obtaining or gathering information about the fate of victims before criminal courts that lacked the authority to apply sanctions' (Filippini 2011: 14).

[13] The acronym stands for Sons and Daughters for Identity and Justice against Oblivion and Silence. The HRO was created by the children of the disappeared, assassinated, or exiled.

[14] The ESMA (Escuela Mecánica de la Armada) was the location of one of the largest clandestine detention and torture camps during the dictatorial rule. It is estimated that around 5,000 people passed through its gates, many of them meeting their end in its torture chambers or in the 'death flights'.

[15] Grassroots initiatives, often led by concerned neighbours, included local memory signs (*baldosas*) located at the homes or places of abduction of the disappeared (Barrios × Memoria y Justicia 2010).

[16] This was the title of the CONADEP's report in 1984 (Comisión Nacional Sobre la Desaparición de Personas 1984) and has become a core demand since.

[17] In 2004, Néstor Kirchner, in the name of the nation-state, asked for forgiveness for the years of silence in the face of the atrocities committed under dictatorial rule.

[18] Congress already annulled the amnesty laws on 2 September 2003 under Law 25,779.

[19] *https://www.fiscales.gob.ar/lesa-humanidad/24-de-marzo-a-46-anos-del-golpe-de-estado-hay-1058-personas-condenadas-en-273-sentencias-por-crimenes-de-lesa-humanidad/* (accessed 28 March 2022).

[20] The 2017 Argentine Episcopal Conference (AEC), which discussed a possible call for reconciliation between families of detained-disappeared and repressors (Uranga 2017), generated extensive rejections, leading to the AEC backtracking and clarifying its use of the term.

[21] Specifically, family members and past officers gathered in organizations such as 'Complete Memory' and 'Association of Relatives and Friends of Argentine Political Prisoners' (Ranalletti 2010; Salvi 2015).

[22] For a detailed argument against Hilb's notions of truth and human rights, see Crenzel (2017: 243).

[23] See the many different critiques levelled at the work of the TRC and its outcomes (e.g. Gready 2011).

[24] See also Stockwell (2014) for an insightful argument about affect and time in women's narratives of the past and its legacies in Argentina.

[25] The book *Hijos de los 70* (Arenes & Pikielny 2016), based on interviews with children of perpetrators and children of the disappeared, can be read as another such attempt that allows for the inconsistencies, contradictions, and ambiguities to coexist in textual form through the 'co-habitation' of contradictory narratives under one literary cover.

[26] The law was passed when the Argentine prisons were overcrowded with people awaiting trial in a very slow and overburdened judicial system.

[27] Text read in the plaza and posted as a news release on Abuelas de la Plaza de Mayo's website (10 May 2017). See *https://www.abuelas.org.ar/noticia/nunca-mas-impunidad-806* (accessed 28 March 2022).

[28] Arendt identifies non-reconciliation as the refusal to reconcile with the world when the crime and the wrongdoer are part of it (Berkowitz 2011; section 3; and Mookherjee's introduction to this volume).

[29] Another clear example is the vigilance that members of H.I.J.O.S. have shown in identifying perpetrators of human rights crimes who do not comply with their house arrests (see Vaisman 2017).

[30] For a very insightful and detailed reading of this text, see Brudholm (2008).

[31] Another example is the numerous *siluetazos*: public artistic interventions where the life-size human silhouettes of the disappeared were pasted on walls and buildings across the city centre, creating an illusion that the bodies or the shadows of the disappeared were everywhere in the city (Longoni & Bruzzone 2008).

[32] Simpson's (2017) notion of 'refusal' resonates strongly with this position. Her question – why continue refusing? – is in part answered by ongoing judicial accountability processes in Argentina, but maybe more poignantly by the slow openness to affective ambivalence and tense, uncomfortable social ties.

REFERENCES

Améry, J. 1980 [1966]. *At the mind's limits: contemplation by a survivor on Auschwitz and its realities* (trans. S. Rosenfeld & S.B. Rosenfeld). Bloomington: Indiana University Press.

Andermann, J. 2012. Returning to the site of horror: on the reclaiming of clandestine concentration camps in Argentina. *Theory, Culture & Society* **29**, 76-98.

Andriotti Romanin, E. 2013. *Memorias en conflicto: el movimiento de derechos humanos y la construcción del juicio por la verdad de Mar del Plata*. Mar del Plata: EUDEM.

Anitua, G.I., N.A. Álvarez & M. Gaitán (eds) 2014. *Los juicios por crímenes de lesa humanidad: enseñanzas jurídico penales*. Buenos Aires: Didot.

Arenes, C. & A. Pikielny 2016. *Hijos de los 70*. Buenos Aires: Sudamericana.

Journal of the Royal Anthropological Institute (N.S.) **28**, 103-117

BALARDINI, L. 2016. Argentina: regional protagonist of transitional justice. In *Transitional justice in Latin America: the uneven road from impunity toward accountability* (eds) E. Skaar, J. Garcia-Godos & C. Collins, 50-76. London: Routledge.

BARRIOS × MEMORIA Y JUSTICIA 2010. *Baldosas × la Memoria II*. Buenos Aires: Instituto Espacio para la Memoria.

BENEGAS, D. 2011. 'If there's no justice …': trauma and identity in post-dictatorship Argentina. *Performance Research* **16**, 20-30.

BERKOWITZ, R. 2011. Bearing logs on our shoulders: reconciliation, non-reconciliation, and the building of a common world. *Theory & Event* **14**, 1-16.

BLEJMAR, J., S. MANDOLESSI & M.E. PEREZ (eds) 2017. *El pasado inasequible: desaparecidos, hijos y combatientes en el arte y la literatura del nuevo milenio*. Buenos Aires: Eudeba.

BOHOSLAVSKY, J.P. & V. OPGENHAFFEN 2010. The past and present of corporate complicity: financing the Argentinean dictatorship. *Harvard Human Rights Journal* **23**, 157-203.

BONNIN, J.E. 2009. Religious and political discourse in Argentina: the case of reconciliation. *Discourse & Society* **20**, 327-43.

———— 2015. Los discursos sobre la reconciliación: variaciones en torno al perdón la verdad y la justicia. In *Democracia, hora zero: actores, políticas y debates en los inicios de la posdictadura* (eds) C. Feld & M. Franco, 225-68. Buenos Aires: Fondo de Cultura Económica.

BORNEMAN, J. 2002. Reconciliation after ethnic cleansing: listening, retribution, affiliation. *Public Culture* **14**, 281-304.

BORRELLI, M. & M.F. OCHOA 2016. Entre la urgencia y la reconciliación: la gran prensa argentina y la sanción de la Ley de 'Punto Final' en 1986. *Revista de Comunicación* **15**, 11-33.

BRUDHOLM, T. 2008. *Resentment's virtue: Jean Améry and the refusal to forgive*. Philadelphia: Temple University Press.

COLECTIVO HISTORIAS DESOBEDIENTES 2019. *Escritos desobedientes: historias de hijas, hijos y familiares de genocidas por la memoria, la verdad y la justicia*. Buenos Aires: Marea Editorial.

COLLINS, C. 2010. *Post-transitional justice: human rights trials in Chile and El Salvador*. University Park: Pennsylvania State University Press.

COMISIÓN NACIONAL SOBRE LA DESAPARICIÓN DE PERSONAS (CONADEP) 1984. *Nunca más*. Buenos Aires: Eudeba.

CRENZEL, E. 2015. Genesis, uses, and significations of the *Nunca más* report in Argentina. *Latin American Perspectives* **42**: **3**, 20-38.

———— 2017. La verdad en debate: la primacía del paradigma jurídico en el examen de las violaciones a los derechos humanos en la Argentina. *Política y Sociedad* **54**, 229-48.

———— 2019. The crimes of the last dictatorship in Argentina and its qualification as genocide: a historicization. *Global Society* **33**, 365-81.

DANDAN, A. & H. FRANZKI 2015. Between historical analysis and legal responsibility: the Ledesma case. In *The economic accomplices to the Argentine dictatorship: outstanding debts* (eds) H. Verbitsky & J.O. Bohoslavsky, 186-200. Cambridge: University Press.

DAS, V. & A. KLEINMAN 2002. Introduction. In *Remaking the world: Violence, social suffering and recovery* (eds) V. Das, A. Kleinman, M. Lock, M. Ramphele & P. Reynolds, 1-30. New Delhi: Oxford University Press.

DERRIDA, J. 1992. The force of law: 'The mythical foundations of authority'. In *Deconstruction and the possibility of justice* (eds) D. Cornell, M. Rosenfeld & D. Carlson, 3-67. New York: Routledge.

———— 2001. *On cosmopolitanism and forgiveness* (trans. M. Dooley & M. Hughes). London: Routledge.

DRULIOLLE, V. 2011. Remembering and its places in postdictatorship Argentina. In *The memory of state terrorism in the Southern Cone: Argentina, Chile and Uruguay* (eds) F. Lessa & V. Druliolle, 15-41. New York: Palgrave Macmillan.

ELSTER, J. 2004. *Closing the books: transitional justice in historical perspective*. Cambridge: University Press.

FABRIS, M. 2013. Perdonar y reconciliarse: la Iglesia católica argentina, el retorno de la democracia y la revisión de las violaciones a los derechos humanos. *Secuencia* **85**, 69-89.

FEIERSTEIN, D. 2006. Political violence in Argentina and its genocidal characteristics. *Journal of Genocide Research* **8**, 149-68.

FIGARI LAYÚS, R. 2015a. *Los juicios por sus protagonistas: doce historias sobre los juicios por delitos de lesa humanidad en Argentina*. Villa María: Eduvim.

——— 2015b. 'What do you mean by transitional justice?' Local perspectives on human rights trials in Argentina. In *Legacies of state violence and transitional justice in Latin America* (eds) N. Schneider & M. Esparza, 3-16. Lanham, Md: Lexington Books.

——— 2018. *The reparative effects of human rights trials: lessons from Argentina.* New York: Routledge.

Filippini, L. 2006. Juicios por la verdad en Argentina. Paper prepared to be delivered to the Latin American Studies Association. (PDF in author's possession).

——— 2011. Criminal prosecution in the search for justice. In *Making justice: Further discussions on the prosecution of crimes against humanity in Argentina* (eds) J. Tiana, L. Filippini, C. Varsky, *et al.*, 11-29. Buenos Aires: Center for Legal and Social Studies (CELS), International Center for Transitional Justice (available online: *https://www.cels.org.ar/web/en/publicaciones/making-justice-further-discussions-on-the-prosecution-of-crimes-against-humanity-in-argentina/*, accessed 28 March 2022).

Fletcher, L.E. & H.M. Weinstein 2002. Violence and social repair: rethinking the contribution of justice to reconciliation. *Human Rights Quarterly* **24**, 573-639.

Galante, D. 2019. *El Juicio a las Juntas: Discursos entre política y justicia en la transición argentina.* La Plata: Universidad Nacional de La Plata.

Garibotto, V. 2019. *Rethinking testimonial cinema in postdictatorship Argentina: beyond memory fatigue.* Bloomington: Indiana University Press.

Gatti, G. 2014. *Surviving forced disappearance in Argentina and Uruguay: identity and meaning.* New York: Palgrave Macmillan.

Gready, P. 2011. *The era of transitional justice: the aftermath of the Truth and Reconciliation Commission in South Africa and beyond.* New York: Routledge.

——— & S. Robins (eds) 2019. *From transitional to transformative justice.* Cambridge: University Press.

Haber, B. & R.A. Wilson 2002. Symbolic closure through memory, reparation and revenge in post-conflict societies. *Journal of Human Rights* **1**, 35-53.

Hayner, P.B. 2011 [2001]. *Unspeakable truths: transitional justice and the challenge of truth commissions* (Second edition). New York: Routledge.

Hendler, A. 2016. ¿Y vos qué hiciste abuelo? *70 y Pico*, un documental íntimo sobre los años de la Dictadura. *Clarín*, 23 February (available online: *https://www.clarin.com/arquitectura/documental-represion-arquitectura-responsabilidad-decano_o_SJGH32uwQg.html*, accessed 28 March 2022).

Hilb, C. 2011. Virtuous justice, and its price in truth in post-dictatorial Argentina. *African Yearbook of Rhetoric* **2**: **1**, 13-20.

——— 2012. Justicia, reconciliación, perdón. *African Yearbook of Rhetoric* **3**: **2**, 41-52.

Jelin, E. 2012. Sexual abuse as a crime against humanity and the right to privacy. *Journal of Latin American Cultural Studies: Travesia* **21**, 343-50.

——— 2017. *La lucha por el pasado: cómo construimos la memoria social.* Buenos Aires: Siglo Vientiuno.

Leebaw, B.A. 2008. The irreconcilable goals of transitional justice. *Human Rights Quarterly* **30**, 95-118.

Longoni, A. & G. Bruzzone (eds) 2008. *El siluetazo.* Buenos Aires: Adriana Hidalgo Editora.

Meyer, A. 2017. Un no a la impunidad en todo el país. *Pagina 12, El país*, 11 May (available online: *https://www.pagina12.com.ar/36998-un-no-a-la-impunidad-en-todo-el-pais*, accessed 28 March 2022).

Mignone, E.F. 1986. *Iglesia y dictadura.* Buenos Aires: Del Pensamiento Nacional.

Ní Aoláin, F. & C. Campbell 2005. The paradox of transition in conflicted democracies. *Human Rights Quarterly* **27**, 172-213.

Pertot, W. 2017. Un rechazo que se convirtió en inmensa multitud. *Pagina 12, El país*, 11 May (available online: *https://www.pagina12.com.ar/36972-un-rechazo-que-se-convirtio-en-inmensa-multitud*, accessed 28 March 2022).

Ranalletti, M. 2010. Denial of the reality of state terrorism in Argentina as narrative of the recent past: A new case of 'negationism'? *Genocide Studies and Prevention* **5**, 160-73.

Robben, A.C.G.M. 2012. From dirty war to genocide: Argentina's resistance to national reconciliation. *Memory Studies* **5**, 305-15.

Ros, A. 2012. *The post-dictatorship generation in Argentina, Chile, and Uruguay.* New York: Palgrave Macmillan.

Rúa, S.C. 2010. Hijos de víctimas del terrorismo de Estado: justicia, identidad y memoria en el movimiento de derechos humanos en la Argentina, 1995-2008. *Historia Crítica* **40**, 122-45.

Salvi, V. 2015. 'We are all victims': changes in the narrative of 'national reconciliation' in Argentina. *Latin American Perspectives* **42**: **3**, 39-51.

Sanford, V. 2003a. The 'grey zone' of justice: NGOs and rule of law in postwar Guatemala. *Journal of Human Rights* **2**, 393-405.

Journal of the Royal Anthropological Institute (N.S.) **28**, *103-117*

———— 2003*b*. *Buried secrets: truth and human rights in Guatemala*. New York: Palgrave Macmillan.

SHAW, R. 2005. Rethinking truth and reconciliation commissions: Lessons from Sierra Leone. United States Institute of Peace Special Report #130 (available online: *https://www.usip.org/publications/2005/02/ rethinking-truth-and-reconciliation-commissions-lessons-sierra-leone*, accessed 29 March 2022).

SIKKINK, K. 2008. From pariah state to global protagonist: Argentina and the struggle for international human rights. *Latin American Politics and Society* **50**, 1-29.

SIMPSON, A. 2017. The ruse of consent and the anatomy of 'refusal': cases from indigenous North America and Australia. *Postcolonial Studies* **20**, 18-33.

SKAAR, E. 2012. Reconciliation in a transitional justice perspective. *Transitional Justice Review* **1**, 54-103.

STOCKWELL, J. 2014. 'The country that doesn't want to heal itself': the burden of history, affect and women's memories in post-dictatorship Argentina. *International Journal of Conflict and Violence* **8**, 30-44.

SUTTON, B. 2007. *Poner el cuerpo*: women's embodiment and political resistance in Argentina. *Latin American Politics and Society* **49**, 129-62.

TURNER, C. 2013. Deconstructing transitional justice. *Law Critique* **24**, 193-209.

URANGA, W. 2017. Los Obispos abrieron el camino al fallo. *Pagina 12, El país*, 4 May (available online: *https: //www.pagina12.com.ar/35508-los-obispos-abrieron-el-camino-al-fallo*, accessed 28 March 2022).

VAISMAN, N. 2017. Variations on justice: Argentina's pre- and post-transitional justice and justice to come. *Ethnos* **82**, 366-88.

———— 2019. Kinship, knowledge and the state: The case of the adult 'living disappeared' in Argentina. In *The Cambridge handbook of kinship* (ed.) S. Bamford, 279-305. Cambridge: University Press.

———— 2020. On (not) coming to terms with the past: forced disappearance, social catastrophe and the different uses of history in Argentina. In *The global crisis in memory: populism, decolonisation and how we remember in the twenty-first century* (eds) E. Spisiakova, J. Mark & C. Forsdick. Liverpool University Press, Modern Languages Open (available online: *https://www.modernlanguagesopen.org/articles/10.3828/ mlo.voio.327/*, accessed 28 March 2022).

———— 2021. Repetitions towards an end: judicial accountability and the vicissitudes of justice. *Ethnos*, 25 May. doi: *10.1080/00141844.2021.1924816*.

———— & L. BARRERA 2020. On judgment: managing emotions in trials of crimes against humanity in Argentina. *Social & Legal Studies* **29**, 812-34.

VAN ROEKEL, E. 2020. *Phenomenal justice: violence and morality in Argentina*. Newark, N.J.: Rutgers University Press.

VARSKY, C. & L. BALARDINI 2013. La 'actualización' de la verdad a 30 años de CONADEP. El impacto de los juicios por crímenes de lesa humanidad. Ministerio de Justicia y Derechos Humanos de la Nación. Dirección Nacional del Sistema Argentino de Información Jurídica. *Derechos Humanos – Infojus* **2**: **4**, 27-54 (available online: *https://ri.conicet.gov.ar/handle/11336/28580*, accessed 28 March 2022).

VERBITSKY, H. 2005 [1996]. *Confessions of an Argentine dirty warrior: a firsthand account of atrocity*. New York: The New Press.

WILSON, R.A. 2003. Anthropological studies of national reconciliation processes. *Anthropological Theories* **3**, 367-87.

ZYLBERMAN, L. 2020. Against family loyalty: documentary films on descendants of perpetrators from the last Argentinean dictatorship. *Continuum* **34**, 241-54.

L'irréconciliation comme pratique : résistance à l'impunité et à la résolution en Argentine

Résumé

En Argentine, l'irréconciliation naît de pratiques quotidiennes de vigilance envers la résolution et de luttes collectives contre l'impunité. Dans le présent article, l'autrice montre comment, dans les décennies qui ont suivi la chute de la dictature (1976-83), activistes des droits humains et membres de la société civile ont conçu des moyens de garder le passé vivant en s'attaquant aux injustices, par le biais d'approches collectives et incorporées de l'histoire du pays et de ses héritages. Par l'examen de mouvements de protestation à grande échelle, de l'expérience quotidienne de l'impunité et d'une exploration filmée des liens de parenté et de leur intrication avec la complicité des civils dans la répression, l'article montre comment l'irréconciliation est matérialisée et mise en actes comme une forme de reconstruction sociale, bien des années après la fin du terrorisme d'État.

Journal of the Royal Anthropological Institute (N.S.) **28**, *103-117*

8

Absence in technicolour: protesting enforced disappearances in northern Sri Lanka

Vindhya Buthpitiya *University of St Andrews*

This essay examines the political uses of photography in the protests of the Tamil families of the disappeared in northern Sri Lanka. Enforced disappearances have long featured as an instrument of state terror. Their lingering effects have been noted as a significant challenge to transitional justice processes in the aftermath of the island's civil war. By examining how protesters make their political demands and grievances known through photography, I explore the tensions between visibility and surveillance. The competing photographies of the protests subvert conceptual understandings of the medium as an ideological tool, but also complicate claims of its capacities for enabling emancipation. Against a backdrop of ethno-nationalist conflict, this mobilization of and through photography serves as a defiant articulation of post-war 'irreconciliation'. It is further tethered to a global visual vernacular of civilian resistance challenging state atrocity, as well as irreconcilable assertions of nation and state.

Photography in the hands of civilians has been central to making visible the violence of a perpetrator's peace that followed Sri Lanka's civil war (1983-2009). By examining the protests of the Tamil families of the disappeared, I consider the limits and the unlikely expansion of Azoulay's assertion of 'photographic citizenship' (2008). The photographies[1] that emerged out of these acts and spaces of resistance were notably diverse. Identity card headshots, formal studio portraits, and family album snaps were shown and displayed alongside grisly trophy images. Further entangled was the photography of journalists and activists, as well as state intelligence personnel who frequented the families' roadside demonstrations. In this setting, Tagg's (1993) claim of photography as an ideological tool and Azoulay's (2008) invocation of photography as a medium for emancipation tussled in a tension of and for visibility. In the shadow of a long-drawn ethno-nationalist conflict, these uses of photography also highlighted how competing claims of nation remained irreconcilable. This troubles and expands photography's possibilities for enhancing 'civic spectatorship' through 'de-territorialization' (Azoulay 2008: 25).

[Correction added on 14 June 2022, after first online publication: The copyright line was changed.]

Journal of the Royal Anthropological Institute (N.S.) **28**, *118-134*
© 2022 The Authors. *Journal of the Royal Anthropological Institute* published by John Wiley & Sons Ltd on behalf of Royal Anthropological Institute.

Dominant theorizations have framed photography as furthering Foucauldian notions of governmentality and surveillance (Tagg 1993). In contrast, Azoulay proposes that photography serves as a mode of political mobilization available to the oppressed (2008: 12). Such a conceptualization transforms photography into 'a tool of a struggle' whereby a citizenship of photography bound to solidarity and responsibility might be fostered (Azoulay 2008: 14). This appeal is hopeful but ultimately idealistic in its formulation. However, it demands empirical investigation precisely because of the ways in which photography is actively utilized by a community seeking to hold the state accountable and reckon with a climate of impunity (see also Vaisman, this volume). Through this example, I highlight how these photographies of protest accrue new meanings and currency in their expedient and/or unexpected social and political mobilization and subversion in a vivid articulation of post-war 'irreconciliation'.

In northern Sri Lanka, the political uses of photography rendered multiple facets of 'irreconciliation' visible, challenging, foremost, the state's assertions of 'peace' achieved out of military victory. The protesters looked to international mechanisms for justice, having been repeatedly failed by successive governments. However, following Brudholm (2008), they were largely uninterested in the core logic of forgiveness that informed the design of such processes and well-meaning civil society initiatives for reconciliation. While 'civic spectatorship' may have succeeded in global visibility for their claims, little progress was achieved locally in terms of their demands to know what happened to their loved ones. The desire for 'never again' in this instance was also inextricable from the nationalist politics of liberation, where freedom from the oppression of an extant sovereign directly informs the political aspirations of another (cf. Azoulay 2008). The protesters' mood was one of resentment and frustration, noting that the war against them still continued by other means as harassment and intimidation by state security personnel persisted.

A short history of 'peace'

Sri Lanka has known 'peace' since the Sri Lankan state forces' military victory over the Liberation Tigers of Tamil Eelam (LTTE) in May 2009. As the self-appointed militant representatives of the Tamil community, the LTTE's demand for self-determination, in response to decades of state violence and discrimination, took the shape of an independent homeland. The group's claim was no less authoritarian or violently contrived than that of the Sri Lankan state, featuring governance structures and a pervasive transnational cultural-ideological project that centred on the necessity for a sovereign Tamil Eelam (see Stokke 2006; Thiranagama 2013).[2]

Between 2006 and 2009, after the breakdown of the 2002 ceasefire agreement, armed hostilities between the military and the LTTE intensified. By 2009, over 300,000 Tamil civilians were trapped in the paradoxically (mis)named 'No Fire Zones' (NFZs) and subjected to indiscriminate shelling and aerial bombardment at the hands of the military. Meanwhile, the LTTE resorted to forced conscription and violently blocking those trying to escape in an effort to use the uprooted population as a human shield. It has been estimated that between September 2008 and May 2009, around 40,000 to 70,000 people were killed in what amounted to a deliberate and catastrophic failure by the Sri Lankan state to protect Tamil civilians. Credible allegations of war crimes and crimes against humanity have been levelled at both the government and the LTTE (Darusman, Ratner & Sooka 2011; International Crimes Evidence Project Sri Lanka 2014; Petrie, UN Secretary-General & UN Internal Review Panel on United Nations

Journal of the Royal Anthropological Institute (N.S.) **28**, *118-134*
© 2022 The Authors. *Journal of the Royal Anthropological Institute* published by John Wiley & Sons Ltd on behalf of Royal Anthropological Institute.

Action 2012). Politically vocal sections of the global Tamil diaspora have called for the atrocities of 2009 to be afforded formal recognition as an act of genocide. These indictments have been resolutely denied by the government, which has maintained the line of a 'humanitarian rescue operation', citing 'zero civilian casualties'.

It is necessary to preface the ensuing discussion on photography in the post-war period by briefly pointing to the wartime image regimes consolidated by both the government and the LTTE. The image world of the aspirant Tamil state was actively engineered by the LTTE as a means for political socialization, recruitment, and fund-raising. It featured elaborate memorial portraiture anointing fallen cadres as martyrs, and the extensive use of atrocity imagery to highlight Sri Lankan state violence as well as the group's own military prowess. Nitharsanam (Truth/Reality), the LTTE's broadcast media unit, included photography and frontline video and film-making divisions. This 'visual economy of the nation' played a crucial role in the LTTE's nation-state building effort and tethering the Tamil community displaced and dispersed across the globe to the promise and necessity of Tamil Eelam (see Poole 1997). While the Sri Lankan state's efforts at mobilizing images were less coherent, it would actively adopt visual and media strategies that had been successfully manoeuvred by the LTTE. The circulation of atrocity images in the mainstream media served an important function in promoting both militarism and what de Mel describes as 'martial virtue' (2007: 13). A virtually cinematic record of what was named 'Eelam War IV' was narrated by embedded journalists who popularized a triumphalist account of the heroic defeat of terrorism and the battlefield benevolence of the armed forces (see Perera 2016).

This period between 2006 and 2009 also marked an important technical development in photography with the transition from analogue film-based practice to digital outputs. An unprecedented volume of images were generated at the frontlines by both victims and perpetrators. Significantly, the advent of mobile phone and compact digital cameras gave rise to graphic contra-narratives that disputed various official untruths concealing the extent of the humanitarian crisis unfolding in the absence of independent witnesses.[3] Thousands of trophy photographs and video clips captured by government soldiers celebrated vicious summary executions and sexual violence. State atrocities were actively documented by LTTE photographers as well as photojournalists and aid workers in the NFZs as the call for an internationally mediated ceasefire mounted to no avail. In the post-war period, these fragments visually enumerating Tamil death and devastation have continued to supplement demands for justice and accountability. They also bolster transnationally consolidated Tamil nationalist political claims sustaining the aspiration for an independent Tamil Eelam.

Nordstrom notes that 'there are layers of invisibility surrounding war' whereby 'complex relationships of truth, untruth and silencing' are produced by deleting frontline actors and actions from formal narratives and official accounts (2004: 25, 28). In the Sri Lankan post-war period, this invisibility was produced through concerted acts of erasure, silencing, spatial (re)organization, and embellishment. These relied not only on infrastructure development, heritage construction, and cultural production, but also on terror and suppression aimed at contriving a consensus of 'peace'. As remnants of the Tamil nationalist-liberationist struggle were assertively expunged, the state's post/war[4] violence against the Tamil community was overlooked or denied. This history-making effort through visual-material manufacture and removal amounted to the cultivation of a 'public forgetfulness' comparable to Feldman's examination of post-apartheid South Africa, where silence was demanded by way of 'fear, intimidation, communal trauma, disinformation and communicative distortion' (2002: 236). Yet in northern Sri Lanka, photography persists as a means of resisting state-mandated amnesia.

The end of the war went hand in hand with international appeals and assistance for establishing mechanisms for reconciliation and transitional justice in line with examples spanning from South Africa to Cambodia. The Sri Lankan government was demonstrably uninterested in such processes, which were also condemned widely by Sinhalese nationalists as a threat to its sovereignty. 'Peace building' had been a part of years of international intervention bound to securing a 'political solution' for the conflict and strengthening civil society for reconciliation (Orjuela 2008). As international pressure to address wartime atrocities mounted, a conciliatory domestic investigation took place in the guise of the 2011 'Lessons Learnt and Reconciliation Commission' (LLRC). The LLRC did not constitute an accountability mechanism and offered instead a series of recommendations that remained unfulfilled emphasizing 'the need for an independent judiciary, a transparent legal process, and strict adherence to the rule of law' (Sooka 2014: 67). Further, the government's denial of war crimes and refusal to accommodate an independent international review, coupled with a pledge to protect its 'war heroes', served an important political purpose in strengthening electoral support from the island's Sinhalese majority.

Disappearing dissent

In the final years of war and its aftermath, thousands of Sri Lankans were forcibly disappeared. A vast majority of victims were Tamil. A large number vanished following their surrender to the state in cases that have been termed 'mass disappearances', while others were detained or abducted in the aftermath of the fighting due to alleged involvements with Tamil militancy, political activism, or criticism of the government.[5] Enforced disappearances have been used extensively as an instrument of terror in Sri Lanka by state security forces and various insurrectionary groups. An estimated 65,000 enforced disappearances affecting Sinhalese, Tamil, and Muslim communities have been reported since the early 1980s, constituting, notoriously, the second-highest caseload globally (UNWGEID 2016).

Women-led civilian resistance against enforced disappearances began in northern Sri Lanka in 1984 with the formation of the Jaffna Mothers' Front and its opposition to the mass arrests and detention of Tamil boys and men (de Mel 2001: 230). De Alwis describes disappearances as 'a site of political contestation' given the violent circumstances within which these took place and the 'insidious practice of making unavailable the violated body as evidence' (2009: 379). The absence of remains results in families being unable to carry out funerary rituals to ensure a peaceful afterlife, rendering this practice particularly malicious. As will be explored later, the positioning of motherhood and gender cannot be disentangled from the visual and political representational dynamics of the protest. In this most recent incarnation, 'The Association for Relatives of the Enforced Disappeared, North and East Provinces' (ARED) was largely made up of mothers whose children had disappeared in the latter stages of the civil war. Activists documenting the government's continued human rights violations and enforced disappearances in the post-war period have themselves been intimidated, imprisoned, or disappeared.

Following several recurrent marches after the end of the war, a short-lived regime change in 2015 enabled the families of the disappeared to confront the government's failure to provide them with information about their loved ones.[6] Sustained protests

Journal of the Royal Anthropological Institute (N.S.) **28**, *118-134*
© 2022 The Authors. *Journal of the Royal Anthropological Institute* published by John Wiley & Sons Ltd on behalf of Royal Anthropological Institute.

Figure 1. Tamil families of the disappeared mark their 500th day of protest. Kilinochchi, 2018. (Photo by the author.)

began in February 2017 based on five demands, including a call to release lists of those who surrendered or were detained by the government forces, the locations of secret detention centres, and the names of detainees held under the Prevention of Terrorism Act (PTA) and various Emergency Regulations (ERs) (ARED 2017). The state undertook a number of piecemeal efforts bound to its vague international commitments to transitional justice by creating various commissions of inquiry, and most notably the Office on Missing Persons (OMP).[7] Established in 2017, the OMP was intended 'to provide appropriate mechanisms for searching and tracing missing persons and to clarify the circumstances in which such persons went missing and their fate' and identify suitable avenues for redress (Parliament of the Democratic Socialist Republic of Sri Lanka 2016). However, the OMP did not possess punitive powers to deal with investigations into testimony identifying perpetrators, its legal enactment patently stating that its findings should not give rise to any criminal or civil liability.

The families, misled and disappointed by various state promises and insincere institutional commitments over the years, demanded a more global audience, appealing to the international community. The iconographies of the protest charted these concerns. Alongside portraits of the disappeared, vinyl banners were printed with the flags of the United States, the United Kingdom, and the European Union. Hand-drawn cardboard signs declared a lack of faith in a domestic process and urged international attention (Fig. 1). Even as these images were mobilized in ways that affirmed Azoulay's theorization of photography's potential to create a 'space of political relations that are not mediated exclusively by the ruling power' (2008: 12), they simultaneously acknowledged the failings of existing mechanisms for redress. As the protests wore on, disappointment in the international community worsened. Despite their defiant visibility in an atmosphere of contempt and intimidation, protesters were left with no practical recourse or access, compounding sentiments of exasperation and

Journal of the Royal Anthropological Institute (N.S.) **28**, *118-134*
© 2022 The Authors. *Journal of the Royal Anthropological Institute* published by John Wiley & Sons Ltd on behalf of Royal Anthropological Institute.

'unforgiveness' (Brudholm 2008: 16). Indeed, many felt that the onus on 'reconciliation', especially as advocated for by international organizations and civil society, was imposed on victims rather than the perpetrators themselves. The forcibly disappeared in Kilinochchi and Maruthankerny were among 23,586 individuals recorded as 'missing' between 10 June 1990 and 19 May 2009. Among the protesters were also those who had lost loved ones to the 'shadow state' well before 1990, and after 2009 through various means, including abductions and arbitrary arrest.[8]

The hollowness of institutional processes such as the OMP, accompanied by dismissive statements made by political figures, were seen by victims as confirmation of the government's disingenuousness and lack of interest in Tamil grievances. This was reinforced by the fact that those who crossed over from LTTE-held territory to government-controlled areas at the end of the war were officially registered. A number of protesters had personally handed over their children and grandchildren to the military in 2009. The political leadership's broken promises to release the names of the detainees and surrendees endured as a significant point of frustration (Rajasingham 2018). Most recently, President Gotabaya Rajapaksa, one of the architects of the final phase of the war in his previous role as Defence Secretary, stated, 'The missing are in fact dead. I cannot bring back the dead' (Abi-Habib & Bastians 2020). The tone of the protests also changed significantly since their beginning, becoming further 'formalized'. The Kilinochchi protest tent, for example, morphed into an office, with continuous protests halting after the 500-day mark and regular demonstrations taking their place.

The failures of visibility

I examine the protests of the families of the disappeared through the photographies that threaded through the site as acts of mobilization, subversion, and surveillance. Here Tagg's (1993) and Azoulay's (2008) contrasting conceptualizations jostle in uneasy contention. Drawing on Foucault (1980) and Althusser (2001 [1970]), Tagg considers photography as solely reflective of 'the power of the apparatuses of the local state which deploy it and guarantee the authority of the images it constructs to stand as evidence or register as truth' (1993: 64). In contrast, Azoulay argues for mobilizing the camera's capacity to create 'powerful forms of commotion and communion' to overcome the confines set by the sovereign (2015: 15). Photography, she argues, is at times 'the only civic refuge at the disposal of those robbed of citizenship' (2008: 121). The use of photography at the protests of the families of the disappeared renders the limits and potentials of the medium visible in an articulation of discontent and irreconciliation. These uses are inextricable from an essential question of visibility, which affords both political possibility and risk where the struggle for self-determination is concerned. Visibility is also central to the design of truth and reconciliation processes, where violations and violences are required to be made visible. These centre either on confession, atonement, testimony, and forgiveness, in line with a Christianized ethos that is intended to foster cohesion, or on the legal, criminological, and forensic reliance on the presentation of 'evidence'. The latter has historically depended on photography in its indexical capacity, informing, in turn, the medium's Foucauldian assumption: as a tool of governance and surveillance.

In Nader's (2001) understanding, processes intended to contrive harmony also involve coercion, which, within the Sri Lankan example determined by complex and impaired citizenship, amounted to the denial of freedom. Reflecting on the experiences of the LTTE's role as a de facto state actor, Brun defines the position of the

Figure 2. Mothers with portraits of their missing children. Maruthankerny, Jaffna, 2018. (Photo by the author.)

northern Tamil community as one of 'complex citizenship', where there is a lack of 'a clear-cut relationship between citizens and the state, but where there are several governing and uncompromising actors that people must relate to' (2008: 401). Tamil demands for self-determination arose out of a situation of 'impaired citizenship', indicating the hierarchies and inequalities that exist within the category of 'Sri Lankan' (Azoulay 2008: 24). Where the aspirant Tamil state was defeated, Tamil citizenship in the post-war period was characterized by renewed complexity, inequality, and impairment, made visible in the protest photographies that punctuated the landscape of northern Sri Lanka.

At the time of publication, the Tamil families of the disappeared in the north and east of Sri Lanka had engaged in over 1,900 days of continuous protest. In meagre tents scattered across six towns pinned with the haunting photographic portraits of those subjected to enforced disappearance, elderly parents, grandparents, spouses, siblings, and sometimes young children sat in roadside vigil (Fig. 2). The images displayed were mostly formal studio portraits, poised, full-length, set against vividly painted backdrops that featured conventions of opulent stage curtains, grand arches, or lush Italianate scenery. Others were enlarged reproductions of National Identity Card (NIC) photographs valued for their frontality: headshots facing right in semi-profile with the left ear fully visible as per the official stipulation. A disconcerting number were pictured in school uniform. Several were more informal, tender moments clipped out of snaps from weddings, birthday parties, or gatherings with friends. In the absence of usable photographs, there were also black and white photocopies of identity documents revealing the interwoven realities of war, displacement, loss, and economic hardship.

In Barthes's poignant terms, 'every photograph [was] a certificate of presence' (2010 [1980]: 87). These indexed lives violently and abruptly disappeared, while drawing attention to the brutalities that necessitated their display. Among those pictured were young men and women who were forcefully conscripted by the LTTE to fill its depleting ranks, surrendered to the government forces, vanished during their internment at squalid 'welfare centres', or were never seen again following their 'rehabilitation' in camps set up for the 12,000 individuals identified as 'ex-combatants'. The portraits also served an important function of signposting for the disappeared. The fear of being forgotten was common among the protesters, especially in instances where the victims were young or wounded when separated from their families. These photographs were not merely visual articulations of resistance for the protesters, but also a guide for those who may not know how to find their way back home.

Photographs of the protesters themselves, mostly elderly parents and grandparents in their various media and civil society circulations, have become visual mnemonics for the failures of Sri Lanka's transitional justice processes. Yet, in contrast to Mookherjee's (2015) exploration of the iconicity of Bangladeshi 'war heroines', these protesters and their images appeared to be largely ignored within the island. The demonstrations were also the subject of a more insidious practice of photography. State intelligence operatives habitually captured the protesters' activities on mobile phones and digital cameras. In mutual awareness, the protesters, their supporters, activists, and government informers, along with their contending photographies, orbited one another. Where 'reconciliation' took the shape of new roads, white-washed government complexes, and grand victory monuments, these transient sites of civilian protest rendered 'irreconciliation' visible. It was incompatible with and opposed to the state's narrative of peace and victory. In these small roadside tents in the island's north and east, violent absence endured in technicolour.

Journalists and activists intermittently visited the sites to compile news items. On certain days, the family members were eager to narrate their stories. Heartbreak was rehearsed on demand for visiting writers and photographers. Each iteration was underpinned by inconceivable despair and desperation, but also a desire to be seen and acknowledged. Correspondence relating to complaints made to the state and the Red Cross and responses that arrived in languages they did not speak (English/Sinhala) were shown in frustration. Private photographs from tucked-away shopping bags emerged during conversations on quieter days to narrate cruelly disrupted lives. On some days, there were no words. Instead, photographs cupped in their hands were held up as offerings to the camera.

At other times, photographs were discouraged, and distaste and apprehensions around their possible uses and commoditization by photojournalists or entrepreneurial immigration brokers were expressed. These concerns hinted at the medium's perceived capacity to contract future protections, entitlements, and citizenships. Foreign correspondents demanded that their fixers organize assembly lines of hands, photos, and tearful faces for their cameras to add colour to global news explainers. These evoked what Kleinman and Kleinman describe as a 'dismay of images' that distilled suffering, situating the protesters within a global visual economy of resistance against state terror (1996: 9). Yet the protesters were anything but passive subjects in the making of these images, thinking through their efficacy and expediency, highlighting importantly the risk and agency involved in the performative politics of 'victimhood'. It was an understanding that demonstrated the global nature of their audience, and the language and visibility required by international apparatuses for attention and perhaps even redress. These photographs also signalled the failures of domestic reconciliation

Journal of the Royal Anthropological Institute (N.S.) **28**, *118-134*
© 2022 The Authors. *Journal of the Royal Anthropological Institute* published by John Wiley & Sons Ltd on behalf of Royal Anthropological Institute.

Figure 3. Demonstration marking 365 days of continuous protest. Kilinochchi, 2018. (Photo by the author.)

processes and international civic spectatorship, as well as global governance and rights ideals and mechanisms.

On demonstration days marking significant international commemorations such as Human Rights Day or the protest's milestones measured by continuity, the families actively presented themselves to be photographed (Fig. 3). The 'chronic mourners' were snapped extensively (Schirmer 1989: 25). Their bodies were situated against photomontages of loss or holding pictures of their disappeared loved ones in their palms. These located the tent's occupants within a broader aesthetic of resistance against state terror and enforced disappearance. The portraits visually linked them to families of the disappeared elsewhere in the world, in a potent formation of Azoulay's (2008) photographic citizenship, transcending and challenging the violences of the sovereign (see also Clarke, this volume). Their defiant presence as a proxy for the absent bodies of the disappeared was also a reminder of the continued absence of justice.

As the protesters faced the cameras, their quiet sadness sometimes gave way to visceral rage and sorrow. They screamed their pain into unblinking lenses. Photographs and footage were compressed and linked to social media posts tethered to a series of dedicated hashtags (#disappearedsl [Disappeared Sri Lanka], #familiesofthedisappeared, #releasethelist, #nojustice, #tamilfod [Tamil Families of the Disappeared]) alongside others denoting ethnicity and location (#tamil, #eelamtamil, #kilinochchi). On Instagram and Twitter, these were re-posted and re-tweeted largely by diasporic Tamils and a small number of local activists. However, the social-media-enabled 'de-territorialization' of these images also reinforced ethno-nationalist claims and interlinked demands for alternative sovereignty rather than necessarily 'civil skills that are not subject to nationality' (Azoulay 2008: 26).

Journal of the Royal Anthropological Institute (N.S.) **28**, *118-134*

Interspersed among the photographs of the disappeared were more patent confirmations of state atrocity in the form of trophy images captured by government soldiers. In a powerful example of photographic contingency, family members found inadvertent confirmation of their loved ones in custody where arrests were denied (see Benjamin 2004 [1931]: 510).[9] In Kilinochchi, an image of a group of men and a young boy in the custody of the army had been printed onto a vinyl banner. It was one of two photographs displayed at the site showing a group of captives huddled around a pit prior to what was believed to be their execution. The still image, one of the hundreds that emerged out of the final months of the war, was used most famously in the Channel 4 documentaries *Sri Lanka's Killing Fields* and *Sri Lanka's Killing Fields: War Crimes Unpunished*. One of the men pictured was known to someone in the group, but they collectively wondered who the anonymous child was and whether he had survived. A year later in London, I learned that he had not. I was shown photographs of the boy's mangled body, identifiable by his blue shorts and a bandaged knee, piled into the back of a truck.

On other days, the protesters requested photographs from visitors to the site. Images of their activism were printed onto demonstration-day banners held up at marches. This was an important act of record-keeping where the progress of the protests was preserved as a part of its iconography. Here, photographs, both personal and those required by the state for identity documents, served as a means for remembering and a reminder of state terror and brutality, especially where government monuments to war victory did not acknowledge the losses of the Tamil community. The premise of photography as an ideological tool of the state, which wields power through documentation and surveillance, was subverted by this mobilization, whereby the protesters made themselves visible to and challenged the state.

The use of photography also permitted the protesters to overcome a language barrier. The state's marginalization of the Tamil language (and citizenship) was one of the most significant tensions of the postwar. 'I have never felt like a citizen of this country!' various interlocutors repeated in frustration, with others describing their status as 'second-class' or 'third-class' citizens. Inequalities instituted within the category of citizenship on account of ethnicity and language were a root cause of the conflict. Photographs enabled those who did not have a common language to communicate to the English- and Sinhala-speaking media and activists who documented and disseminated their stories and their losses. They offered an arresting visual to the largely uninterested or hostile mainstream refusing to overlook possible associations with the LTTE.

Anti-politics of solidarity

Media attention afforded to the protests was not without strain. While international transmissions elicited solidarity and support, little progress was made with regard to the protesters' actual demands. Photography of the protests, especially on demonstration days, was cautiously strategized by its proponents. Where the 'chronic' state of grief and devastation in which these protesters were suspended was largely unacknowledged by the state as well as the majority of their fellow citizens, its outpouring was directed towards the camera, where it might be acknowledged and recorded for posterity. This expands on Seoighe's consideration that these acts of resistance constitute a form of collective performative politics aimed at challenging the established 'state architecture of domination' (2016: 1, 3). It also echoes Clarke's consideration in this volume of *victim visibilization* in Colombia as a refusal of state-sponsored truth commissions, signalling a new kind of accountability politics of the collective, which in this instance is made possible by photography.

The un/intentional centring of gender as well as 'victimhood' permitted an assertion of what was 'counter-political' in appearance, but inextricable from the anti-politics of the ethno-nationalist conflict within which the protesters' grievances were rooted (Spencer 2007). The protests were predominantly led by women, and certainly described as such. 'Motherhood' was notably emphasized. I highlight here Spencer's differentiation between the counter-political and the anti-political. The former seeks to defuse the effects of the political whereas the latter 'is rooted in paradox – the exploitation, for political purposes, of popular unease with the moral implications of actually existing politics' (2007: 177). The foregrounding of women – elderly mothers and grandmothers – and young girls in the protests and their photographic representations in terms of 'victimhood' sometimes afforded a counter-political veneer to what were perceived to be anti-political Tamil nationalist claims. As was the case during the war years, 'victimization' was a visual trope that was consciously mobilized to supplement the necessity for liberation and sovereignty. While the protesters exercised important, if ambivalent, agency in presenting themselves to the camera, the subsequently unruly circuits within which these images were transmitted varied in their political inscription, which troubled the ways in which the protests were received in Sri Lanka in particular.

Referring to the protesters as *Tamil amma*s (Tamil mothers) fortified expressions of solidarity, especially among activists in the Tamil disapora, where the emphasis on Tamilness and motherhood affirmed kinship in ethnicized terms. The figure of the protesting mother was not without Tamil nationalist resonance, evoking particularly Annai Poopathy (1932-88), a mother of ten from Batticaloa who was a part of the Mothers' Front, having lost two sons to Sri Lankan state atrocity. In 1988, she fasted unto death demanding a ceasefire between the Indian Peace Keeping Forces (IPKF) and the LTTE. Her death was assimilated into the Tigers' nationalist rhetoric on martyrdom, including annual commemoration events. Against the militarized, masculinized material incarnations of the Sri Lankan state, the largely elderly women comprised a transitory feminized formation.

In reality, the feminized nature of the protest was also determined by socioeconomic practicalities, where the elderly who were not employed or did not have care responsibilities were able to spend long periods at the protest site. It was these distressing realities of undertaking continuous protest that rendered the censure directed at the protesters deeply saddening. The photographies of the protests thus visually encompassed the tension between the counter-political and the anti-political permitted by the ambivalence of photography. Kannan Arunasalam captured this anxiety in his poignant film installation *The Tent* (2019). This consisted of two screens set up side-by-side. The first recorded a quiet day at the Mullaitivu protest camp, with the camera looking outwards from a tent onto the road as its residents contemplated the mundane, the war, and their future. On the second, by contrast, the camera turned to the 500th Day demonstration at Kilinochchi, where the protesters wailed in visceral grief, holding up photos of their loved ones.

In spite of the political risk and agency that underlies participation in these protests, the demonstrators consciously foregrounded their 'victimhood', a category that is often viewed as apolitical or marginalized because of its centrality to the discourses of

Journal of the Royal Anthropological Institute (N.S.) **28**, 118-134
© 2022 The Authors. *Journal of the Royal Anthropological Institute* published by John Wiley & Sons Ltd on behalf of Royal Anthropological Institute.

reconciliation and transitional justice. As noted by Jeffrey and Candea, '[V]ictimhood can be a prime way of suspending or attempting to suspend the political through an appeal to something non-agentive and "beyond" or "before" politics', although it also 'establishes a space for a specific kind of politics' (2006: 289). Terwindt, meanwhile, highlights how victim mobilization reliant on interlinked terminology can serve as an effective driver for processes of criminalization (2020: 66). However, where the state was the perpetrator, the centring of victimhood appealed most directly to international truth and justice mechanisms dominated by legal, criminological, and medical lexica and practice that are inevitably reminiscent of photography's Foucauldian co-option within these fields. Feldman critiques such mechanisms for 'truth', noting that they amount to the imposition of a pathologization on countries struggling with the aftermath of oppression, political terror, and violence. In the process, geopolitical inequalities and hierarchies are played on and exacerbated, permitting those in the Global North to absolve themselves from examining their own past, whereas the process ultimately needs to be 'transnational' to be effective (Feldman 2002: 235).

After many years of being ignored by the state within a context of complex and impaired citizenship, the protesters' demands for justice were directed not at the sovereign, but at the global as mediated by photography and its capacities for amplifying visibility, which powerfully speaks to its potential to de-territorialize 'citizenship' (Azoulay 2008). Here 'victimhood' must be performed, where photographs that situate protesters holding images of their loved ones as 'victims' position them in a new kind of globally determined and recognizable seriality that glosses over 'political' incompatibilities. Within the neoliberal framework of world peace and contexts of 'genocidal cosmopolitanism' emphasized by Mookherjee (2011), Azoulay's suggestion of solidarity and responsibility emboldens advocacy and accountability networks. Here, the photographs of these protesters demanded international governance commitments and action.

In this context of ethno-nationalist conflict, redress and solidarity were further complicated by the lingering effects of Tamils 'othered' by war, where ethnicity was conflated with 'terror' in the categorization of politically active Tamils as terrorists. Former in/voluntary affiliations to the LTTE have been a dominant reason as to why the protests have been dismissed, overlooked, or censured. Even though southern Sri Lanka was plagued with enforced disappearances, there was little compassion or solidarity and overwhelming silence. Perceived sympathy and support from the Tamil diaspora was also seen as a cause for doubt and criticism. Indeed, the protests were supported by various Tamil diaspora groups who, for example, sponsored representatives' travel to make submissions at the UN Human Rights Council sessions in Geneva as well as participate in a demonstration in London. These connections were both ambivalent and inevitable given the transnational character of the Tamil community, and were not without political expediency for various parties. However, 'the diaspora' had also long been demonized by the state and Sinhalese nationalists alongside civil society activism, non-governmental organizations, and international governance mechanisms during the war, and in relation to international pressure for investigations into war crimes in its aftermath.

Confronting the sovereign

Critiquing Tagg's theory that photographs are 'merely a "screen" onto which more powerful primary ideologies are projected', Pinney argues for photography's 'subversive and unpredictable potential', the 'new kinds of juxtaposition and seriality' it affords that enable the world to be seen in fresh ways (2015: 24, 28). Similarly, Kalantzis stresses the ambivalence of the photographic image, the 'continuous [social] repossession and use' of the image that 'destabilizes the initial inscriptions, making them culturally [and, in this setting, politically] salient objects' (2019: 82). This observation resonates in relation to the assembly of photographs at the protest sites, but also in relation to the ways in which the protesters understood and wielded the potential powers of their images. They were intimately aware of the ambivalence of photography, fearing and desiring the power and the visibility afforded by the medium. The 'appropriation' of photographs both in Strassler's work on Indonesia (2010) and in these observations of post-war Sri Lanka highlights a departure from the 'official' narrative that photography has been theorized to reflect (cf. Tagg 1993). At the site of the protests, these theoretical leanings coexist in uneasy contention. Photographs of these photographs and their movement in expanded, globalized circuits of protest and resistance offered continuity not only to the images, those whose moments of life they captured, but also to the hope and struggle of these families of the disappeared in their quest to find answers. Yet the photographs of the protests also reveal inequalities of global news-image economies, producing distressing 'formative fictions', as explored by Gürsel (2016: 113).

The confrontation of the sovereign was enacted through the subversive use and political mobilization of identity documents and photography. Elsewhere, the NIC was actively appropriated into personal use by inclusion in family albums and reframed as memorial images in a manner comparable to the Indonesian *pasfoto*, whereby the state-bureaucratic and sentimental, repressive, and honorific became entangled (Strassler 2010: 145). This was further complicated by an ethno-nationalist conflict, securitization, and competing nation-state and citizen-making projects. Informed by this, the defiant use of the NIC asserted an absent presence that evoked an obvious strain of nation, state, and citizenship. NIC photographs and sometimes NICs and passport pages were wielded by protesters on demonstration days, evidencing the photographic image and presence of the disappeared as was once recognized and authorized by the state. The gazes of NIC portraits were reverted back at the state in a demand for accountability and justice. Here, photography's co-option into governmentality was defiantly appropriated and subverted. The state's narratives of reconciliation are actively challenged through images of its own making in this transient shrine for lives lost in a conflict precisely intended to weaken the state. The recasting of identity photographs was not simply about individual loss, but a collective, implicitly *national* confrontation of the politically constituted erasure instrumented by the Sri Lankan state.

Conclusion

> They have not given us one reason to trust them and it is not for the lack of trying because we have done everything they have asked of us – write letters, go to this commission hearing there, this meeting here. We have been begging them for years. But what have we got? Nothing. We are looking to the UN, the international community, to give us answers, and they are our only hope now, but they, too, continue to disappoint us. Where can we go from here?

Such was the angry declaration of one protesting *amma* in Kilinochchi. Her son had been detained by the military in 2009 and was never seen again. The protesters resolutely confirmed their lack of interest in a local mechanism, explicitly articulated in the previously discussed iconography of the protests. Their mobilization of photographs and their presenting of themselves to be photographed immediately evoked conscious participation in Azoulay's call to enact a new form of civil relations that was not mediated by the sovereign power (2008: 143). However, what of that enactment where mechanisms for justice and redress have been founded on global systems of accountability that are made up of and privilege the extant state? If accountability is contingent on states holding other states accountable within partial and unequal geopolitical relations, what justice and redress might civic spectatorship practically yield?

The aftermath of the Second World War was framed by a forward-looking global language of peace and aesthetic of governance bound to the establishment of an internationalized regime of responsibility espousing the idealized values of the declaration of human rights. It was also designed in a manner such that states would hold one another accountable for violations. While these circulations were intended to supplement promises of peace and dignity bound to international co-operation and governance, however, for those who were looking to such institutions for protection the realities were tenuous. Especially for populations in civil conflicts such as the Tamil families of the disappeared, 'reconciliation' remained elusive and improbable as it was left to the design and operation of state actors who were perpetrators of violence and faced little to no pressure for justice and accountability. Meanwhile, the families' mobilization of the visual intensifed, signalling a recognition of the medium's powers to confront a peace constructed of erasure. The anger and devastation of these families in the deliberate making visible of irreconciliation thus pointed to the failures of responsibility and civic spectatorship.

Acknowledgements

This research is a part of 'Photodemos: Citizens of Photography – The Camera and the Political Imagination' at UCL Anthropology. This project has received funding from the European Research Council (ERC) as part of the European Union's Horizon 2020 research and innovation programme under grant agreement No 695283.

NOTES

[1] The term 'photographies' follows from Tagg (1993: 119) indicating a set of discursive practices informed by Foucault and Batchen's (2000: 57) consideration of vernacular photographies. I use 'photographies' in this instance to indicate the multiplicity of everyday photographic practices relevant to the protests of the families of the disappeared.

[2] About a quarter of the island's Tamil population live outside Sri Lanka, predominantly as a consequence of conflict-induced displacement and dispersal (Maunaguru 2019: 7).

[3] The final months of fighting have been described as a 'war without witnesses' given the withdrawal of United Nations staff from the war zone in September 2008 and the government's prohibition on international media from entering the NFZs.

[4] I use post/war as an abbreviation to combine war and postwar.

[5] The International Truth and Justice Project and the Human Rights Data Analysis Group note that in a three-day period between 17 and 19 May 2009, a total of 503 individuals, including 443 persons named in various cross-referenced, crowd-sourced lists, were disappeared upon surrender to the state forces (Ball & Harrison 2018).

[6] The opposition-led *Yahpalanaya* (good governance) coalition government of the United National Party (UNP) and Sri Lanka Freedom Party (SLFP) led by President Maithripala Sirisena and Prime Minister Ranil Wickramasinghe was in power between 2015 and 2019. The 2015 presidential election marked an unexpected regime change from the previous government led by President Mahinda Rajapaksa (2005-15).

[7] Since 1994, successive Sri Lankan governments have established at least eight Presidential Commissions of inquiry into 'removals' and disappearances, including three zonal commissions. The most recent, the 2013 'Presidential Commission to Investigate Complaints Regarding Missing Persons', known as the 'Paranagama

Commission', and its subsequent expansions, which underpinned the formation of the OMP, inquired into abductions and disappearances related to the civil war between 10 June 1990 and 19 May 2009. The Paranagama Commission received 23,566 complaints, including approximately 5,000 from families of armed forces personnel.

[8] Thomson-Senanayake (2014) describes the establishment of a 'shadow-state' by way of an economic, political, legal, and socioeconomic framework under which disappearances were carried out.

[9] Walter Benjamin describes how the photographic image contains the 'spark of contingency, of the here and now, with which reality (has so to speak) seared the subject, . . . the inconspicuous spot where in the immediacy of that long-forgotten moment the future nests so eloquently that we, looking back may rediscover it', which in turn permits re-readings beyond what was framed and intended by the photographer (2004 [1931]: 510; see also Pinney 2012).

REFERENCES

ABI-HABIB, M. & D. BASTIANS 2020. 'I can't bring back the dead': Sri Lanka leader ends search for war missing. *New York Times*, 21 January (available online: *https://www.nytimes.com/2020/01/21/world/asia/ sri-lanka-civil-war.html*, accessed 26 March 2022).

ALTHUSSER, L. 2001 [1970]. Ideology and ideological state apparatuses. In *The Norton anthology of theory and criticism* (ed.) V.B. Leitch, 1483-508. New York and London: W. W. Norton.

ARED 2017. *Release of lists of surrendees/detainees*. Kilinochchi: Association for Relatives of the Enforced Disappeared.

AZOULAY, A. 2008. *The civil contract of photography*. New York: Zone.

——— 2015. *Civil imagination: a political ontology of photography*. London: Verso.

BALL, P. & F. HARRISON 2018. *How many people disappeared on 17–19 May 2009 in Sri Lanka?* San Francisco: Human Rights Data Analysis Group, International Truth and Justice Project.

BARTHES, R. 2010 [1980]. *Camera lucida: reflections on photography* (trans. R. Howard). New York: Hill & Wang.

BATCHEN, G. 2000. *Each wild idea: writing photography's history*. Cambridge, Mass.: MIT Press.

BENJAMIN, W. 2004 [1931]. Little history of photography. In *Selected writings*: vol. 2, part 2: *1931-1934* (ed. M.W. Jennings, H. Eiland & G. Smith; trans. R. Livingston *et al.*), 507-30. Cambridge, Mass.: Harvard University Press.

BRUDHOLM, T. 2008. *Resentment's virtue: Jean Améry and the refusal to forgive*. Philadelphia: Temple University Press.

BRUN, C. 2008. Birds of freedom. *Critical Asian Studies* **40**, 399-422.

DARUSMAN, M., S. RATNER & Y. SOOKA 2011. *Report of the Secretary General's Panel of Experts on accountability in Sri Lanka*. New York: United Nations Secretariat.

DE ALWIS, M. 2009. 'Disappearance' and 'displacement' in Sri Lanka. *Journal of Refugee Studies* **22**, 378-91.

DE MEL, N. 2001. *Women and the nation's narrative: gender and nationalism in twentieth-century Sri Lanka*. Lanham, Md.: Rowman & Littlefield.

——— 2007. *Militarizing Sri Lanka: popular culture, memory and narrative in the armed conflict*. New Delhi: Sage India.

FELDMAN, A. 2002. Strange fruit: the South African Truth Commission and the demonic economies of violence. *Social Analysis: The International Journal of Anthropology* **46**, 234-65.

FOUCAULT, M. 1980. *Power/knowledge: selected interviews and other writings 1972-1977* (ed. C. Gordon; trans. C. Gordon, L. Marshall, J. Mepham & K. Soper). New York: Pantheon.

GÜRSEL, Z.D. 2016. *Image brokers: visualizing world news in the age of digital circulation*. Berkeley: University of California Press.

INTERNATIONAL CRIMES EVIDENCE PROJECT SRI LANKA 2014. *Island of impunity? Investigation into international crimes in the final stages of the Sri Lankan civil war*. Sydney: Public Interest Advocacy Centre Ltd.

JEFFREY, L. & M. CANDEA 2006. The politics of victimhood. *History and Anthropology* **17**, 287-96.

KALANTZIS, K. 2019. *Tradition in the frame: photography, power, and imagination in Sfakia, Crete*. Bloomington: Indiana University Press.

KLEINMAN, A. & J. KLEINMAN 1996. The appeal of experience; the dismay of images: cultural appropriations of suffering in our times. *Daedalus* **125**, 1-23.

MAUNAGURU, S. 2019. *Marrying for a future: transnational Sri Lankan Tamil marriages in the shadow of war*. Seattle: University of Washington Press.

Journal of the Royal Anthropological Institute (N.S.) **28**, 118-134
© 2022 The Authors. *Journal of the Royal Anthropological Institute* published by John Wiley & Sons Ltd on behalf of Royal Anthropological Institute.

MOOKHERJEE, N. 2011. 'Never again': aesthetics of 'genocidal' cosmopolitanism and the Bangladesh Liberation War Museum. *Journal of the Royal Anthropological Institute* (N.S.) **17**: **S1**, S71-91.

———— 2015. The raped woman as a horrific sublime and the Bangladesh War of 1971. *Journal of Material Culture* **20**, 379-95.

NADER, L. 2001. Harmony coerced is freedom denied. *Chronicle of Higher Education* 47: **44**, 1-4.

NORDSTROM, C. 2004. *Shadows of war: violence, power, and international profiteering in the twenty-first century*. Berkeley: University of California Press.

ORJUELA, C. 2008. *The identity politics of peacebuilding: civil society in war-torn Sri Lanka*. New Delhi: Sage India.

PARLIAMENT OF THE DEMOCRATIC SOCIALIST REPUBLIC OF SRI LANKA 2016. *Office on Missing Persons (establishment, administration and discharge of functions) Act, No. 14 of 2016*. Colombo: Department of Government Printing.

PERERA, S. 2016. *Warzone tourism in Sri Lanka: tales from darker places in paradise*. New Delhi: Sage India.

PETRIE, C., UN SECRETARY-GENERAL & UN INTERNAL REVIEW PANEL ON UNITED NATIONS ACTION 2012. *Report of the Secretary-General's Internal Review Panel on United Nations action in Sri Lanka*. Geneva: United Nations.

PINNEY, C. 2012. Seven theses on photography. *Thesis Eleven* **113**, 141-56.

———— 2015. Civil contract of photography in India. *Comparative Studies of South Asia, Africa and the Middle East* **35**, 21-34.

POOLE, D. 1997. *Vision, race and modernity: a visual economy of the Andean image world*. Princeton: University Press.

RAJASINGHAM, K. 2018. Can OMP deliver justice when Sri Lanka's president won't? JDS, 12 June (available online: *http://www.jdslanka.org/index.php/news-features/human-rights/782-can-omp-deliver-justice-when-sri-lankas-president-wont*, accessed 26 March 2022).

SCHIRMER, J.G. 1989. 'Those who die for life cannot be called dead': women and human rights protest in Latin America. *Feminist Review* **32**, 3-29.

SEOIGHE, R. 2016. Nationalistic authorship and resistance in northern Sri Lanka. *Society and Culture in South Asia* **2**, 1-30.

SOOKA, Y. 2014. *An unfinished war: torture and sexual violence in Sri Lanka 2009-2014*. London: The Bar Human Rights Committee of England and Wales (BHRC)/The International Truth & Justice Project, Sri Lanka.

SPENCER, J. 2007. *Anthropology, politics, and the state: democracy and violence in South Asia*. Cambridge: University Press.

STOKKE, K. 2006. Building the Tamil Eelam state: emerging state institutions and forms of governance in LTTE-controlled areas in Sri Lanka. *Third World Quarterly* **27**, 1021-40.

STRASSLER, K. 2010. *Refracted visions: popular photography and national modernity in Java*. Durham, N.C.: Duke University Press.

TAGG, J. 1993. *The burden of representation: essays on photographies and histories*. Minneapolis: University of Minnesota Press.

TERWINDT, C. 2020. *When protest becomes crime*. London: Pluto Press.

THIRANAGAMA, S. 2013. *In my mother's house: civil war in Sri Lanka*. New Delhi: Zubaan.

THOMSON-SENANAYAKE, J. 2014. *A sociological exploration of disappearances in Sri Lanka*. Hong Kong: Asian Human Rights Commission.

UNWGEID 2016. *Report of the Working Group on Enforced or Involuntary Disappearances on its mission to Sri Lanka*. New York: United Nations.

L'absence en Technicolor : protestations contre les disparitions forcées dans le nord du Sri Lanka

Résumé

Le présent article examine les usages politiques de la photographie dans les protestations des familles de Tamouls disparus dans le nord du Sri Lanka. Les disparitions forcées sont depuis longtemps un instrument de la terreur d'État. On sait que leur retentissement durable est un obstacle notable aux processus de justice transitionnelle qui ont suivi la guerre civile sur l'île. En examinant comment les protestataires font connaître leurs exigences politiques et leurs doléances par la photographie, l'autrice explore les tensions entre visibilité et surveillance. Les photographies de protestations concurrentes subvertissent la compréhension conceptuelle de ce support comme outil idéologique, tout en compliquant ses aspirations

Journal of the Royal Anthropological Institute (N.S.) **28**, *118-134*
© 2022 The Authors. *Journal of the Royal Anthropological Institute* published by John Wiley & Sons Ltd on behalf of Royal Anthropological Institute.

à devenir un moyen d'émancipation. Dans le contexte d'un conflit ethno-nationaliste, cette mobilisation de la photographie et par la photographie constitue la mise en forme vindicative d'une « irréconciliation » d'après-guerre. Elle est également liée à un langage visuel global de résistance de la société civile face aux atrocités commises par les États, ainsi qu'à des affirmations irréconciliables de la nation et de l'État.

9

Rendering the absent visible: victimhood and the irreconcilability of violence

KAMARI MAXINE CLARKE *University of Toronto*

Contemporary justice-making processes often focus on reconciliation or legal retribution, but not on the complexity of victimhood beyond individual subjectivity or refusals of state propositions for social repair. In Colombia, where drug cartels and state-sponsored violence had terrorized the population for over fifty years, it was not forgiveness and acceptance that punctuated the turn of the twenty-first century, but the refusal to reconcile with the state's duplicity regarding the disappearance and death of thousands. This essay illustrates how irreconciliation as an affective sentiment is taking shape in Colombia through forms of reattribution that take the form of *victim visibilizations*. In analysing the strategic use of *victim visibilizations as a refusal of state accountability*, their expansion of the notion of victimhood, and their politics of irreconciliation, I show how even with the state's remorse-driven discourses, the public's understanding that political, judicial, and social accountability was not possible and pushed them to chart new strategies for disclosure and healing.

Displayed on a busy street in Bogotá, Colombia, in February 2020 was a controversial mural of five Colombian generals of the National Army identified as directly responsible for 5,763 cases of 'false positives' (ODHDH 2012; Rojas Bolaños & Benavides Silva 2017), a practice of misrepresenting civilians as guerrilla fighters killed in combat, reported from 2000 to 2010. Painted by the group known as Movimiento Nacional de Víctimas de Crímenes de Estado (MOVICE, National Movement for Victims of Crimes of the State), this work was a visible and shocking representation of demands for state accountability. It publicly exposed high-ranking officials who had been associated with the murder and disappearance of thousands, but who had not accepted responsibility. Among the most explicit forms of public refusal of state violence have been attempts to use artistic visibilizations to tell alternate stories about responsibility for violence (see Echavarría 2018). The mural featured the inscription 'Who gave the order?' and not only suggested the officers were to blame, but also condemned the state's participation, particularly that of Álvaro Uribe, President from 2002 to 2010, and Juan Manuel Santos, Minister of Defence under Uribe from 2006 to 2009 and President from 2010 to 2018 (Bruno & Carrilo 2009; *El Tiempo* 2019). Santos was paradoxically awarded the Nobel

Journal of the Royal Anthropological Institute (N.S.) **28**, *135-152*
© Royal Anthropological Institute 2022.

Peace Prize in 2016 after leading the peace talks with FARC while also having been the Minister of Defence during the time of the false positives.

Beyond documenting these atrocities, MOVICE – an organization that represents victims and focuses on developing strategies to obtain truth, justice, and comprehensive reparation, and guaranteeing that crimes against humanity are not repeated – works with victims of violence to rearticulate memories in ways that are in sync with the realities of state power. By articulating the claim that the Colombian military has been the principal perpetrator of violence, the organization not only works with victims of forced disappearance to vindicate the memory of disappeared citizens, but also condemns the state for its lack of action (MOVICE 2020b). It attempts to *visibilize* questions such as: why were the missing detained? Why were they disappeared? Who ordered their disappearance? And what was the purpose of their disappearance? The imagery has been presented in galleries and exhibitions; in parks, city plazas, and universities; on the internet; and, in the era of COVID-19, it has been printed on personal face masks.

In response to the blatant accusations and through a human rights protection action, one of the officers demanded that MOVICE's Bogotá mural be removed, and a judge ordered it to be painted over and for the image to stop circulating. By the time this decision was made, members of the 13th Brigade of the National Army had already covered the generals' images with white paint (MOVICE 2020a).[1] Despite the physical removal of the public mural, the image had an afterlife as people circulated it on the internet with impunity, rendering the attempt to remove it futile. Instead, online chats, WhatsApp postings, and Twitter and Instagram feeds discussed the need for state actors to take responsibility for the murders, disappearances, and cover-ups, without which these publics would refuse to accept the prevailing state explanations.

On 12 February 2021, the Special Jurisdiction for the Peace (SJP) presented its report, No. 033/2021,[2] on 'deaths unlawfully presented as in combat'. This case is part of the struggle of dozens of mothers and victims of the false positives who led the 'Who gave the order?' campaign. The document became a key element in the investigation and an element of national controversy. Although it sought to present to the public how the cases were being prioritized, it announced that after the verification of new sources and databases, the total number of victims of this crime had increased to 6,402 people killed by the Colombian army. This was 4,154 more individuals than the 2,248 that the Office of the Attorney General had originally announced. The report found that 78 per cent of the cases occurred between 2002 and 2008, and that 66 per cent of the victims who were extra-judicially executed by state agents died in ten of the country's thirty-two departments. The magnitude of such a finding encouraged the victims' organizations that led the 'Who gave the order?' campaign to launch a new campaign of irreconciliation known as the 'Campaign for the Truth' (MOVICE 2017). On 7 March 2021, they reproduced the mural in recognition of the revised number of victims and the expectation that it will continue to increase. MOVICE's statement of irreconciliation is clear: as long as the SJP does not produce results or uncover where the order came from, the campaign will continue to question the responsibility for these crimes and to render forgiveness a matter of irreconcilability.

By 'irreconcilability' here I am referring to the practices of refusal in which, following Mookherjee (introduction to this volume), one refuses to carry out magnanimous performances of forgiveness. What we see are refusals to engage on those terms and instead attempts to address the ongoing impunity for decades of injustice through the resistance of what Buthpitiya (this volume) refers to as the resistance of the violence of 'peace'. In this essay, this resistance takes the form of irreconciliation as an aesthetic, political, and conceptual engagement with injustice through ongoing demands for greater accountability and the call for new domains for inscribing justice using contextually relevant strategies. The decade of false positives on which the mural focuses is just one of many violent periods that many Colombians have endured and that have shaped people's senses of there being lack of accountability for ongoing violence.

A significant period of mass violence began in Colombia in the mid-1960s as a sustained war between the Colombian government, various paramilitary groups, and left-wing guerrilla groups, one of which is known as the Revolutionary Armed Forces of Colombia (FARC), as well as drug and crime organizations (Leech 2011; LeGrand 2003; Wickham-Crowley 1991). Between 1964 and 2020, over 3 million people were displaced and 220,000 were killed; between 1970 and 2015, there were approximately 60,630 victims of forced disappearances in Colombia (CNMH 2014a). Understood as a crime against humanity, forced disappearances infringe on the basic right to life, human dignity, liberty, autonomy, and personal security; the right not to be arbitrarily detained; the right to due process; the right to recognition as a person before the law; and the right to humane treatment in detention (Amnesty International 2020; CNMH 2013; Trial International 2020). It involves cruel and degrading treatment of both the victim and their family members, who are condemned to the uncertainty of not knowing the whereabouts of their loved one (CNMH 2014a). These disappearances, followed by state truth, reconciliation, and forgiveness projects, allow us to reflect on how contemporary state projects narrativize the transition from violence to its eradication.

By criticizing what they see as a lack of appropriate state measures to make perpetrators of mass violence accountable for their crimes, various publics in Colombia have engaged in memorializations to visibilize wrongdoing as refusals of both the state-sponsored truth commission and the subsequent peace agreement between the Colombian government and the FARC in 2016 (Calle 2015; Marín 2018; Wallace 2017: 24-57). These visibilizations reflect public acts of reattribution that refuse not only the state's articulations of supreme legality, but also its overtures to reconcile past violence through new hybrid judicial initiatives, unless those initiatives recognize the responsibility of high-ranking leaders for that violence.

When, having conversations during a research exchange with the Transformative Memory Project, I asked Seth from MOVICE whether taking over large swathes of city walls for graffiti visibilizations was legal, he quickly responded, 'It was not legal for the military to kill civilians, so why should they worry about the legality of their graffiti?'[3] Instead, he insisted, 'Future victims have the right to protect themselves with information and murdered victims have the right to express themselves in the symbolic worlds of their loved ones'. What was important for Seth was that families see their loved ones vindicated in the identification of those responsible for the crimes.

In March 2020, the MAFAPO[4] mothers, an organization affiliated with MOVICE, worked with designer Eduard Barrera to create a face mask featuring images of the generals and the inscription 'In the face of so much silence, we will not be quiet' (SEMANA 2020). This very bold, visible, and personal refusal to accept the legitimacy of false positives might also be seen as an attempt to personalize a narrative about violence, corruption, and concealment and open it to public scrutiny. As we shall see, this form of refusal rejects the law's narrow focus on individual perpetrators, instead demanding the unveiling of state complicity, while calling for an expanded

Journal of the Royal Anthropological Institute (N.S.) **28**, 135-152
© Royal Anthropological Institute 2022.

understanding of victimhood that narrows the distance the law has wedged between victims and their surviving families. Ultimately, this refusal demands a rethinking of the limits of reconciliation in mass-atrocity contexts.

For forgiveness and social transitions from state-led violence to be deemed legitimate, those who have suffered its consequences need to see governmental initiatives as worthy of supporting (Andrews 1999; Pettigrove 2006; Riaño-Alcalá & Baines 2017). However, the opposite happened in Colombia's 2016 referendum, when 50.2 per cent voted against a peace deal with the FARC. Many Colombians said they voted 'no' because it was too lenient towards both the rebels and the state. In the absence of reckonings, the families and loved ones of those victimized by violence have taken a politico-affective approach that I call 'reattributive irreconciliation'. This form of irreconciliation is not simply a benign response to perceived injustice. Rather, by counteracting the 'theatre of reconciliation' that state agents are seen as staging, it reflects a call for accountability in relation to and beyond the state. It also insists on an expansion of victimhood from the individual to a collective politics through which the families of the murdered and disappeared are promoting a new type of accountability (Mendeloff 2009).

This involves transforming the presumably corporeal dead from their status as materially absent to asserting their central presence in the family and region's body politic. Thus, both the refusal of the singular subject as the only 'victim' and the disclosure of truth about the lives of the disappeared are interrelated in ways that extend their physical existence with the lives of those who represent them. By expanding the domain of victimhood to include families and loved ones, survivors refused the narrow concept of an individualized victim, expanding the category to include those who suffered loss as proximate victims (Crapanzano 2011; LeGrand, van Isschot & Riaño-Alcalá 2017; Riaño-Alcalá 2006; 2013). Victimhood came to be seen not as passive loss or a discursive performance but as the material transference of the deceased to the bodies of the living. What unfolded was irreconciliation – a form of refusal to accept the status quo and to forgive – and demands to learn from and narrate the struggles of those who lost their lives. Victimhood was displayed and asserted with emotional force, a manifestation of embodied refusals that I have elsewhere referred to as 'affective attribution' (Clarke 2019).

Affective attribution takes place when people protest and re-signify assignations of culpability and come to terms with loss. It can also involve displacing state structures and narratives with other formations, such as people's courts, alternative policing, new adages, extraordinary forms of visibilization, and so forth. These formations compel people to contend with loss, anger, and the memory of violation. In this regard, this essay explores how through extraordinary forms of visibilization, affective attribution can lead to the refusal to forgive as well as a politics of irreconciliation that holds out for a better outcome in terms of justice. By exploring the deployment of victim visibilization in Colombia, instead of telling a story about the reconciliation of loss and suffering that accompanied many state truth and reconciliation projects, this essay examines the refusal to accept violence as an epistemological assertion. This is an approach that demands a new conception of humanity through a new road to justice.

In Colombia, where drug cartels and state-sponsored violence terrorized the population, it was not forgiveness and acceptance that punctuated the turn of the twenty-first century, but the refusal to reconcile with the state's duplicity regarding the disappearance and death of thousands (McCormack 1999; Sánchez & Camacho

Journal of the Royal Anthropological Institute (N.S.) **28**, *135-152*
© Royal Anthropological Institute 2022.

2008). Even with the state's remorse-driven discourses on the need for accountability for the violence, the public's expectation that political, judicial, and social accountability was not possible pushed them to chart new strategies for disclosure and healing. In Colombia, irreconciliation reigned and people found new ways to forge a path forward.

Irreconciliation: embodying humanity through the lifeworld of another

Over the past twenty years, the human rights literature has expanded to explore institutions and social movements focused on both retributive and restorative justice as the answer to how people reconcile material loss and transformations of the missing following mass-atrocity violence (Garbett 2017; Llewellyn & Howse 1998; Llewellyn & Philpott 2014; Rotberg & Thompson 2000). These strategies of reparation of sociohuman relationships have spanned truth-based reconciliation strategies as well as various acknowledgements of wrongdoing, forgiveness, remorse, and renunciation (Amstutz 2007). However, in Colombia, the state is not seen as having disclosed the full truth, admitted wrongdoing, or held its agents responsible for the violence they committed.

Many scholars interested in forgiveness in relation to truth and reconciliation commissions (TRCs) remind us that forgiveness does not involve denial. Instead, it involves 'giving up hope for a better past' and 'a means by which the legacy of past wrongdoings is redeemed' (Amstutz 2007: 561; see also Andrews 1999; Bartel 2018; Jeffery 2017). These authors argue that through a combination of truth telling, repentance, remorse, renunciation of vengeance, as well as the cancelling of what is seen as a deserved penalty, forgiveness can be a useful tool in addressing/managing histories of political violence and oppression. Yet many agree that the application of forgiveness presents challenges in the political realm. These challenges range from confusion over who should offer forgiveness to who should receive it (Amstutz 2007; Bartel 2018; Crocker 2000), as well as how victimhood should be articulated and what its limits are (Andrews 1999; Lupton 2014).

These ambiguities are not insignificant. Many scholars, including Hannah Arendt (1958), Donald Shriver (1998), and P.E. Digeser (1998; 2003; 2004), had previously explored this role of forgiveness in politics. For Arendt, forgiveness was linked to human action and agency. Humans are unable to control the outcomes of processes that initiate with an action. Thus, the consequences of actions are unpredictable and irreversible. These unexpected outcomes may result in unhappy or unfortunate consequences for others. Arendt, therefore, finds a solution to the predicament of human action, suggesting that the antidote is presented as forgiveness (Lupton 2014). For her, forgiveness is offered as a way of making amends for the harm caused by the action. In this regard, Shriver suggests that there are four dimensions of forgiveness: the first is given in an agreement between the parties about something from the past that is best left behind; the second is an abandonment of the feeling of revenge; the third is empathy towards the humanity of the enemy that allows for a healthy coexistence in the future; and the fourth seeks to renew the fractures generated by an enmity. For Digeser, forgiveness re-establishes a relationship after a transgression has occurred. Thus, forgiveness becomes a mechanism by which the victim acknowledges the harm and decides to release the transgressor from the moral debt that has been owed. Here forgiveness implies a change of heart which casts doubt on its application to a political context. And forgiveness in politics entails leaving resentment aside. Once forgiven, the transgressor is treated differently. These approaches to forgiveness can be seen, following Mark R. Amstutz (2007), as missing a key element of forgiveness: the cancellation or mitigation of penalty, remorse, or repentance. In this light, many view the acknowledgement of wrongdoing through these elements as the foundation of forgiveness and without them see any attempt to reconcile wrongdoing as falling short of this goal. Thus, as noble as such aspirations for political forgiveness may be, a slow and growing interest in questioning reconciliation and forgiveness projects has begun to take root and has led to increasing attention to the politics of unforgiveness. This exploration of unforgiveness has highlighted the moral dimensions of resistance and resentment. Among the most compelling work on this topic has been the introduction of irreconciliation through the language of refusal.

Audra Simpson's (2017) anatomy of refusal offers insights into the ways that long-standing dispossession of Indigenous lands is engaged through a politics of refusal to be folded into settler colonial lifeworlds. Others, such as Martha Minow (2002), examine the successes and shortcomings of the South African TRC and highlight the way that particular moral, psychological, and religious responses produced the ideal tropes that drove its work. This, along with works by Thomas Brudholm (2006) and Jean Améry (1980 [1966]), as well as various critical interventions by Jacques Derrida (2001), Michael Herzfeld (2009), and Walter Reich (1990), point to important scholarly questions about unforgiveness. They also raise the need to explore what it means to feel, refuse, and embody those components of ourselves that speak to our humanity and the affective strategies through which people engage in acts of unforgiveness. As we will see in Colombia, affective displays of refusal through unforgiveness manifest in widespread memorializations aimed to counter the state's inaction.

Public mobilizations represent ways of reckoning with irreconcilability of a social condition that lacks accountability for violence. Part of the problem is that criminal law and its related legality presumes that law works on behalf of society. This sphere of justice making also produces displays and performances of justice. It carries legal rules through which to render decisions on guilt and to parse accountability, but what it does not do is to provide the ability to narrate that loss in affectively structured ways. The law does not exist to eradicate that pain and replace the loss. The law exists to ascertain the culpability of the accused. Who committed the crime? When? And how? And though legal accountability of perpetrators is symbolic of the state's commitment to address violence against the violated, family members understood that Colombia's history required a way to address criminal responsibility for violence that not only narrativized the role of rebel groups and child soldiers as perpetrators, but also identified the state and its complicity as core considerations in the complexities of responsibility for violence.

Histories of violence and attempts at justice

While forced disappearance has been a recurrent phenomenon in armed conflicts, the situation in Colombia has been placed in the spotlight because of its magnitude and consequent impact on the daily life of Colombians (Bushnell 1993; Shultz et al. 2014). According to the National Centre for Historical Memory (Centro Nacional de Memoria Histórica) in Colombia, there are 55,012 cases of people who have been disappeared (CNMH 2014b). Of these, eight out of every ten people who are reported to have gone missing have disappeared in the last twenty years (CNMH 2014a).

Between 1970 and 2000, reports of missing people were prosecuted as kidnapping or understood as 'presumed dead' (CNMH 2014b).[5] After 2000, forced disappearance was

Journal of the Royal Anthropological Institute (N.S.) **28**, 135-152
© Royal Anthropological Institute 2022.

incorporated into the Colombian Penal Code to describe an individual who is deprived of his or her liberty by another person followed by the refusal to inform others about the victim's condition or whereabouts (Albaladejo Escribano 2009). Forced disappearance can be perpetrated by the state, a political organization, individuals who belong to illegal armed groups,[6] state security forces, or public officers.[7]

In general, violence in Colombia has been perpetrated by both state and non-state actors: drug-trafficking organizations, residents, the paramilitary, and some military forces all played an important role in shaping this crime. According to the CNMH, in 51.4 per cent of the cases recorded (between 1970 and 2015), it has not been possible to establish who the perpetrator was (CNMH 2014a). Their data show that approximately 13,562 people (46.1 per cent) disappeared because of the illegal action of paramilitary groups; another 5,849 (19.9 per cent) due to guerrilla action; 2,598 (8.8 per cent) at the hands of demobilized groups; and 2,368 (8 per cent) as a result of the actions of the military forces. Finally, there were approximately 4,686 (15.9 per cent) cases that corresponded to unknown armed organizations in the country (CNMH 2014a). The narratives that accompany these statistics suggest that the violence was not arbitrary but emerged from a history of displacement, forced labour, inequality, and the ongoing resort to various illegal activities such as drug trafficking by members of rebel movements and by agents of the state (Cotte Poveda 2007; Pecaut & González 1997).

Despite the development of transitional justice mechanisms in Colombia during the 1980s and 1990s, they were not seen as producing emancipatory possibilities (LeGrand 2003). Nor did they enable transitions from violence to peace. Rather, by leaving unanswered questions about the responsibility for violence and the location of the missing, the mechanisms reified otherness and created distance from the actual histories of violence. Families, civil society organizations, and members of the public involved in activism demanded that the state be held accountable for the missing, and that in the absence of declarations of responsibility, they should contribute to the search for the missing (Barrera Berrio & Medina Alvis 2011; Dejusticia 2010; SEMANA 2014).

In addition to applying pressure to contend with the problem of forced disappearance as a crime, Law 589 of 2000 established mechanisms for the prevention of crime and protection of victims' rights. One important development was the Commission for the Disappeared, established as a permanent body to locate people who are presumed missing. Constituted by judicial organizations, such as the Attorney General's Office, non-governmental organizations, associations of families of missing persons, and forensic institutions, its objective was the investigation of the crime of forced disappearance, designing and implementing the National Plan for the Search for Disappeared Persons, and setting up investigation groups for specific cases related to missing people (FGN 2017). Owing to the number of corpses recovered from mass graves, Law 589 also mandated a National Register of Disappeared Persons. This data reference information system has as its main objective the identification of non-identified bodies that are taken to the Institute of Forensic Medicine.[8] The law created a mechanism for the protection of the property of missing persons and, through this system, family members can administer and dispose of the victim's property. This law was important as it enabled the recognition of enforced disappearance as an independent crime, leading to the development of mechanisms such as the National Register of Disappeared Persons. Such actions were made possible through the government's issuance of Law 1448 of 2011, known as the

Victims' Law, which recognized victims' rights and guarantees. By recognizing the need to guarantee memory reconstruction as a right to the production of truth (Monroy 2019), the Victims' Law defines judicial and administrative actions aimed at assisting victims and repairing harm using economic means. It also recognized the importance of symbolic reparation by creating a National Day of Memory and Solidarity with Victims. Celebrated each year on 9 April, it assigns the status of 'victim' to those people who suffered individual or collective harm as of 1 January 1985.

Yet many victims refused this overture and argued that the implementation of these measures was slow and insufficient due to the lack of political will, limited resources, and legal shortcomings. In response, wide-scale public mobilizations contributed to significant institutional, social, and judicial reckoning, starting with various demobilizations of the FARC and leading to the commencement of the 2012 negotiations towards a Peace Agreement, which lasted for at least four years.[9] The negotiations ended with the signing of an historic agreement on the end of conflict and cessation of hostilities and surrender of weapons on 26 August 2016. On 2 October 2016, the Colombian people voted in a referendum asking if they wanted to implement the agreements signed in Havana. A slight majority of 50.21 per cent of the population opted for 'no', rejecting the original text. Finally, on 24 November 2016, a General Agreement for the Termination of the Conflict and the Construction of a Stable and Lasting Peace was signed (Colombian National Government & FARC-EP 2016). Among the agreements was a plan for comprehensive rural development, political participation, and an end to drug trafficking.

Following the signing of the Peace Agreement, the Colombian state established a mixed transitional justice project that combined various administrative institutions with judicial and extra-judicial measures. They established a Truth, Coexistence, and Non-Recurrence Commission (Truth Commission); a Unit for the Search for Persons Presumed Disappeared in the Context and by Reason of the Armed Conflict (UBPD in Spanish); and the SJP. Ultimately propelled by public engagements, the peace deal led to governmental commitments to mechanisms for economic and political rights, universal education in rural regions, subsidies for the development of former rebels, and access to clean drinking water.

Despite these measures of the last four decades, some Colombians refused to engage with the theatres of the TRCs and insisted on highlighting the state's failure to protect those whose lives were wrongly taken and to account for their whereabouts – irrespective of their revolutionary or non-revolutionary goals. From that indignation emerged a counter-movement demanding not only the right to know about the conditions of violence that led to the loss of loved ones, but also that state actors locate the bodies of the disappeared and allow for proper burials of those victimized (LeGrand et al. 2017; Riaño-Alcalá 2006; 2013; Riaño-Alcalá & Baines 2012). Part of this movement was built through the representational labour of those loved ones who remain. This labour has been central to calls for state action and accountability in Colombia throughout the decades of armed conflict, especially in regions that have been most violently impacted. In what follows, however, I will focus on just a few contemporary efforts that prioritize the essential role of ending state impunity and stamping out the exceptionalism of leaders whose actions were seen as contributing to Colombia's violence and enforced disappearances, while also asserting their own status as 'victims' under particular circumstances.

Journal of the Royal Anthropological Institute (N.S.) **28**, *135-152*
© Royal Anthropological Institute 2022.

Visibilizing victimhood: the response to false positives

Fair Leonardo Porras, a 26-year-old male who suffered from learning difficulties and had the cognitive capacity of a 12-year-old, was an inhabitant of Soacha, Colombia, a predominantly working-class municipality on the outskirts of the city of Bogotá. In 2008, state agents reported him and eleven other individuals to be insurgency rebels who roamed the country killing innocent people. The Second Division of the army in Norte de Santander killed them at least 600 kilometres away from their home (CNMH 2017). Upon realizing that the Porras situation was not an isolated case, nineteen mothers from Soacha who had lost their children during this period and under the same circumstances mobilized hundreds of mothers, fathers, wives, sons, and daughters to spread the word that their relatives had also disappeared or were killed in so-called operations against criminality (MAFAPO 2018). They began a struggle to reclaim the names of their sons whom the National Army had murdered and then presented as guerrillas who had been killed in combat.

In response to the production of state misrepresentations, MAFAPO has used various acts of refusal, including mobilizations, artistic representations, and symbolic commemorations to resist state narratives of who was to blame for the violence. One of its most representative activities is known as the 'Costurero de Memoria' (Sewing Box of Memory). This is a collective that sees itself as victims of enforced disappearances. It emerged from the initiative of a mother whose three daughters had been disappeared. To help her heal from this loss, she made a blanket out of their clothes, and the practice spread. During weekly gatherings, members of the group offered participants the opportunity to share stories of the disappearance of their children, husbands, or brothers while they sewed as a form of catharsis (Agamez 2019a).[10] MAFAPO mothers also made and embroidered fabrics representing the criminal events that surrounded the fictionalized story the state told about their loved ones. The mothers insisted that while it may be useful to speak using statistics, they wanted their work to lead to the visibilizations of the lived worlds of the missing, and in doing so allow their sewing to reflect their suffering, to reflect the way that they, too, were victims of mass-atrocity violence. These acts of refusal illustrate how feelings about and perceptions of justice can be communicated through presenting, signalling, performing, and remembering the missing or murdered.

In one photographic series, 'Madres Terra', fifteen MAFAPO mothers undressed and covered all but their faces and arms with soil, symbolizing the resistance and rebirth of women who lost their families, with whom they engaged in re-narrativizing their memories (Agamez 2019b). These portrayals were compiled by artist Carlos Saavedra to represent what many within their constituencies saw as the ancestral relationship between mothers and the earth as sources of life, while others described it as an act of burying. Whatever the interpretation of the imagery, the depictions were shocking and emotionally laden with loss. Indeed, it was not just the disappeared who suffered the indignities of unfreedom but also those who remained behind.

These visibilization projects open up spaces for making sense of the way that women's suffering, survivors' suffering, stands in for a new formulation of victimhood. For example, Blanca, a member of the MAFAPO Foundation, stressed how being part of this association has helped her healing process:

> The fact is that I have changed 100 per cent. Yes, I am not the same as I used to be. I used to laugh, I used to make fun, I used to go out, but not anymore. I want to be here in the house locked up …

> You know what makes me happy? When I meet the mothers of Soacha. Sometimes we cry together, sometimes we laugh, sometimes we fight, and that is my happiness … They are the engine of my life. My 'cuchi Barbies' [old Barbies]. I am happy with them. I meet them and we talk, we talk, but then I leave, and I feel sad again, melancholy.

Cecilia, also a member of MAFAPO, emphasized accountability when she spoke of the group's importance to her: 'Why have I not withdrawn from MAFAPO? Because I will continue in my fight until I find out who the Army Chief was, I mean, who gave the order to kill my brother. I will not rest until I know'.

In the visibilizations and statements about their feelings of loss, victimization, and state duplicity in regard to the false-positive narrative, the members of MAFAPO reinscribe culpability, or reattribute guilt, onto members of the state. This act of reattribution was also a strategy used by MOVICE, the group behind the controversial mural. Prior to the COVID-19 pandemic, we witnessed MOVICE collaborating with artists and galleries to display photos that exposed Colombia's history of violence. After the National Government implemented a COVID-19 lockdown, MOVICE helped facilitate a project called 'Memoria en Casa' (Memory at Home), in which participants in various cities set up altars in their homes, displaying pictures and objects of their missing loved ones and exhibited them on social media and the organization's website.[11] By using photos of those victimized as tools of visibilization, truth, and transformation, their surviving family saw themselves as advancing memories that they feared the state would erase through false representations. And while these memorializations were erected to preserve the memories of loved ones, they also sought to extend the memory of the missing into the pain of those left behind (Ortiz Cassiani 2015). As one member of MOVICE said, 'We display the garments and trinkets and photos of the missing in order to show that their disappearance continues to cause us sorrow and pain. The display of our loved ones in this way is our effort to share our suffering with each other'. Such visualizations of loss are also social claims to suffering (Riaño-Alcalá & Baines 2017).

These practices have a long history in the tradition of Catholic memorializations of the dead in Latin America that actively engage in rituals to connect the corporally dead with the living (Cherry 2004). Various vigils and life celebrations attempt to bring comfort and accompany the family in their grief and to negotiate the future direction of the soul so that it may reach peace and resurrection. These rituals include erecting altars in dedicated public places or in individual homes, as well as gathering at the graves of loved ones and bringing personal objects of the departed such as T-shirts, caps, photos, trinkets, food, and drinks to honour the memory of their dead. What emerges through these activities and their regional variations is a ritualized notion of suffering as an affective burden of the living, but, in the case of contemporary visibilizations of victimhood, articulated within everyday practices. These practices take shape across kinship networks and especially in the context of families of women. Through these kinship networks, we see an analytic linkage between the role of the divine, social respectability, and the suffering of individual women and mothers.

Memorializations are produced in spaces within which people can recognize each other through the dynamics of kinship relations. These spaces involve the co-presence of the corporally dead and the living as well as the omnipresence of suffering. Colombian healing networks position the visibilization of art as central to the journey of suffering. They show that the 'victimhood' narratives being articulated through the visibilization movement in Colombia and other parts of Latin America reflect the transference of memories of the disappeared to mechanisms (photos, trinkets, etc.)

that are embodied and used to keep the disappeared alive. What such visibilizations offer us, then, are everyday ways that people reattribute responsibility towards the state, and while doing so they create openings through which to engage with each other in the aftermath of violence. These various initiatives create a space of remembrance that is also a contested domain and does two things at once. It allows for the memory of the disappeared to be displayed and worn with honour, but it also allows the disappeared to be embodied in the lifeworlds of living agents, who, through a call to rectify their pain, refuse state solutions and instead demand the re-narrativization of their story. It is no surprise, therefore, that the emergence of such grand and co-ordinated victim visibilizations have led to the reclaiming of space in the name of the disappeared, following Catholic traditions of symbolic representation. From large museum exhibits to grand murals on city streets to in-home memorials, large-scale victim visibilizations articulate a form of irreconciliation that is not merely about the binary distinction between individual death and suffering from that loss. Rather, the intersubjective nature of suffering allows us to see how loss is expressed through new formations of personhood and how those recalibrations of personhood shape new sociopolitical realities, new support structures, and multiple perspectives through which to understand the paradoxes of loss and new configurations of possibility. Such arguments allow us to consider the limits of forgiveness and the need to consider new forms of reckonings that are at play. They involve the transformation of the category of victimhood from a passive position of loss to a kinship network of affectively constituted empowerment that asserts the irreconcilability of violence.

Historically, the classification of a criminal transgression involved a single victim as a legal category and the assumption was that, despite the existence of social suffering, determinations of harm were not transferable (Frost & Hoggett 2008). For example, the Colombian legal system clearly and specifically incorporates the concept of victim in Law 975 of 2005, known as the Justice and Peace Law. However, MOVICE, among others, criticized this definition because it did not include the rights of victims to truth, justice, and reparation. Consequently, with the issuance of Law 1448 of 2011, the concept of the victim was taken up again. Through expanding the legal definition of victimhood, it gave legal recognition to those who also suffered the loss of a loved one during the armed conflict (Delgado 2011). With the recognition of the demand for the expansion of victimhood, we see a theory of embedded personhood that departs from the singular rights-endowed victim-actor to what the law refers to as 'indirect victims'. This re-conceptualization moves from victimhood as impacting a singular actor to a rendering of an agentive victimhood in which the disappeared can be actively counted and their whereabouts interrogated for the purposes of evidence or witness testimony.

According to Indress, one of the MAFAPO mothers we interviewed,

> I think we were victims too, because, as I told you before, they took away a very important person from me, because when Jorges was ... five days old, I promised him that I would never turn my back on him, that I would be with him through thick and thin, that I would never be separated from him. [But] they took him from my arms, they vilely murdered him, and it was a very big pain, a pain that they caused me, they caused all of us mothers, and it is a pain that one cannot heal.

As for her memory and reconciliation efforts, Indress stated,

> To remember my son, there is no need to do so many things; just looking at his picture there I am seeing him, there I am remembering him. I see him, I breathe deeply, and I say: 'God, do your holy will' ... Right now, I am making the quilt to describe when he left San Nicolas, of the road he followed,

when he arrived at the place where he was murdered, I am making that quilt. Sometimes it takes me eight or fifteen days, or a month, to look at it, take it out, I sew a little bit, then I put it away, and so on. But it's something that you keep with that person at all times, and you think: well, the person died, he's already buried, he's going to be forgotten, but that is a lie, as time goes by, that person is more remembered.

These memorializations of the lives of the disappeared and the visibilizations of loss demand recognition and terms for a radically reconfigured future in which the dead, the buried, are seen as continuing through various ongoing visual remembrances.

Through victim visibilization, both the missing and the conditions of their disappearance become the terms on which a new future is possible. Though that aspiration is manifest in domains of loss, in the bodies of the missing, the disappeared are also seen as being transformed. Their memory and cause live through the refusal of indirect victims to accept justice meted out within the same conditions of violence. A new future can be imagined that requires that we re-envision presumptions about the liberal subject and that we rethink the basic principles upon which democracy functions. This re-narrativization of the trope of the liberal subject as a single = individual whose injury lies only within their person emerged as a critical philosophical tenet on which transformative memories were politicized. For when one element of the social whole is taken away, the entire whole is affected by that loss. This principle of social harm is part of the basis upon which irreconciliation has taken shape for various constituencies in Colombia.[12]

Senator Ivan Cepeda, popularly seen as one of the most influential authorities on the political left and a victims' representative, recounted his own story and mapped out for us what a different future could entail. On 8 August 2019, twenty-five years after his father, Manuel Cepeda Vargas, was assassinated, Ivan Cepeda asked the SJP to determine the individual responsibility for this murder. Among the requests that Cepeda made to the SJP was to subpoena Jose Miguel Narvaez, who was the Director of the Administrative Department of Security in 1994. This was because, according to other perpetrators and defendants in this case, the former director was alleged to have participated in the assassination. In response to his request and the work of the court, Cepeda was accepted and recognized by the SJP as a victim of case No. 06, 'Victimization of Members of the Patriotic Union'. In recognition of this principle of the social unity of the disappeared and the living, he spoke with us in the MOVICE office about his vision for change.

In a nod to, yet disavowal of, law as the answer for transforming society, Cepeda emphasized that the transformative value of MOVICE's visibilization strategies was to produce retold memories of the past. As he explained, 'MOVICE's visibilization strategies to testify and confront power are critically important for individual and social healing and rectifying abuses in truth telling about our violent past'. But though he emphasized its importance, in response to my question about whether visibilization as a strategy of social change was effective, he warned against using individual healing in ways that ultimately remove us from political power. Instead, he insisted,

The public has a major role to play in taking steps to being subjects of power. We must use these artistic visibilizations to both testify and confront power. But we also need to take power, to build a new reality that allows us not only to use victimhood to change narratives about violence, but also to use it to claim power.

Ultimately, he saw these memory-making visibilization strategies as essential political vectors that were far from marginal. Every society dealing with post-violence contexts, from illegal settlements to civil wars to ongoing forms of violence, plays a critical role in confronting memories and reattributing them for particular ends. And because false positives produce misinformation about the conditions of death of thousands, insisting on new modalities to 'socialize these memories differently is critical', added Henri, a MOVICE comrade who spoke after Cepeda. As he nodded and agreed that it was important to refuse illegitimate power, he reminded us that those who testify through victim visibilizations become witnesses in the narrativization of new discourses of power.

Our conversation ended with a call to remember that it is important to maintain a sustained voice; that the issue is not what position is valid but what the plurality of positions are in the quest to refuse impunity and to reallocate power towards positive ends. What my interlocutors communicated that day is that the resultant narrative texts that speak through victim visibilizations to the sustained life of the living are deeply political. They are necessary to tell a different truth. This refusal of particular 'truths' and the rearticulation of other truths can be deployed in impactful ways.

Proximity and differentiation: the limits of forgiveness

In relation to those victimized by violence beyond Colombia, by the twenty-first century a 'victim' discourse emerged that tended to decontextualize the pain and suffering of those who were victimized by violence and recontextualize them in a theatre of justice that formed the basis for the work of international justice writ large. Indeed, although the promise of justice offered victims solace, the reality was that law's emancipatory power did not address the temporality of the pain and enduring absence. This is because the legal doctrine was seen as producing distance and differentiation between perpetrators and victims. Understood as such, distance represents the objectification of suffering so that it can be documented and rendered rational for the law to engage with it. Differentiation, as a practice of legal identification, allows for the parsing of culpability for violence to a given person. It was this dual presence of distance and differentiation that contributed to some of the public's refusal of the Colombian justice mechanism. The differentiation erased the nature of victimhood and in doing so it led to the refusal to reconcile. Indeed, the temporality of loss cannot always be addressed with a brief apology or a bid for forgiveness. Nor can it be adequately addressed through retributive justice. Victim visibilizations developed as a response to the state's unwillingness to admit to its complicity in violence and the way it distanced surviving victims from victimhood. These displays and performances insist that victims who lost loved ones, as agents of representation, do not want distance from the missing. And they want the sacrifice of the life of their loved ones to have meant something.

What is important to reckon with are not only the ways that the family and loved ones of the disappeared have become an extension of the body of the disappeared who was victimized, but also the way that the disappeared are made to live through the refusal practices of those who carry their legacy. For the experience of the loss of the life of a loved one results in a visceral response that is felt and embodied with feeling and pain. The daily reminders of loss cannot be easily heard or felt or seen. The insistence on victim status for the family and loved ones of the disappeared provided a domain for the recognition of their loss. It also highlighted a way of thinking of the extension of the loved one's continuity of life. This form of refusal of traditional modes of personhood

Journal of the Royal Anthropological Institute (N.S.) **28**, 135-152
© Royal Anthropological Institute 2022.

was a form of irreconciliation that enabled the family as proxy victims to negotiate loss through the maintenance of an afterlife for those who had been taken from them. These practices are shaping a set of principles that refuse the distancing between legal justice and the pain of the violation. As statements of power about the refusal to transition to 'business as usual', they render reconciliation impossible without the return of the disappeared, a prospect that becomes less likely as the years pass.

What we see in the theatres of justice in the contemporary period are shifts from a focus on justice for victims to calls for a new future that insists that the lives of the disappeared matter, that information about the missing matters, and that society has a role in sharing in the restoration of the life of those who survive them. In claiming the status of *victims* and participating in the extraordinary visibilization of loss, the living engage in dialogue with the life of the dead. They, like the wave of victim visibilizations across the region, are building counter-narratives that articulate the terms on which demands for humanity are emerging and refusals of business as usual are in circulation.

The disappeared remain alive in the afterlife of the imagery that is meant to shock our sensibilities and enable new truths to be told in different registers. The visibilizations have their own agency to articulate a story about justice. Various struggles against state brutality or demands for accountability are underway in the contemporary period. To take seriously victim visibilizations as extensions of 'victims' themselves and a form of political action requires that we rethink the nature of the social. This involves moving beyond notions of individual subjectivity and interrogating personhood through a unity of collective being. That unity combines the disappeared and contemporary personhood with the practices of representation. To miss this cycle of interconnection as a progression to retributive justice is to miss the philosophical tenets that undergird the radical aspirations that drive it.

For as the argument of the introduction to the special issue suggests, irreconciliation emerges from the lack of recognition and acknowledgement of a harm, the lack of truth telling that allows for the assignment of responsibility for wrongdoing, and the absence of an explanation for that wrongdoing. Despite the fate of the disappeared in Colombia, the shaming of the five generals is alive in the world and gives voice to the violated. Through the public disclosure of violence, we see, following Derrida (2001), that recognizing calls for humanity through forgiveness does not account for the place of vulnerability that people feel. Rather, in this study, various members of MOVICE and the families engaged in the emotional reparation of violence aspire to the possibility of reparations and reconciliation. Through demands for change and community efforts to recast injustice, we see refusals to accept inaction and attempts to re-narrate new social truths. As a statement about the irreconcilability of the loss of lives, the description of the mural with which we opened this essay speaks through the public display of those it sees as accountable but who are protected by corrupted power. This is the public's refusal of impunity, the irreconciliation of state violence.

Acknowledgements

This essay is based on research done while in Colombia in February 2020 and followed up by a research team in April and May 2020. Thank you to Muff Anderson for her initial insights, which helped me to consider this comparative case. And appreciation goes to research assistants, Laura Acosta Zarate and Sara Ali, as well as colleagues, Pilar Riano-Alcala, Bronwyn Leebaw, Muff Anderson, and also Anitra Grisales for their tremendous input into this essay. Also thank you to the blind reviewers and the volume's editor, Nayanika Mookherjee, for their insights and direction.

NOTES

¹ Photos of the original mural and the one covered in white paint can be consulted at *https://www. eltiempo.com/justicia/investigacion/mural-sobre-falsos-positivos-fue-borrado-en-bogota-424764* (accessed 24 March 2022).

² 'Auto 033/2021. Objetivo: hacer de público conocimiento la priorización interna del Caso 03 denominado "muertes ilegítimamente presentadas como bajas en combate por agentes del Estado"'. 12 February 2021.

³ This essay is based on fieldwork observations conducted in Bogotá in February 2020 and subsequent interviews with members of MOVICE, MAFAPO, and BeligerArte, which are all involved in memorializations and victims' rights. Pseudonyms are used for interviewees.

⁴ MAFAPO stands for the Madres de los Falsos Positivos de Colombia (Mothers of the False Positives of Colombia).

⁵ According to article 97 of the Civil Code, after an individual has been missing for more than two years without notice of his or her whereabouts, a judge starts a presumed death proceeding with three summonses to appear in court. In the absence of a response, the person's death is confirmed.

⁶ See Constitutional Court, decisions C-587/1992 and C-317/2002.

⁷ See Constitutional Court, decision C-317/2002.

⁸ The idea was that anyone can access this instrument as soon as they have news of their loved one's disappearance. Once this is known, judicial actors are expected to immediately order all the necessary steps to locate them.

⁹ The creation of specialized units within the Comprehensive System of Truth, Justice, Reparation, and Non-Repetition emerged with the purpose of fulfilling the commitment acquired by Colombia to guarantee the rights of the victims of forced disappearance and their families. This is the core sense of what is stated in the final agreement for ending conflict (Colombian National Government & FARC-EP 2016: 110).

¹⁰ Some photos of this work are available at *http://experiencias.centromemoria.gov.co/costurero-de-la-memoria-kilometros-de-vida-y-de-memoria/* (accessed 24 March 2022).

¹¹ The gallery is available at *https://movimientodevictimas.org/galeria-memoria-en-casa-movice/nggallery/page/4* (accessed 24 March 2022).

¹² For a similar argument, see Vaisman (2014).

REFERENCES

Agamez, J.M. 2019*a*. Costurero de la Memoria: kilometros de vida y de memoria. Centro Nacional de Memoria Histórica, 19 July (available online: *http://experiencias.centromemoria.gov.co/costurero-de-la-memoria-kilometros-de-vida-y-de-memoria/*, accessed 24 March 2022).
——— 2019*b*. Madres Terra. Centro Nacional de Memoria Histórica, 22 May (available online: *http://experiencias.centromemoria.gov.co/madres-terra/*, accessed 24 March 2022).
Albaladejo Escribano, I. 2009. *La desaparición forzada de personas en Colombia*. Bogotá: Oficina en Colombia del Alto Comisionado de las Naciones Unidas para los Derechos Humanos (OACNUDH).
Améry, J. 1980 [1966]. *At the mind's limits: contemplation by a survivor on Auschwitz and its realities* (trans. S. Rosenfeld & S.B. Rosenfeld). Bloomington: Indiana University Press.
Amnesty International 2020. Enforced disappearances (available online: *https://www.amnesty.org/en/what-we-do/enforced-disappearances/*, accessed 24 March 2022).
Amstutz, M. 2007. Human rights and the promise of political forgiveness. *Review & Expositor* **104**, 553-77.
Andrews, M. 1999. Truth-telling, justice, and forgiveness: a study of East Germany's Truth Commission. *International Journal of Politics, Culture and Society* **13**, 107-24.
Arendt, H. 1958. *The human condition*. Chicago: University Press.
Barrera Berrio, A. & Y.A. Medina Alvis 2011. El estado colombiano frente al delito de desaparición forzada. Unpublished manuscript, Universidad Milita Nueva Granada.
Bartel, R. 2018. Confession and the anthropology of forgiveness: reflections on Colombia's processes of transitional justice. *Journal of Latin American and Caribbean Anthropology* **24**, 145-61.
Brudholm, T. 2006. Revisiting resentments: Jean Améry and the dark side of forgiveness. *Journal of Human Rights* **5**, 7-26.
Bruno, S. & D. Carrilo (dirs.) 2009. *Falsos positivos*. Film.
Bushnell, D. 1993. *The making of modern Colombia: a nation in spite of itself*. Berkeley: University of California Press.

CALLE, A. 2015. Pueblo Bello lucha por su memoria (available online: *https://centrodememoriahistorica.gov. co/micrositios/pueblo-bello/*, accessed 30 March 2022).

CHERRY, S. 2004. Forgiveness and reconciliation in South Africa. In *Forgiveness in context: theology and psychology in creative dialogue* (eds) F. Watts & L. Gulliford, 160-77. London: Continuum.

CLARKE, K.M. 2019. *Affective justice: the International Criminal Court and the pan-Africanist pushback.* Durham, N.C.: Duke University Press.

CNMH 2013. *Huellas y rostros de la desaparición forzada (1970-2010)*, vol. II. Bogotá: Centro Nacional de Memoria de Histórica.

———— 2014*a*. *Hasta encontrarlos: el drama de la desaparición forzada en Colombia* (available online: *http://centrodememoriahistorica.gov.co/descargas/informes2016/hasta-encontrarlos/hasta-encontrarlos-drama-de-la-desaparicion-forzada-en-colombia.pdf*, accessed 24 March 2022).

———— 2014*b*. *Normas y dimensiones de la desaparición forzada en Colombia*, vol. I. Bogotá: Centro Nacional de Memoria de Histórica.

———— 2017. Por Fair Leonardo Porras, ¡nunca más! (available online: *https://centrodememoriahistorica.gov. co/por-fair-leonardo-porras-nunca-mas/*, accessed 24 March 2022).

COLOMBIAN NATIONAL GOVERNMENT & FARC-EP 2016. Final agreement for the ending of the conflict and the construction of a stable and lasting peace (available online: *https://www.refworld.org/docid/5b68465c4. html*, accessed 24 March 2022).

COTTE POVEDA, A. 2007. Pobreza, desigualdad y crecimiento: una interpretacion de las causas de la violencia en Colombia (available on-line: *https://ideas.repec.org/p/col/000137/003328.html*, accessed 24 March 2022).

CRAPANZANO, V. 2011. *The Harkis: the wound that never heals.* Chicago: University Press.

CROCKER, D.A. 2000. Truth commissions, transitional justice, and civil society. In *Truth v. justice: the morality of truth commissions* (eds) R.I. Rotberg & D. Thompson, 99-121. Princeton: University Press.

DEJUSTICIA 2010. Exigen reconocer a desaparecidos como víctimas. 22 April (available online: *https://www. dejusticia.org/exigen-reconocer-a-desaparecidos-como-victimas/*, accessed 24 March 2022).

DELGADO, M. 2011. Las víctimas como sujetos políticos en el proceso de justicia y paz en Colombia: Discursos imperante y disruptivos en torno a la reconciliación, la justicia y la reparación. Doctoral thesis, FLACSO México.

DERRIDA, J. 2001. *On cosmopolitanism and forgiveness* (trans. M. Dooley & M. Hughes). London: Routledge.

DIGESER, P.E. 1998. Forgiveness and politics: dirty hands and imperfect procedures. *Political Theory* **26**, 700-24.

———— 2003. Justice, forgiveness, mercy, and forgetting: the complex meaning of executive pardoning. *Capital University Law Review* **31**, 161-78.

———— 2004. Forgiveness, the unforgiveable and international relations. *International Relations* **18**, 480-97.

ECHAVARRÍA, J.M. 2018. *Works* (ed. D.E. Schmeichler). Mexico City: Editorial RM Mexico.

EL TIEMPO 2019. Controversia por mural sobre falsos positivos que borraron en Bogota (available online: *www.eltiempo.com/justicia/investigacion/mural-sobre-sobre-falsos-positivos-que-borraron-en-bogato-424764*, accessed 30 March 2022).

FGN 2017. Mecanismo de Búsqueda Urgente (MBU) (available online: *https://www.fiscalia.gov.co/colombia/ noticias/destacada/que-es-el-mecanismo-de-busqueda-urgente/*, accessed 24 March 2022).

FROST, L. & P. HOGGETT 2008. Human agency and social suffering. *Critical Social Policy* **28**, 438-60.

GARBETT, C. 2017. The International Criminal Court and restorative justice: victims, participation and the process of justice. *Restorative Justice* **5**, 198-200.

HERZFELD, M. 2009. *Evicted from eternity: the restructuring of modern Rome.* Chicago: University Press.

JEFFERY, R. 2017. The Solomon Islands Truth and Reconciliation Commission Report. In *Transitional justice in practice: conflict, justice, and reconciliation in the Solomon Islands* (ed.) R. Jeffery, 113-39. New York: Palgrave Macmillan.

LEECH, G. 2011. *The FARC: the longest insurgency.* London: Zed Books.

LEGRAND, C. 2003. The Colombian crisis in historical perspective. *Canada Journal of Latin America and Caribbean Studies* **28**, 165-209.

————, L. VAN ISSCHOT & P. RIAÑO-ALCALÁ 2017. Land, justice, and memory: challenges for peace in Colombia. *Canadian Journal of Latin America and Caribbean Studies* **42**, 259-76.

———— & R. HOWSE 1998. Restorative justice: a conceptual framework. Paper prepared for the Law Commission of Canada.

LLEWELLYN, J. & D. PHILPOTT 2014. *Restorative justice, reconciliations, and peacebuilding.* Oxford: University Press.

LUPTON, J.R. 2014. Judging forgiveness: Hannah Arendt, W.H. Auden, and *The Winter's Tale*. *New Literary History* **45**, 641-63.

MAFAPO 2018. Una década sin respuesta para las madres de Soacha. Centro Nacional de Memoria Histórica, 10 October (available online: *https://centrodememoriahistorica.gov.co/una-decada-sin-respuesta-para-las-madres-de-soacha/*, accessed 24 March 2022).

MCCORMACK, L. 1999. *Colombia: a cultural profile*. Anti-Racism, Multiculturalism and Native Issues Centre, Faculty of Social Work, University of Toronto.

MARÍN, M.E.G. 2018. La ecosofía: un aporte a la memoria de Pueblo Bello. *Revista Lasallista de Investigación* **15**, 143-51.

MENDELOFF, D. 2009. Trauma and vengeance: assessing the psychological and emotional effects of post-conflict justice. *Human Rights Quarterly* **31**, 592-632.

MINOW, M. 2002. Between vengeance and forgiveness. *Negotiation Journal* **14**, 319-55.

MONROY, J.P. 2019. La reparación simbólica a víctimas de desaparición forzada, olvido o perdón. *Agora USB* **19**, 244-52.

MOVICE 2017. Carta abierta a la Comisión de la Verdad en el Dí de la dignidad de las ví de crímenes de Estado (available online: *https://movimientodevictimas.org/en/carta-abierta-a-la-comision-de-la-verdad-en-el-dia-de-la-dignidad-de-las-victimas-de-crimenes-de-estado/*, accessed 1 April 2022).

——— 2020a. Mural '¿Quién dio la orden?' ya es patrimonio de la sociedad: Movice (available online: *https://movimientodevictimas.org/en/mural-quien-dio-la-orden-ya-es-patrimonio-de-la-sociedad-movice/*, accessed 24 March 2022).

——— 2020b. Las despariciones forzadas no son una historia del pasado, son una realidad del presente (available online: *https://coeuropa.org.co/las-desapariciones-forzadas-no-son-una-historia-del-pasado-son-una-realidad-del-presente/*, accessed 24 March 2022).

ODHDH 2012. *Ejecuciones extrajudiciales en Colombia, 2002-2010* (available online *https://coeuropa.org.co/wp-content/uploads/2017/05/Documentos-tematicos-8-FINAL-1.pdf*, accessed 24 March 2022).

ORTIZ CASSIANI, J. 2015. La memoria incómoda: Afrodescendientes y lugares de memoria en Cartagena de Indias. Ministerio de Cultura de Colombia.

PECAUT, D. & L. GONZÁLEZ 1997. Presente, pasado y futuro de la violencia en Colombia. *Desarrollo Económico* **36**, 891-930.

PETTIGROVE, G. 2006. Hannah Arendt and collective forgiving. *Journal of Social Philosophy* **37**, 483-500.

REICH, W. 1990. *Origins of terrorism: psychologies, ideologies, theologies, states of mind*. Washington, D.C.: Woodrow Wilson Center Press; Baltimore: Johns Hopkins University Press.

RIAÑO-ALCALÁ, P. 2006. *Dwellers of memory: youth and violence in Medellin, Colombia*. Piscataway, N.J.: Transaction Publishers.

——— (ed.) 2013. *Remembering and narrating conflict: resources for doing historical memory work*. Centro Nacional de Memoria Historica and the University of British Columbia.

——— & E. BAINES (eds) 2012. Special Issue: Transitional justice and the everyday. *International Journal of Transitional Justice* **6**: **3**.

——— & ——— 2017. How do we be together? Opening Remarks, International Roundtable on Memories and Responsibilities, Vancouver, 8 February.

ROJAS BOLAÑOS, O.E. & F.L. BENAVIDES SILVA 2017. Lealtades impuestas, obediencia ciega: en las profundidades de campos de batalla ficticios. In *Ejecuciones extrajudiciales en Colombia, 2002-2010*. Bogotá: Ediciones Universidad Santo Tomas.

ROTBERG, R.I. & D. THOMPSON 2000. *Truth v. justice: the morality of truth commissions*. Princeton: University Press.

SÁNCHEZ, G. & Á. CAMACHO 2008. *Trujillo una tragedia que no cesa*. Bogotá: Editorial Planeta Colombiana SA.

SEMANA 2014. Desaparecidos: el estado el gran responsable. 26 May (available online: *https://www.semana.com/nacion/articulo/desaparecidos-el-estado-el-gran-responsable/389173-3/*, accessed 24 March 2022).

——— 2020. Con tapabocas con mensajes, madres de Soacha piden justicia por sus hijos. 9 May (available online: *https://www.semana.com/nacion/articulo/con-tapabocas-con-mensajes-madres-de-soacha-piden-justicia-por-sus-hijos/670317/*, accessed 24 March 2022).

SHRIVER, D.W. 1998. *An ethic for enemies: forgiveness in politics*. Oxford: University Press.

SHULTZ, J.M., D.R. GARFIN, Z. ESPINEL, ET AL. 2014. Internally displaced 'victims of armed conflict' in Colombia: the trajectory and trauma signature of forced migration. *Current Psychiatry Reports* **16**, 1-16.

SIMPSON, A. 2017. The ruse of consent and the anatomy of 'refusal': cases from indigenous North America and Australia. *Postcolonial Studies* **20**, 18-33.

TRIAL INTERNATIONAL 2020. Enforced disappearance (available online: *https://trialinternational.org/topics-post/enforced-disappearance/*, accessed 24 March 2022).

VAISMAN, N. 2014. Relational human rights: shed-DNA and the identification of the 'living disappeared' in Argentina. *Journal of Law and Society* **41**, 391-415.

WALLACE, C. 2017. *Colombia insight guides*. Lochem: Uitgeverij Cambium B.V.

WICKHAM-CROWLEY, T.P. 1991. *Exploring revolution: essays on Latin American insurgency and revolutionary theory*. New York: Routledge.

Rendre l'absent visible : victimes et irréconciliabilité de la violence

Résumé

Les processus contemporains de fabrique de la justice se concentrent souvent sur la réconciliation ou le dédommagement en justice, mais mésestiment la complexité du statut de victime, au-delà de la subjectivité individuelle ou des refus de propositions de réparation sociale par l'État. En Colombie, où la population est terrorisée à la fois par les cartels de la drogue et par la violence couverte par l'État depuis plus de cinquante ans, ce n'est pas l'oubli ni l'acceptation qui ont marqué le début du XXIe siècle, mais un refus de conciliation avec la duplicité de l'État à propos de la disparition et de la mort de milliers de personnes. Le présent article illustre la manière dont l'irréconciliation, en tant que sentiment affectif, prend forme en Colombie à travers les formes de réattribution par la *visibilisation des victimes*. En analysant l'usage stratégique de la *visibilisation des victimes comme refus de la responsabilité de l'État*, l'élargissement de la notion de victime et la politique d'irréconciliation, l'autrice montre comment c'est après avoir compris l'impossibilité de la responsabilisation politique, judiciaire et sociale malgré le repentir discursif de l'État que le public a trouvé de nouvelles stratégies de divulgation et de guérison.

Journal of the Royal Anthropological Institute (N.S.) **28**, *135-152*
© Royal Anthropological Institute 2022.

10

Irreconcilable times

Nayanika Mookherjee *Durham University*

In *Denktagebuch* (*Thought diary*, 1950-73), Hannah Arendt wrote that acts which cannot be forgiven are beyond punishment and hence cannot be reconciled to. In this essay, I draw from Arendt to further theorize and extend the concept of irreconciliation. I draw together ethnographic material, historical material, documents, media reports, and reviews during this era of irreconcilability which includes Black Lives Matter; the memorialization debates on the removal of statues of enslavers; the history of slavery in the United Kingdom; and the 'harmony ideology' experienced by BAME (Black, Asian, and minority ethnic) academics within UK organizations linked to long-term discrimination. I argue for the concept of irreconciliation as a bulwark against impunity, against a 'window-dressed', symbolic performance of redress, and to be able to echo Arendt's words that 'this' – any original cause of injustice – 'ought never to have happened'.

On 23 July 2020, the New York Democrat Representative Alexandria Ocasio-Cortez delivered a speech condemning Republican Representative Ted Yoho, who, following a discussion about their differences in opinion concerning the link between poverty and crime, was accused of accosting her within hearing range of a reporter and calling her a f***ing b**ch. While Yoho has denied using these words, the media and social media furore which followed attacking either Yoho or Ocasio-Cortez shows how divisive this event was. The *New York Times* labelled Ocasio-Cortez as disruptive as she repeated in Congress the names she said Yoho had called her. So, while she was attempting to point out the complexity of the patriarchal dynamics women face in their public lives, the response to her speech in turn highlighted the abuse received by women – a point that she was seeking to shed light on (Traister 2020). On the other hand, the wide praise she received for identifying the patterns of dehumanizing language used against women, who are frequently accosted abusively at work and with impunity, indicated the increasing spaces available in which to speak out and the support for such actions.

Journal of the Royal Anthropological Institute (N.S.) **28**, 153-178
© 2022 The Authors. *Journal of the Royal Anthropological* Institute published by John Wiley & Sons Ltd on behalf of Royal Anthropological Institute.

This also turns our attention to how irreconciliation is increasingly being brought to the fore by those who are suffering discrimination, not least many BAME (Black, Asian and minority ethnic)[1] academics within UK higher education (HE). The Yoho-Ocasio-Cortez illustration also indicates two common experiences among many BAME academics: namely how they are treated in their place of work, and that if they raise a problem, *they* are deemed to be the problem.

BAME colleagues have tried to raise issues of discrimination because their lives have been affected by various expressions of organizational power and the complicity of colleagues. I, as a co-founder of the first BAME network of academic staff and postgraduate students in Durham University, have been told of many instances of discrimination across different institutions. These can include claims of larger teaching and administrative load; lack of acknowledgement of the contribution being made; ignoring long-term in-depth expertise of BAME colleagues; gender and racial pay gaps; being reprimanded for the smallest of issues compared to others whose serious transgressions are not addressed; circulation and reiteration of racial stereotypes when issues are raised by BAME colleagues; general and everyday harassment; and, above all, bystanderism.[2] BAME academics who raise issues of injustice are also (like Ocasio-Cortez) labelled as 'combative' and 'scary' by their line managers. This ends with them becoming caught in 'the tiredness of the loop of repetition' (Ahmed 2019: 148) of unresolved injustices, such as those discussed in this volume's essays.

Generally, it is incumbent upon survivors to forgive, reconcile, and seek closure as a demonstration of peacefulness, as various essays in this special issue note. The Ocasio-Cortez illustration is a reminder of how the processes of conciliation and mediation are also used to their advantage by organizations and institutions in instances of conflict among colleagues. Such manipulations and limitations become apparent especially when grievances and concerns are suppressed or remain unaddressed, or when successful grievance cases and their results are not upheld by the organization's human resources (HR) departments. These include perceptions recounted to me by certain departmental heads across academia who feel HR exists only to protect management. In such organizational instances, the aggrieved person needs to be passive, accept 'that cup of tea' (Ahmed 2019: 188) of conciliation and harmony ideology (Nader 1991).[3]

In instances of persistent denial of, and impunity from dealing with, past injustices, or of 'staged' processes that claim to address injustice, reconciliation is similarly suggested as a solution to those who raise their voices in protest. As ethnographic data from essays in this volume show, survivors can refuse to reconcile and decline to carry out the coercive normativity of forgiveness. When they do so in the face of unacknowledged injustices, and particularly in response to what is perceived as a performative redress of inequality, I have theorized this negation as irreconciliation. I consider ethnographic material alongside historical material, reviews, and reported news events to look at the debates surrounding statues which commemorate enslavers and colonial figures. I also include in this discussion the unsatisfactory responses of HR departments and HE management to complaints of bullying by BAME employees. I extend the concept of irreconciliation to describe the responses of BAME colleagues and others to the microaggressions of ordinary life. First, I bring in the experiences of the bullying of BAME academics through my intersectional, privileged positionalities of being a South Asian/BAME female professor in anthropology. Owing to issues of confidentiality and sensitivity linked to wider BAME networks, I draw on these experiences – both my own and others' – but, to preserve anonymity, present them

Journal of the Royal Anthropological Institute (N.S.) **28**, 153-178

predominantly through a third-person narrative, and where possible cite examples from published sources and reports. Second, I juxtapose these debates with the discussions on the history of memorializing slavery based on my research and teaching on memorialization. [Correction added on 14 June 2022, after first online publication: This paragraph has been updated in this version.]

'This ought never to have happened'

As noted in my introduction, for Hannah Arendt, writing about the Nazi war criminal Adolf Eichmann in her *Denktagebuch* (*Thought diary*) (2002; see also Berkowitz 2011), acts which cannot be forgiven are beyond punishment, and hence cannot be reconciled to. In her argument for non-reconciliation, she claims that 'this ought never to have happened' (Berkowitz 2011: 3). In this she rejects the world that harbours such acts and calls for a new world through the denial of that which currently exists. What Arendt refers to as 'non-reconciliation', which we have termed 'irreconciliation' in this volume, seeks to redraw the frameworks of reconciliation to highlight the prevalent (unclear) impacts and responses to injustices. I draw from Arendt's *Thought diary* to further theorize and elaborate on an ethnography of irreconciliation by extending the concept to include protests against the memorialization of slave owners, and the complaints of BAME academics in British HE. Since 2007, I have carried out fieldtrips with students exploring Britain's history of slavery as part of my undergraduate module 'Violence and Memory'. The trips focus on the 'trade' and 'philanthropy' of the enslavers who are depicted as Britain's 'virtuous sons' (see also Fig. 3 below), and so I will also examine the practices of displacement which indicate Britain's 'aphasic' relationship with its imperial past (Gapud 2020: 331). The concept of aphasia allows us to track processes of displacement and goes beyond the idea of 'historical amnesia' (Tyler 2012), or invisibility, in relation to the history of slavery and colonialism (Wemyss 2016). Burch-Brown (2020) also proposes that we examine the debate about the statues of enslavers within a transitional justice framework but is uncritical of the framework itself.

What the Black Lives Matter (henceforth BLM) movement has brought to centre-stage is a *public secret* (see Mookherjee 2006): that of the existing discrimination around both the memorialization of slavery's history and the experiences of BAME academics. Rather than equating them, I am drawing out the similarities in the processes through which injustices in both instances are thwarted rather than addressed. HE's biases and discriminatory behaviour have been broached many times in the past, but have been unheeded, ignored, and enabled by bystanderism and obfuscation. That these situations are analogous can be seen in the following example: in an event hosted by the Irish Museum of Modern Art in March 2021, during a discussion of Professor Sara Ahmed's (2017) work on complaints, other speakers compared the vilification of the complainants in HE that Ahmed described to a similar resistance to the complaints brought by women whose children were put up for adoption without their consent by Irish mother-and-baby homes. Ahmed's work speaks well to how bureaucracy and institutions re-create hierarchies and resist responding meaningfully to grievances. I also show the institutional tactics of 'equivalence', 'due process', and 'balancing' which are deployed in responses to complaints. Continued complaints in the face of unheeding bureaucracies thus emerge as forms of irreconciliation. Thus, participants at the event in Ireland saw a correspondence between the experiences of complaints of Irish mothers and that of BAME academics who protested against institutional injustices. These discussions, while at a different level, might be related to the resistance that is implicit in the attempts to reveal the truth in post-genocidal contexts, in the history of slavery, or in experiences of racial discrimination in British HE. Regulations are used by organizations to discount the staff experiences of bullying, harassment, microaggression, sexism, and racism that are the result of long-term discriminatory practices. The phrase 'due process' is also invoked in various institutional responses to bullying and harassment complaints in order to stymie them. In each of these instances, codes of rules, regulations, and practices as determined by HR set the remit within which violations are determined and have to be resolved. In innumerable instances, these regulations enable impunity and the letter of the law is often not enforced, thereby enabling the continuation of the status quo. Or law itself is used to sustain the status quo. Here, Derrida's commentary on Benjamin's theorization on violence – that 'force is essentially implied in the very concept of justice as law (*droit*)' (Derrida 1992: 5) – is helpful to think through the role of law in parallel with some of the discussions in the introduction and in this volume related to contexts of state violence.

Despite official statements from organizations espousing anti-racist positions in 2020 after George Floyd's death, the institutional pushbacks against BLM and anti-racist movements have been constant. Here, ethnographic work on memorialization and post-conflict contexts allows for linkages that enable understanding of the concerted organizational efforts at obfuscation. This is alongside what I call 'institutional window dressing' in relation to racial and colonial histories in the United Kingdom and is similar to the tactics involved in diversions and 'aphasia' (Gapud 2020). It is best captured by what Allen Feldman refers to as 'exclosure', which, as we noted in the introduction, is 'the self-defacement of this appearing non-appearance of violence' (2015: 12). Exclosure here (like the discussions of genocidal instances elsewhere in this volume) refers to when the institutional structures meant to redress injustices do so performatively and instead work to undermine the search for justice. I add to the examples to indicate certain institutional performances in British HE where there is continuing discrimination against academics and how these are met with irreconciliation and vigilance. On the one hand, irreconciliation emerges against continuing institutional impunities and their obfuscation of anti-racist movements vis-à-vis performative anti-racist messaging. On the other, it emerges alongside the public outcries and debates relating to statues celebrating slavery. In the following section, I explore the institutional responses and practices around the 2020 BLM events as part of the contexts of current irreconciliation.

Black Lives Matter and institutions

On 25 May 2020, George Floyd was killed in Minneapolis by a white police officer who knelt on his neck for nearly eight minutes while Floyd continuously said: 'I can't breathe'. Floyd's death, Breonna Taylor's death in a raid on her apartment,[4] and the subsequent BLM protests that have taken place across the globe since May 2020 exemplify the everyday realities of racisms. This, alongside the COVID pandemic, is powerfully and irrefutably exposing the inequities in societies. Experiences of racism have been felt intensely during the COVID epidemic, within which carrying out anti-racist protests has also faced criticism. One example of such protests after Floyd's death took place at the base of the 1890-installed statue of Confederate General Robert E. Lee (an enslaver) on Monument Avenue in Richmond, Virginia (see Moreno 2020). After witnessing the police tear gas protesters in Richmond on 30 May 2020, Dustin Klein, a Richmond-based lighting designer, and Alex Criqui, a photojournalist, sought

Figure 1. Image of Harriet Tubman projected upon a Confederate monument venerating Robert E. Lee in Richmond, Virginia. (Photo credit: Regina H. Boone/Richmond Free Press, with permission.)

to amplify the messages of BLM through projecting the movement's images onto the bronze statue. The takeover of the Lee monument for peaceful protest by activists and the light installations depicting intersectional, ingrained injustices exposed the peaceful yet resolute irreconciliation that exists among Black American communities with regard to the contemporary police violence they experience. Here and in other instances, monuments and activities around them are a reflection of an engagement with the past from the vantage point of current predicaments rather than a position on that past alone (Rao 2016). Looking at the occupation around the monument, Aaron Parker, a native of the area, commented: 'This is what monuments could be' (Moreno 2020). Opponents of the Governor of Virginia's attempts to remove the Lee memorial successfully sought an injunction blocking the move. On 26 June, as police in riot gear surrounded the memorial, the image of the abolitionist and activist Harriet Tubman was projected on the Lee monument along with the line: 'Slavery is the next thing to hell' (Fig. 1).

Journal of the Royal Anthropological Institute (N.S.) **28**, *153-178*
© 2022 The Authors. *Journal of the Royal Anthropological* Institute published by John Wiley & Sons
Ltd on behalf of Royal Anthropological Institute.

I was extremely upset by these events in May-June 2020 and the worldwide news. I found that this resonated with the messages I was receiving from BAME colleagues about their experiences, and the contradictory BLM messaging being sent by institutions and line managers while at the same time remonstrating against anti-racist protests. The death of George Floyd and the subsequent pain and outrage felt by the injustice of the innumerable deaths due to police brutality in the run-up to 25 May 2020 sparked a fuse across the world as well as many discussions among British BAME colleagues. Much of the discussion of this section is based on personal communications from these colleagues, mainly anonymized, and supported, where possible, by examples from published sources and reports.

The mobilization after Floyd's death was such that various organizations and line managers who had not paid any attention to race issues and had ignored the bullying and harassment of BAME colleagues felt the need to send out 'blacked-out' anti-racist messages in support of BLM. Overnight, BLM had made it trendy to be anti-racist. Suddenly, everyone wanted to 'decolonize' the curriculum as a panacea without thinking through the foundations necessary to put decolonization into action. This was considered by many BAME academics to be hypocritical, seasonal, and a form of virtue signalling whereby institutions sent BLM-related messages without addressing the issues of bullying and structural racism among their personnel. As a result, social media became inundated with discussions of the numerous occasions that the same organizations had ignored racist incidents. This led to various networks and communities writing open letters demanding an end to endemic racism in their institutions and highlighting the need for changes in practices and policies relating to the representation, recruitment, and support of BAME individuals.

In spite of the distressing context of BLM, these letters and communications by BAME colleagues were often deemed to be 'combative' by line managers. The epithet 'combative' reminds us that BAME individuals did not want to go 'back to the cup of tea' (Ahmed 2019: 188) and this was an expression of their irreconciliation to long-term daily microaggressions. Terming BAME communications as 'combative' also parallels the debate about the need for 'democratic decision-making' in the case of the removal of statues, as discussed below. It is worth recalling that the removal of many statues happened after years of trying to follow procedures, of signing petitions, of having polite conversations and cups of tea with councils and authorities – all of which were not heeded. The case with BAME networks is analogous: they have been raising the issues of racial discrimination, bullying, and harassment through formal procedures, and have been thwarted continually. Various EDI (equality, diversity, and inclusion) heads and committees felt they could not support any BAME open letters as that would be a conflict of interest. Others queried the request for greater representation and raised the issues of 'merit', 'criteria', and 'competitiveness', as if the demands for BAME representation were asking for anything more than the parameters of employment outlined in their contracts. BAME networks also pointed out the hypocrisy of these official messages given the way institutions have turned a blind eye or paid lip-service to various grievance cases. In some instances, it is claimed that institutions have preferred to promote and reward those carrying out various discriminatory acts. These include incidences of bullying, harassment, and microaggressions against BAME colleagues (see Devlin & Marsh 2018; Universities UK 2020) in total disregard of various 'respect at work' policies. This has included rewarding those who have had successful, as well as multiple, grievance cases upheld against them.

Journal of the Royal Anthropological Institute (N.S.) **28**, *153-178*
© 2022 The Authors. *Journal of the Royal Anthropological* Institute published by John Wiley & Sons Ltd on behalf of Royal Anthropological Institute.

Owing to such factors, sometimes those at the receiving end of bullying and harassment tend to go off sick or even leave their university rather than engage in a lengthy and formal grievance process which itself often encourages the issues to simply 'go away'. Alternatively, there was a concern expressed to the Durham Commission on Respect, Values, and Behaviour about the perceived practice of paying the responsible party to leave the university, with a perception that this occurs particularly at a senior level, rather than acknowledging that bullying behaviour is unacceptable and deserving of action up to and including dismissal without compensation (Report of the Durham Commission on Respect, Values, and Behaviour 2020: 25).

Separately, some who were believed to be promoting and rewarding bullies are now understood to be tasked with implementing the findings of various commissions and reports. In the process, institutions have subsequently been perceived as congratulating themselves for having initiated investigations, commissions, and reports on actions that their own managerial practices caused. This seems to be the ultimate manifestation of 'a lousy diversity doublespeak' (Doharty, Madriaga & Joseph-Salisbury 2021: 233). Part of this doublespeak includes, as I mentioned earlier, the processes of conciliation, or mediation, which are used by organizations and institutions. These are deployed in instances of conflict among colleagues and even if grievances and concerns are suppressed, remain unaddressed, or when successful grievance cases and their results are not upheld by an organization's HR. The use of terms like 'equalizer' and 'due process' deployed by HR and institutions also enables impunity. As Ahmed (2017) notes in her discussion of these complaints: 'Indeed, many of those I have spoken to have spoken of how they became the complained about; a complaint can be redirected to the complainer; as if she says something is wrong because something is wrong with her'.

The bullying and harassment of BAME colleagues show that they are seen to be trespassers who have risen above the station they are meant to stay in. In accounts from numerous grievance cases, claims indicate how 'bureaucracy' is used to control and bully colleagues. A BAME colleague told me that their line manager had said: 'I did not show them how angry and irritated I was with them [the said BAME colleague]. I just used bureaucracy against them'. These bureaucratic manoeuvres can include an insistence on organizing in-person meetings soon after 9 a.m. (even though guidelines prescribe that those meetings should not start before 9.30 a.m.) despite participants' requests to move it to 9.30 a.m. because of their caring duties and/or transport timings; using performance management as a stick against colleagues whose teaching evaluations are deemed to be negative; getting mentors to report to promotion committees when the role of mentoring is meant to be based on trust and confidentiality; and line managers escalating email discussions frequently with the threat of consulting HR to instigate a more formal process of investigation. Increasingly, one finds that the issues raised by BAME colleagues are being raised *against them* in turn, while, sometimes, senior colleagues find that their race and gender are being discounted when they are mistreated. As Ahmed puts it:

> Racial harassment can be the effort to restore a hierarchy: how someone is being told you are not where you should be or you are above where you should be, or you are where I should be or even you have taken my place. Some of us in becoming professors become trespassers; you are being told you need permission to enter by being told you do not have permission (2019: 188).

The law again works efficiently to stop a complaint by declaring that 'a complaint is "not a complaint"' because it does not fulfil the technical requirements for being a

Journal of the Royal Anthropological Institute (N.S.) **28**, *153-178*
© 2022 The Authors. *Journal of the Royal Anthropological* Institute published by John Wiley & Sons
Ltd on behalf of Royal Anthropological Institute.

complaint' (Ahmed 2019: 161) As in truth and reconciliation commissions (TRCs), the law sets the 'parameters within which conflict must be resolved' (Turner 2016: 45) and hence helps to serve the status quo. Ahmed cites a powerful and familiar example:

> For example, a member of staff made a complaint about bullying from the head of her department. The experience of bullying had been devastating, and she suffered from depression as a result. It took her a long time to get to the point where she could write a complaint. She described what happened once she was able to file a complaint: 'I basically did it when I was able to because I was just really unwell for a significant period of time. And I put in the complaint and the response that I got was from the deputy VC [Vice-Chancellor] and HR. He said he couldn't process my complaint because I had taken too long to lodge it'. Some experiences are so devastating that it takes time to process them. And the length of the time taken can be used to disqualify a complaint (2019: 161).

Grievance processes can be similar to other conflicts discussed in this volume. As I have argued in this volume's introduction, the South African TRC's moral equalization of the suffering of black and white communities as forsaking revenge was deemed to be necessary for the liberation of the nation. Similarly, in essays by Josephides (Northern Ireland), Bertelsen (Mozambique), Buthpitiya (Sri Lanka), and Clarke (Colombia) in this volume, there has been a process of equalizing blame if violence was carried out by both sides. This moral equivalence has been greeted with anger in various instances as this equalizing position did not recognize the suffering of victims and families. As elaborated by Visser (Bangladesh) and Vaisman (Argentina), processes of amnesties (known as the 'two-demon theory')[5] have equalized victimhood, ensuring a long period of silence and almost complete impunity. We also find this process of equalizing in the memorialization of slavery. For example, as we discuss further below, when a long-awaited memorial to the enslaved was finally built in Lancaster in 2005 at the peripheral quayside of the city, it was 'equalized' with the setting up at the same time of a pub with the name of the enslaver Robert Gillows in the city centre. [Correction added on 14 June 2022, after first online publication: The year in the last sentence of this paragraph has been corrected from '2018' to '2005' in this version.]

Similarly, institutions are now willing to allow BAME communities to articulate their experiences of bullying and harassment in the light of BLM and the rebranding opportunity linked to the buzzwords of 'diversity' (Ahmed 2012) and 'decolonization'. BAME colleagues note that those who were often silent bystanders and active abettors of the bullying and harassment of BAME colleagues in the past are overnight wanting to be part of the decolonizing project. This is evidenced in the proliferation of decolonization workshops led by staff without any relevant expertise or life experience, and the promotion of research projects as 'decolonized'. Moreover, decolonization like 'diversity might be "just used now," because of its affective qualities as a happy or positive term' (Ahmed 2019: 148). It might explain the keenness of various organizations today to readily use the word 'diversity' and attempt to implement it after years of such requests by BAME individuals. I turn to the debates linked to the statues, memorials, and names linked to slavery in the following sections.

The landmarks and resonance of slavery

On the evening of 7 June 2020, I had watched the video of the slave trader Edward Colston's statue being removed in Bristol, in southwest England, as part of an anti-racism protest which ended with four individuals being arrested for criminal damage. They were acquitted in December 2021. In the United Kingdom, slavery was abolished in the British Empire by the Slavery Abolition Act of 1833 and the further brutal

Journal of the Royal Anthropological Institute (N.S.) **28**, 153-178
© 2022 The Authors. *Journal of the Royal Anthropological* Institute published by John Wiley & Sons Ltd on behalf of Royal Anthropological Institute.

apprenticeship of the enslaved ended in 1838. I felt that the removal of Colston's statue was a historic event, like so many others that were happening around the world. From 2007 and during fieldtrips I carried out with students, my own awareness had heightened of the presence of various everyday structures related to slavery within the United Kingdom. Following the Colston figure's removal, June 2021 saw the head of a bronze statue of Egerton Ryerson – architect of Canada's residential school system – sawn off and thrown into Lake Ontario following the discovery of the buried remains of 215 First Nations children on residential school grounds (see Niezen, this volume). Red paint was daubed on both the statues, and graffiti reading 'DIG THEM UP' was written on Egerton's pedestal, hinting at other undiscovered children's graves.

In the seventeenth and eighteenth centuries, Colston's Royal African Company sold more than 200,000 people from West Africa as slaves – including women and children – and some 19,000 died en route. Many thousands were branded on their chests with the name of his company (Clarke 2020). As I watched the video of the 7 June event (YouTube 2020a), I saw that protesters not only removed his statue from its pedestal, but also rolled the red-paint-covered effigy down the road, before a protester knelt on Colston's neck, enacting George Floyd's death. Then the statue was thrown into the River Avon in a powerful symbolic gesture of consigning Colston to a 'watery grave' – giving him the same burial as the dead and dying slaves who were tossed overboard. The removal of Colston's statue was evocative of Arendt's comments (see Berkowitz 2011: 13): given that such crimes (in this case, slavery) are irreconcilable, should not the world in which they existed be rejected? Here, the very process of 'defacing' (Taussig 1999: 7) these statues exposes a public secret: that of the unaddressed legacies of slavery which constitute the material foundations of many British institutions and charities. The Colston event also revealed how, since 1990, there had been a democratic, formal – albeit fruitless – attempt to have Bristol's city council add a plaque to the statue that identified its connections to slavery. The protesters, thus, reignited the conversation in the United Kingdom about rejecting a society in which the statues of enslavers are allowed to tower over its citizens.

This rejection has already been taking place in different parts of postcolonial Africa, where statues of colonial figures have been toppled as a first step in addressing racism. As South African constitutional lawyer Lwando Xaso has noted: 'Statues represent so many ideas that are wrapped up in the physical object itself, and that by toppling them, you are saying that those ideas that they represent no longer have a place in society' (as quoted in Patta 2020). Such removals have included the statue of Cecil Rhodes in South Africa, as well as statues in Ghana, Kenya, and Cameroon. Andre Blaise Essama, for example, has been toppling colonial statues in Cameroon (Akwei 2017; YouTube 2020b) and is being called a local hero. Self-described as an activist, Essama aims to replace all the colonial statues and monuments built by French colonialists in the capital city Douala with those of national heroes who fought for the bilingual country's independence. In 2015, he launched his campaign when he repeatedly beheaded the statue of French colonial hero General Philippe Leclerc de Hauteclocque and was imprisoned each time. The Cameroonian government has now placed this statue within an iron-grilled complex to protect it from Essama. Similarly, the artist Jimmy Ong has been deconstructing and beheading the statue of the colonialist Stamford Raffles, who is alleged to have founded Singapore (BBC News 2019).

In the United Kingdom, following the removal of Colston's figure, a statue of merchant and slave trader Robert Milligan was removed by the Tower Hamlets Council

Journal of the Royal Anthropological Institute (N.S.) **28**, 153-178
© 2022 The Authors. *Journal of the Royal Anthropological* Institute published by John Wiley & Sons Ltd on behalf of Royal Anthropological Institute.

Figure 2. Base of Colston statue in the M Shed Museum, Bristol, 11 June 2021. (Photo credit: @ProfDanHicks, Twitter, with permission.)

from West India Quay East London;[6] a new plaque has been added to Edinburgh's statue of Henry Dundas; Churchill's statue in London was graffitied as being racist; and the petition calling for removal of Shrewsbury's statue of Robert Clive (also known as Clive of India) was narrowly defeated. Scottish First Minister Nicola Sturgeon has acknowledged that street names and statues in the United Kingdom continue to honour those who profited from human misery. Prime Minister Boris Johnson, however, has said that one cannot edit or censor a nation's past. Prior to a BLM protest, the statue of Winston Churchill – who is also known as Johnson's and the Conservative Party's hero – was completely boarded up to avoid it being defaced again. The Turner Prize-winning sculptor Anish Kapoor described the Prime Minister's opinion on statues negatively, adding: 'Statues are not history; they are emblematic monuments to our past which can be thought to represent how we see ourselves and our history' (as quoted in Stewart, Walker, Mohdin & Quinn 2020).

The well-known historian William Dalrymple has created controversy on Twitter by referring to the removal of statues as an 'erasure' of history and compared it to the attacks on historic structures by the Taliban and Hindu right-wing supporters of the BJP in India. He clashed with the British Black historian David Olusoga, who tweeted that the removal of Colston was 'making history'. The removal of Colston and the subsequent curation of that statue in the M Shed Museum in Bristol have indeed made history, and the graffitied and red-painted statue was exhibited horizontally lying down (Fig. 2).

That the material wealth of the British Empire was built on its trafficking of slaves has long been known. Since 2007, I have been carrying out a fieldtrip on the history of slavery in the United Kingdom with students which is linked to a module I taught in Lancaster and teach now in Durham. This involves a tour of a city (e.g. Lancaster,

Journal of the Royal Anthropological Institute (N.S.) **28**, *153-178*
© 2022 The Authors. *Journal of the Royal Anthropological* Institute published by John Wiley & Sons Ltd on behalf of Royal Anthropological Institute.

Liverpool, Newcastle, or Durham) led by a cultural historian that identifies its visible but barely noted landmarks, as well as examines documents in archives that links the city to slavery. In this way we have learnt how to look at a city, its buildings, doorways, and roads differently in the light of the city's link with slavery and how that contributed to both its and Britain's material wealth. Rare are the monuments such as the 'Captured Africans' sculpture, created in 2005 by the artist Kevin Dalton-Johnson with support from the mosaic artist Ann McArdle, which was unveiled as the first memorial to mark the history of slavery in Lancaster – the fourth largest port city in the United Kingdom (after London, Bristol, and Liverpool) that had engaged in slavery.[7]

Students were often surprised to find the 'Captured Africans' memorial tucked away on St Georges Quay in Lancaster, in a spot not visited by many. In 2018, when my 8-year-old son visited this memorial with me, he mentioned that he imagined he would see more people there, expected it to be in the middle of the city, and also thought it would be bigger, 'like a steeple', similar to Second World War memorials. Apart from the politics of location, what was striking is that soon after this memorial was set up, a new pub was opened in the city centre named after the famous furniture maker and enslaver Robert Gillows, who became rich from the mahogany wood brought in by the ships carrying the enslaved. Again, we see that most enslavers are commemorated as 'most virtuous and wise' sons of the empire (see the epitaph in Figs 3 and 4 as visible in the plaque under Colston's statue). Apart from naming the pub after the 'voyager' (as per the website)[8] Gillow, also emblazoned on the pub's front window were these unabashed words: 'trading in the unusual since 1720' (see Figs 5 and 6). All these instances of displacement through naming, semantics, and structural prominence highlight the deeply entrenched processes of 'aphasia' (Gapud 2020: 331): that is, processes through which occlusions of knowledge, of national histories, occur.

The commemoration of enslavers through statues and landmarks such as this pub is worth noting. In May 2021, following a campaign by a group called Black History Lancaster, which was formed in response to BLM, the name of the pub was changed to Jailor's Barrel because of its proximity to the Lancaster castle and prison, where nine individuals accused of witchcraft were hung in 1612 as part of the Pendle witch trial. On 14 May 2021, with the name change a contentious issue, discussion ensued online in open, local forums. While some lamented that the best sign in the town had gone due to 'wokeism' and 'political correctness', others joked sarcastically that the witch community might want the name 'cancelled'. Many were critical of those who argued in favour of the pub's original name, Robert Gillows, and applauded the name change with a 'well done' and further added:

> Making a decision to stop celebrating a man who thought it was acceptable to own other human beings isn't ridiculous; thinking that there is something wrong in that choice is ridiculous.

Others pointed to the various name changes the place has had:

> Gutted! It will always be Robert Gillow!

> It's been robert gillow for about 5 minutes!

> I remember it being a restaurant, Elliott's I think. It's had a few names.[9]

In 2021, schools, buildings named after Colston in Bristol were renamed, most prominently Colston Hall, now Bristol Beacon. The plaque under the Henry Dundas statue in Edinburgh has also been changed and now it reads: 'He was instrumental in

Journal of the Royal Anthropological Institute (N.S.) **28**, *153-178*
© 2022 The Authors. *Journal of the Royal Anthropological* Institute published by John Wiley & Sons Ltd on behalf of Royal Anthropological Institute.

Figure 3. Epitaph under Colston statue, Bristol, 11 June 2021. (Photo credit: @ProfDanHicks, Twitter, with permission.)

deferring the abolition of the Atlantic slave trade. Slave trading by British ships was not abolished until 1807. As a result of this delay, more than half a million enslaved Africans crossed the Atlantic'. There are innumerable architectural remnants of slavery in Lancaster and in other cities in Britain. Around the stasis of COVID, there has been more participation at BLM demonstrations and there are increased calls for a change of these landmarks that are seen to be arrogantly celebrating, on a pedestal and without remorse, what is a problematic British, colonial past. While I have explored the role of memorials as standing in for remorse (Mookherjee 2007; 2019), the statues of enslavers and colonizers like Robert Clive represent a pride in an imperialistic past full of injustices. A lack of reckoning with this history is believed by many BAME individuals, and others, to constitute part of the setting for contemporary racism. This

Figure 4. Empty pedestal of Colston statue. (Photo credit: @ProfDanHicks, Twitter, with permission.)

pride in history obscures the foundational violence (see the introduction and Visser and Niezen, this volume) blanketed under amnesia and the 'celebration and sublimation of the grand beginnings' (Derrida 2001: 57). Turning to the debates on memorialization as oblivion or pedagogy, I interrogate the role of historical inquiry, which, according to Renan (1896: 163), brings to light the deeds of violence that took place at the origin of all political formations.

Memorialization as oblivion or pedagogy?
Memorialization has various purposes. On one hand, the need to memorialize is based on the externalization and communication of private pain as public and is an injunction against forgetting on the part of communities and governments. However, in the examples I have discussed so far, the mercantile capitalism of slavery and colonialism

Figure 5. 'Captured Africans': Lancaster's slavery memorial. (Photo by the author, 2018.)

are being memorialized for the British public as a history of which to be proud. But the public secret that the material wealth of Britain is rooted in slavery and colonialism often remains unacknowledged in these statues. It has been argued that as soon as we affix a meaning to an object, the memory of it slowly becomes consigned to oblivion (Forty 1999; see Mookherjee 2007; 2019). Thus, in the case of the statues of enslavers, the people they portray could be seen to have been consigned to oblivion after being put on their pedestal. Yet the very fact that the replica of an individual enslaver has been put on a pedestal, overlooking people and a city, decentres the oblivion argument. This returns to Anish Kapoor's point above that these statues 'are emblematic monuments to our past which can be thought to represent how we see ourselves and our history'. The choice of these statues highlights a pride in empire which seems to be embodied in

Figure 6. Front window of the Robert Gillows pub with the words 'Trading in the unusual since 1720'. (Photo by the author, 2018.)

these statues. That BLM also demands and acts on the removal of these statues is further indicative of the relationship between material objects (Forty 1999: 8) and history. It is assumed that the durability of such objects enables the prolongation and preservation of a history and its values – here of slavery. However, in other instances of the history of slavery, the call for the removal of slavery's artefacts from our daily cityscapes is being refuted by Liverpool activists like the late Eric Lynch as an injunction against forgetting. I examine this discussion below.

In 2017, as part of the slavery fieldtrips that I have undertaken with students on my 'Violence and Memory' module, we came across an image (Fig. 7) of enslaved children in a doorway in Liverpool which was pointed out to us by Eric Lynch, who was leading

Journal of the Royal Anthropological Institute (N.S.) **28**, *153-178*

Figure 7. Image of enslaved children in a doorway in Liverpool. (Photo by the author, February 2017.)

the slavery history tour. In 2017, we had to do this tour without making it obvious and without blocking pavements as Eric advised this caution, citing difficult experiences he had encountered.[10]

On our trip, Eric pointed to this image in the doorway and said there were plans for its removal in line with gentrification of the city and making it a tourist destination for the Beatles. He was against the removal of this and other innumerable architectural remnants (which are distinctively different from statues of slave owners) relating to the slave trade embedded in Liverpool. Here, erasing evidence of historical events can also be about erasing symbols that point to a violent, inglorious past. This is in practice another form of aphasia, another obfuscation of knowledge through urban gentrification.

Journal of the Royal Anthropological Institute (N.S.) **28**, *153-178*

In the case of the city of Durham,[11] the landscape and visitor footfall (apart from students and their families) are connected to visits to the gothic cathedral and the various ecclesiastical landmarks linked to Christianity. Yet the link with slavery and the wealth accrued, which can be identified within these religious edifices, remains unmarked. The histories of slavery and mining are, however, intrinsically intertwined in Durham. So far, when exploring Newcastle and Durham's history of slavery, we see that it is dominated by an abolitionist narrative. However, the slavery fieldtrips with students further demonstrated that, given the North East had connections to slavery, there is a process of 'remembering to forget' (Mookherjee 2006; Rowlands 1999). This is when the focus is on how abolition was fought for in the past. The North East region, including the Palatinate and County of Durham, had connections to slavery in the Caribbean and the North American colonies and then the United States through emigration, resident and absentee sugar plantation ownership, executors/trustees of dead owners, plantation overseers, shipping, trading, coal mining, clergymen, colonial administrators, and military personnel (army and navy). Coal from the North East was sent to Jamaica, where it was used to heat raw sugar cane, harvested by slaves, to turn it into sugar, which was then exported to Britain. The Crowley ironworks on Tyneside made shackles and neck collars worn by the slaves, and specialist agricultural tools for the plantations in the West Indies and the North American colonies (Creighton 2020: 3).

As part of the Anglican Church hierarchy, the Bishops of Durham were involved in running the Society for the Propagation of the Gospel in Foreign Parts (SPG), which had been set up in 1701 (Fig. 8). The SPG had been left two slave plantations in Barbados by Christopher Codrington, to be developed for a college funded by the plantations in the 1710s. Personnel at the College had Durham connections. In 1835, when the British government paid £20 million (some £17 billion today) to slave owners as part of emancipating the enslaved, the Society received compensation (over £500,000) for the 410 enslaved people[12] on the plantation attached to the college. Speaking in 2006 at the Church of England's synod, in the context of the church's apology for the role it played in the eighteenth century in benefiting from slave labour in the Caribbean, the Rt Rev. Tom Butler, Bishop of Southwark said,

> The profits from the slave trade were part of the bedrock of our country's industrial development. No one who was involved in running the business, financing it or benefiting from its products can say they had clean hands. We know that bishops in the House of Lords with biblical authority voted against the abolition of the slave trade. We know that the church owned sugar plantations on the Codrington estates (Bates 2006).

The SPG became the United Society Partners in the Gospel (USPG) when in 1965 it merged with the Universities' Mission to Central Africa (UMCA; founded by David Livingstone in 1857).[13] So the USPG as a Christian mission agency has had a long history of rebranding. Significantly, in 2022, the USPG has opened up its archives and is seeking to come to terms with its past (Sadgrove 2022). Many individuals in the SPG had remained enslavers until abolition in 1833-4 and were beneficiaries of the government compensation. A search on the UCL Legacies of British Slave-Ownership database[14] shows 252 clergymen (Church of England reverends) who owned slaves or were associated with slavery at abolition.

Durham University was set up in 1842 after the compensation payout in 1835 and in 1875 Durham University became affiliated to the University of Codrington College in

Figure 8. List of Bishops in Durham Cathedral who were part of the Society for the Propagation of the Gospel in Foreign Parts (SPG). All Bishops in the House of Lords voted against abolition of slavery (Bates 2006). (Photo by the author, February 2020.)

Barbados (named after the well-known enslaver Christopher Codrington) for degree-granting purposes (Simmons 1972). The next year, Fourah Bay College in Sierra Leone was also affiliated. The colony had been established to settle the London Black poor, and was supported by Granville Sharp, a member of the Durham County-based family. County Durham's history is closely linked in with slavery and the campaigns against the slave trade. Post emancipation, the links with the Codrington and Fourah Bay Colleges pose a distinct question concerning Durham's role in the spread of colonial education and involvement in various types of imperial enterprise in the late nineteenth and early twentieth centuries (Nwauwa 1996: 26).

Journal of the Royal Anthropological Institute (N.S.) **28**, 153-178

Coal was crucial to the development of British industrialization, which underpinned colonialism and imperialism. So, in Durham's history, slavery, ships, coal mining, clergymen, and the various links to sugar plantations are intrinsically intertwined. Within Durham City, the only memorials to mining are the copper artwork in the Palatine café in the university, and the 1947 memorial and the Haswell Lodge banner in the cathedral. All other mining memorials are located outside the city. In contrast, there is the statue in the Market Place to the Marquess of Londonderry, which seems to contravene the history of mining, trade unionism, and leftist tradition and pride intrinsic in the county. He supported the use of child labour in the mines, was against strikes, unions, and tenancy rights, and was an uncaring landlord of estates in Ireland (Castleton 2019).

The debate around the continued ignorance about objects in buildings and cities and names of streets, buildings, businesses, and organizations related to slavery, which exist alongside statues and names of enslavers that exist throughout the United Kingdom, highlights the role of aphasia. The statues and monuments connote a historical arrogance through the ideas they embody and the choice made to put them on pedestals as 'philanthropists'. This is an attempt to glorify them as well as obliterate the violent histories they are linked to. Children watching the removal of the Colston statue with me also assumed that the statue of anyone must be that of a good person. The debate around the removal of statues has raised interesting questions about the significance and banality of memorialization, and the mode of oblivion that is intrinsic to the process.

This oblivion serves the status quo in enabling the statue of an enslaver to overlook our cities. Most people might not have been aware of these statues' history or of their presence in their cities. However, the debate over their removal has made their histories known. So, removing these statues could remove the horrific ideals these enslavers could be said to symbolize, but could it also erase their dark histories for future generations, as Eric Lynch argued? That there is resistance to such removals is seen in the fact that in January 2021 the UK's Secretary of State for Housing, Communities and Local Government, Robert Jenrick, passed a law to ensure that historic statues should be 'retained and explained' for future generations as a source of pride and not to reveal a violent past. Individuals who want to remove any historic statue, whether listed or not, will now require listed building consent or planning permission (BBC Sounds 2021: 16 mins; UK Government 2021). Many academics and public intellectuals argue against the idea of plaques for reasons like those of Xaso and Kapoor quoted above. Gary Younge (2021) powerfully notes that these statues are lazy and ugly, and he demands that all of them should be removed. In their place, he argues, the histories of the enslaved should be made part of the UK school curriculum, from which it is currently conspicuously absent.

That said, some cities commemorate the history of slavery differently. Hence, as we have seen, Lancaster attempts to balance the building of a slavery memorial on the periphery of the city and a pub named after an enslaver in the city centre. Yet today, even after the name change to the pub, the traces of the history of enslavers are retained through the tagline and RG (standing for Robert Gillow) symbol. Liverpool wants to remove the signs of slavery at Albert Dock and make the city a destination for Beatles tourism. But activists would rather retain these structures so that the memory of slavery is not erased from the city. In Durham, there is no visible presence of this past, and the city is renowned for its gothic cathedral. There is also no acknowledgement that the wealth of this city was

Journal of the Royal Anthropological Institute (N.S.) **28**, *153-178*
© 2022 The Authors. *Journal of the Royal Anthropological* Institute published by John Wiley & Sons Ltd on behalf of Royal Anthropological Institute.

founded on the links between the cathedral, mining, and slavery. Instead, this proud mining city houses a towering statue of a man who was against the well-being of miners.

The student responses to these fieldtrips were particularly insightful. They were often stunned by the prevalence and sites that marked the history of slavery in cities. The stories mentioned by the cultural historians leading the students through Lancaster, Liverpool, Newcastle, and Durham also allowed them to join the dots between different figures and protagonists. The presence of the images of the children as slaves (Fig. 7 above) was particularly poignant and the ensuing discussion on memorialization and removal was insightful because it highlighted the ethical challenges related to these themes.

The slavery tours also allowed students to reflect on the role of walking through urban spaces as a performative act and to think through how to memorialize slavery when there is no statue and no official record of slavery, even if it is visible in road signs, plaques in churches and cathedrals, and carvings on doorways and buildings, as we see in Durham, Liverpool (which has a slavery museum), Newcastle, and Lancaster (which has a slavery memorial). Along with a focus on the politics of exhibition and display, remembering and forgetting, and remembering what to forget, students followed Wallace in undertaking 'a performative understanding of human subjectivity, one recognizing that the idea of "the experiencing body located in time and space" is crucial to any process of historical reckoning' (2006: 47). What was significant in the process was for students to discern how various decisions made around depicting the history of slavery had repercussions at an individual and global scale. As I discussed above and also noted in a discussion of a Radio 4 programme, *Descendants*, on 4 June 2021, many abolitionists were paid compensation for their enslaver status when abolition took place. Many married into enslaved money and inherited properties accrued due to slavery. The £20 million that the UK government spent to reimburse the owners of slaves – who themselves were some of Britain's richest businessmen – took the British taxpayer 182 years (until 2015) to pay off. These discussions led many students to become proactive in exploring their family backgrounds and some of them also came to feel pride about their grandparents' mining background, which they would have otherwise not revealed to their peers.

In a particularly interesting debate, students raised the question of responsibility and what their role might be in addressing racial injustice. Following Hannah Arendt (2003 [1968]), we asked what should the relationship be between collective responsibility and individual culpability? Rather than a self-gratifying guilt, we discussed how collective responsibility can be aimed for through an informed critique of the system: in short, we must not be reconciled and instead sensitively take forward the discussion of responsibility. I had been undertaking these trips since 2007 without using the explicit vocabulary of decolonization and BLM. However, students identified these discussions as exemplary examples of decolonization in the faculty. By engaging with these sites, I have followed Wallace (2006) in addressing historical presence/absence and our role as critical, reflexive agents in relation to historical atrocity. The ethnography has also highlighted the need to reflect on our locational complexities within the history of slavery. Here Derrida's (1992: 5) commentary on Benjamin's theorization on violence and the relation between force and law (*droit*) is instructive. As we see in the various essays in the volume, perpetrators already had impunity in the system, and in recent juridical contexts the rule of law has further enabled their impunity by deciding the

Journal of the Royal Anthropological Institute (N.S.) **28**, *153-178*
© 2022 The Authors. *Journal of the Royal Anthropological Institute* published by John Wiley & Sons Ltd on behalf of Royal Anthropological Institute.

boundaries of the cases, which at the outset shuts down, forecloses, the possibilities of truth and justice. Consequently, victims have refused to reconcile. I turn, finally, to what I refer to as the 'window dressing' of our current epoch, which makes irreconciliation an essential framework for the work ahead.

Window dressing and irreconciliation: Mahatma Gandhi as 'diversity'

On 2 August 2020, it was revealed that Mahatma Gandhi would feature as the first BAME person on a British commemorative, but uncirculated, coin to be produced by the Royal Mint. This was thanks to the support of the Chancellor, Rishi Sunak (McGleenon 2020), in response to the debates on race and equity, and the BLM and Rhodes Must Fall movements. However, accusations of racism have also been levelled against Gandhi relating to his time in South Africa, leading to his statue being removed in Ghana. There have been calls to remove his statue from Manchester and Leicester. Historians like Professor Faisal Devji have, however, pointed out that although Gandhi was a fallible man, his record was mixed as he supported Africans during the Boer and Zulu wars, and he was more radical and progressive than most contemporary compatriots (Regan 2020). Hence, according to Devji, it is 'absurd' to compare him with slaveowners and his statue represents the Gujarati communities in the United Kingdom who were ousted by Idi Amin from East Africa. Claudia Webbe – Leicester's Black British MP – also considers these criticisms against Gandhi a 'massive distraction' from the BLM movement. Chancellor Rishi Sunak and Home Secretary Priti Patel are of Hindu, South Asian descent and part of the East African flight of Indians to the United Kingdom. They are part of the core of the 'diverse' Conservative government whose hero Churchill also reviled and demonized Gandhi. The inclusion of Gandhi on the coins is therefore deeply paradoxical. Gandhi was not only an anti-colonial campaigner, who led the protest against British rule in India and exposed the moral impoverishment of British colonialism, he was also a critic of capitalism.

The use of Gandhi here reminds us that diversity can become a 'commitment to something, including a commitment to change, change as diversification' (Ahmed 2019: 148). Such window dressing is also reflected in institutions' BLM support messages; their new focus on creating institutional BAME networks, and calls for 'respect' at work; and the use of the buzzword 'decolonization' – all in contradistinction to years of them disregarding the bullying and harassment of minority colleagues. The many passive bystanders or fence-sitters who ignored the discrimination of colleagues also add to the toxicity of institutional life. Is this sudden focus on decolonization a form of rebranding of institutions, a 'Schindlerization', to create a feel-good, upbeat vibe (Reich 2006: 466; as mentioned in the introduction to this volume)? It is in this context that the figure and principles of Gandhi and decolonization seem to be up for appropriation into institutions whose practices have been absolutely antithetical in the near past.

Decolonization needs to be about everyday practices and beyond the curriculum, while involving active bystanders and allies. As Achille Mbembe points out (Patta 2020), decolonization has to be done for posterity's sake and must be backed up with socioeconomic justice, material change, and engagement with the intersectional injustices within institutions. This is particularly true in anthropology, where the study of historical gaps in the British educational system (Wemyss 2016) is not deemed to be a matter for disciplinary focus. Yet, in spite of or because of the security of jobs and salaries, many feel unable to raise concerns about injustices within our home institutions. There are likely other varied reasons. This then makes it difficult to teach or discuss anti-racism with students or to act on it within the obstructive organizations one works in, among other factors.

The recent outcries relating to racial injustice and statues in the United States (Lee memorial), the United Kingdom (Colston, Rhodes), and Canada (Ryerson linked to residential schools) has highlighted clearly to me the similarities between the processes through which any redress related to genocidal injustices have been stalled, and the legal means through which the debate around statues has been curtailed. I have explored the links between the debates on statues and staff experiences in HE institutions. I noted above that in Bristol, a petition was submitted in the early 1990s to address the controversy of the Colston statue and the various landmarks linked to it. Yet any change was stalled by the wealthy Society of Merchant Venturers, who ensured that Colston's plaque mentioned only his 'philanthropy' (Steeds & Raval 2020). The debate about removing the statue of Ryerson (in lieu of changing its name) in Canada at X University (students called it X University in order to not use the name Ryerson) has gone on for decades, as has the university's attempt to 'pacify' the movement. This is captured in the aptly named Instagram account @wreckonciliation_x_university. The removal of the statue only took place after the discovery of the graves of the resident school First Nations children in 2021. Similarly, in the case of the Rhodes Must Fall movement in Oxford, all 'due process' was followed with inquiries and investigations. After Oriel College initially backed its removal, in May 2021, it was announced that the statue would not be taken down due to the cost and complex logistics (Race 2021). Any decision to move the statue would require planning permission from Oxford City Council, Historic England, and the relevant minister, Robert Jenrick. In October 2021, a plaque was added to 'contextualize' the debates around the statue in Oxford. The removal of the Lee statue in the United States was also stopped by two injunctions, but the statue was finally removed in September 2021.

As I mentioned above, in January 2021, Robert Jenrick passed a law to ensure that historic statues should be 'retained and explained' for future generations. This celebration of pride in all the violent and unjust events of the past is also reflected in the decision to make the 'retain and explain' policy a test for board appointments for trustees of museums to ensure that their views on heritage align with government policy (Barker & Foster 2021). Academics interviewing for these jobs thus have their public statements and social media posts examined to ensure that they agree with 'the retain and explain' policy (Barker & Foster 2021). Contrary to Derrida (2001: 57), there is no amnesia about the foundational violence which is being celebrated as grand beginnings. The attempt to retain and explain highlights the need to celebrate the spoils of colonialism, empire, and slavery. As Spivak asks, '[W]hen does the love for one's corner of the ground become the nation thing?' (2010: 13). Today, rather than just forgetting, as Renan (1896) argued, being necessary in order to create a nation, it is pride in nations' dark histories that also seem to be foundational for states across the world.

In all these instances, our three formulations of irreconciliation are apparent: it occurs when past historical injustices have not been addressed in spite of the issues having been raised; when historical injustices have been symbolically addressed through committees and investigations only to strengthen the status quo and resist the truth; and when the protests continue against such virtue-signalled and performative redress.

Journal of the Royal Anthropological Institute (N.S.) **28**, 153-178

I have drawn together an ethnography and review of documents, media material, and events relating to BLM, the debates on the removal of statues of enslavers, the absent presence legacy of slavery in the United Kingdom, and the intransigence and long-term discrimination in institutions. It becomes obvious how the prevalence of the drawing out of the processes of equalizing, the use of the law (*droit*) and bureaucratic regulations, and 'harmony ideology' all sustain injustices. We see how inequalities are consigned to oblivion in instances relating to legacies of slavery, institutional bullying, and harassment relating to BAME colleagues and BLM. In demonstrating this, I have tried to identify the need for the concept of irreconciliation to be employed as a form of vigilance against impunity, against the 'window-dressed', symbolic performance of redress. Irreconciliation is also 'the absolute willingness to register the impact of violence, so that that registering is also the creation of a possibility for being otherwise' (Ahmed as cited in Binyam 2022), beyond the corrosive subjectivity that injustice and its lack of acknowledgement engender. We should build on Hannah Arendt (Berkowitz 2011: 3) and say 'this ought never to have happened'. As Josephides suggests in her essay in this special issue, irreconciliation is about being held accountable, which is a necessary aspect of a mature, enlightened self and enables care for one's person.

Acknowledgements

Thank you for all the anonymous comments from the reviewers and from the *JRAI* editorial team. I am grateful to the members of the Durham BAME network, which has been such an amazing space for sharing stories, giving strength to each other, and creating friendships. Thanks also to various students on my third-year undergraduate 'Violence and Memory' module, which I have been lucky enough to teach for many years. I am grateful to many colleagues (whose identities I am keeping confidential) for sharing documents, links, information, comments, and feedback. I am also very grateful to Regina H. Boone/Richmond Free Press and Professor Dan Hicks for giving me permission to use their photographs within this essay. Finally, I am thankful for Ronald Niezen's translation of the German version of Hannah Arendt's *Denktagebuch* (*Thought diary*).

NOTES

[1] BAME is an umbrella term with which many within that collective do not feel comfortable as it homogenizes experiences and hierarchies. The term is often used interchangeably with black (which refers to those who see themselves as being politically black) or BIPOC (Black, indigenous, people of colour) used in North America. I use BAME while cognizant of the criticism against it as well as its bureaucratic connotations. It nonetheless brings into focus the broad and varied intersectional experiences of non-white people facing racism in the United Kingdom. In my experience, the term BAME has allowed individuals to share and support each other in their experiences of racism.

[2] To protect confidentiality and the precarious/fragile status of the affected persons, among other matters, I have deliberately withheld some of this material. I hold additional material and sources to substantiate these claims.

[3] Here, as in Nader's (1991) example of 'harmony ideology' in genocidal injustices, the institutional contexts prevented complaints from being voiced.

[4] Breonna Taylor, a 26-year-old African-American woman, was fatally shot on 13 March 2020 when police officers entered her Kentucky apartment as part of an investigation into drug dealing. The details of the case are hugely contested. None of the officers involved in the raid have been charged with Taylor's death.

[5] This phrase is used pejoratively among the left in Argentina and refers to the rhetorical efforts of 'reconciliation' based on ideas of forgiveness and forgetting, which seek to absolve military perpetrators.

[6] See Wemyss (2016) for a history of this statue.

[7] See Rice (2007) and Wallace (2006) for the histories of slavery in Bristol, Lancaster, and Liverpool.

[8] *https://www.robertgillow.co.uk/doing_wp_cron=1597391486.2163779735565185546875_www.ucl.ac.uk/lbs* (accessed 28 March 2022).

[9] I have paraphrased comments and not cited the references of these forums to keep them confidential.

[10] This seems to have changed as in 2018 Eric Lynch was awarded the Citizen of Honour by Liverpool City Council in recognition of his exceptional contribution to the city and to the International Slavery Museum. In fact, on Tripadvisor, Lynch's slavery history tours were considered as one of the 'top things to do in Liverpool' (*https://www.tripadvisor.co.uk/Attraction_Review-g186337-d215463-Reviews-Slavery_History_Trail-Liverpool_Merseyside_England.html*, accessed 28 March 2022). On 2 November 2021, Lynch sadly passed away and there are plans to create the 'Eric Lynch Slavery Memorial Plaque' in recognition of his life spent drawing attention to the city's slavery history when it was not supported by the authorities. William Brown Street is one of the first of around ten streets in Liverpool which will become home to an 'Eric Scott Lynch Slavery Histories' plaque.

[11] This section on Durham draws on Charlton (2008).

[12] A database of those awarded compensation for being enslavers can be found at the Centre for the Study of the Legacies of British Slavery website: *https://www.ucl.ac.uk/lbs//*, accessed 28 March 2022). The details of the payout to Codrington can be found here: *https://www.ucl.ac.uk/lbs/claim/view/6568* (accessed 28 March 2022).

[13] See *https://www.uspg.org.uk/about/history/* for more (accessed 28 March 2022).

[14] See *https://www.ucl.ac.uk/lbs/search/* (accessed 28 March 2022).

REFERENCES

AHMED, S. 2012. *On being included: racism and diversity in institutional life*. Durham, N.C.: Duke University Press.

———— 2017. Complaint as diversity work. Feministkilljoys, 10 November (available online: *https://feministkilljoys.com/2017/11/10/complaint-as-diversity-work/*, accessed 29 March 2022).

———— 2019. *What's the use? On the uses of use*. Durham, N.C.: Duke University Press.

AKWEI, I. 2017. This Cameroonian nationalist is chopping off heads of colonial statues in his country. Face2faceAfrica, 8 December (available online: *https://face2faceafrica.com/article/cameroonian-nationalist-chopping-off-heads-colonial-statues-cameroon*, accessed 29 March 2022).

ARENDT, H. 2002. *Denktagebuch*, vol. 1: 1950-1973 (eds U. Ludz & I. Nordmann). Munich: Piper Verlag.

———— 2003 [1968]. Collective responsibility. In *Responsibility and judgement: Hannah Arendt* (ed.) J. Kohn, 147-54. New York: Schocken Books.

BARKER, A. & P. FOSTER 2021. The battle over Britain's history. *Financial Times*, 12 June.

BATES, S. 2006. Church apologises for benefiting from slave trade. *Guardian*, 9 February (available online: *https://www.theguardian.com/uk/2006/feb/09/religion.world*, accessed 29 March 2022).

BBC NEWS 2019. Singapore: the artist cutting off the head of a British colonialist. 28 October (available online: *https://www.bbc.co.uk/news/av/world-asia-50134723/singapore-the-artist-cutting-off-the-head-of-a-british-colonialist*, accessed 29 March 2022).

BBC SOUNDS 2021. *The week in Westminster*, 23 January (available online: *https://www.bbc.co.uk/sounds/play/mooormdw*, accessed 29 March 2022).

BERKOWITZ, R. 2011. Bearing logs on our shoulders: reconciliation, non-reconciliation, and the building of a common world, *Theory & Event* **14**, 1-16.

BINYAM, M. 2022. You pose a problem: a conversation with Sara Ahmed. *Paris Review*, 14 January (available online: *https://www.theparisreview.org/blog/2022/01/14/you-pose-a-problem-a-conversation-with-sara-ahmed/*, accessed 29 March 2022).

BURCH-BROWN, J. 2020. Should slavery's statues be preserved? On transitional justice and contested heritage. *Journal of Applied Philosophy*, 20 November. *https://doi.org/10.1111/japp.12485*.

CASTLETON, D. 2019. Durham Market Place's controversial equestrian statue: tantrums, suicide and bankruptcy. *Durham Magazine*, 15 November (available online: *https://durhammagazine.co.uk/featured/durham-market-places-controversial-equestrian-statue-tantrums-suicide-bankruptcy/026095/*, accessed 29 March 2022).

CHARLTON, J. 2008. *Hidden chains: the slavery business and North East England*. Newcastle upon Tyne: Tyne Bridge Publishing.

CLARKE, E. 2020. Who was Edward Colston? The problematic legacy of the Bristol slave trader. *Evening Standard*, 8 June (available online: *https://www.standard.co.uk/news/uk/who-edward-colston-slave-trader-a4462256.html*, accessed 29 March 2022).

Journal of the Royal Anthropological Institute (N.S.) **28**, *153-178*

CREIGHTON, S. 2020. Slavery and abolition and people of African descent in the North East. Part 2. History and Social Action Publications (available online: *https://seancreighton1947.files.wordpress.com/2020/09/part-5-the-involvement-of-people-of-african-heritage-in-the-north-east-2.pdf*, accessed 29 March 2022).

DERRIDA, J. 1992. Force of law: the 'mythical foundation of authority'. In *Deconstruction and the position of justice* (eds) D. Cornell, M. Rosenfeld & D. Carlson, 3-67. London: Routledge.

———— 2001. *On cosmopolitanism and forgiveness* (trans. M. Dooley & M. Hughes). London: Routledge.

DEVLIN, H. & S. MARSH 2018. Hundreds of academics at top UK universities accused of bullying. *Guardian*, 28 September (available online: *https://www.theguardian.com/education/2018/sep/28/academics-uk-universities-accused-bullying-students-colleagues*, accessed 29 March 2022).

DOHARTY, N., M. MADRIAGA & R. JOSEPH-SALISBURY 2021. The university went to 'decolonise' and all they brought back was lousy diversity double-speak! Critical race counter-stories from faculty of colour in 'decolonial' times. *Educational Philosophy and Theory* **53**, 233-44.

FELDMAN, A. 2015. *Archives of the insensible: of war, photopolitics and dead memory*. Chicago: University Press.

FORTY, A. 1999. Introduction. In *The art of forgetting* (eds) A. Forty & S. Kuchler, 1-18. Oxford: Berg.

GAPUD, A.J. 2020. Displacing empire: aphasia, 'trade', and histories of empire in an English city. *History and Anthropology* **31**, 331-53.

McGLEENON, B. 2020. Royal Mint to produce a new coin with the first BAME person to feature in UK history. *Express*, 2 August (available online: *https://www.express.co.uk/news/uk/1317661/British-coin-royal-mint-Mahatma-Gandhi-rishi-sunak-bame-black-lives-matter*, accessed 29 March 2022).

MOOKHERJEE, N. 2006. 'Remembering to forget': public secrecy and memory of sexual violence in Bangladesh. *Journal of the Royal Anthropological Institute* (N.S.) **12**, 433-50.

———— 2007. The 'dead and their double duties': mourning, melancholia and the martyred intellectual memorials in Bangladesh. *Space and Culture* **10**, 271-91.

———— 2019. 1971: Pakistan's past and knowing what not to narrate. *Comparative Studies of South Asia, Africa and the Middle East* **39**, 212-22.

MORENO, S. 2020. Projections at Lee Monument offer peace in times of violence. *Washington Post*, 5 July (available online: *https://www.washingtonpost.com/local/projections-at-lee-monument-offer-peace-in-times-of-violence/2020/07/05/477f79c4-bec8-11ea-8908-68a2b9eae9e0_story.html*, accessed 29 March 2022).

NADER, L. 1991. *Harmony ideology: justice and control in a Zapotec mountain village*. Stanford: University Press.

NWAUWA, A.O. 1996. *Imperialism, academe and nationalism: Britain and university education for Africans, 1860-1960*. London: Frank Cass.

PATTA, D. 2020. In Africa, toppling statues is a first step in addressing racism, not the last. CBS News, 19 June (available online: *https://www.cbsnews.com/news/in-africa-toppling-statues-is-a-1st-step-in-addressing-racism-not-the-last/*, accessed 29 March 2022).

RACE, M. 2021. Cecil Rhodes: refusal to remove Oxford statue a 'slap in the face'. BBC News, 20 May (available online: *https://www.bbc.co.uk/news/uk-england-oxfordshire-57189928*, accessed 20 March 2022).

RAO, R. 2016. On statues. The Disorder of Things, 2 April (available online: *https://thedisorderofthings.com/2016/04/02/on-statues/*, accessed 29 March 2022).

REGAN, A. 2020. Calls to remove 'racist' Gandhi statue in Leicester. BBC News, 12 June (available online: *https://www.bbc.co.uk/news/uk-england-leicestershire-53025407*, accessed 29 March 2022).

REICH, W. 2006. Unwelcome narratives: listening to suppressed themes in American Holocaust testimonies. *Poetics Today* **27**, 463-72.

RENAN, E. 1896. What is a nation? In *The poetry of the Celtic races and other studies* (trans. W.G. Hutchinson), 163-76. London: Walter Scott Ltd.

REPORT OF THE DURHAM COMMISSION ON RESPECT, VALUES, AND BEHAVIOUR 2020. (available online: *https://www.dur.ac.uk/resources/respect.commission/5774_Respect_Report_Final_2020.pdf*, accessed 29 March 2022).

RICE, A. 2007. Naming the money and unveiling the crime: contemporary British artists and the memorialization of slavery and abolition. *Patterns of Prejudice* **41**, 321-43.

ROWLANDS, M. 1999. Remembering to forget: sublimation as sacrifice in war memorials. In *The art of forgetting* (eds) A. Forty & S. Kuchler, 129-46. Oxford: Berg.

SADGROVE, J. 2022. Understanding our archives: why engaging with history is essential but painful. *Koinonia*, 8 January: 12-13.

Journal of the Royal Anthropological Institute (N.S.) **28**, 153-178
© 2022 The Authors. *Journal of the Royal Anthropological* Institute published by John Wiley & Sons Ltd on behalf of Royal Anthropological Institute.

Simmons, G.C. 1972. Western Indian higher education – the story of Codrington College: the question of continued affiliation between Codrington College and Durham University. *Caribbean Quarterly*, **18**: **3**, 51-72.

Spivak, G.C. 2010. *Nationalism and the imagination*. Kolkata: Seagull Books.

Steeds, M. & P. Raval 2020. The problematic past of the Merchant Venturers. *The Bristol Cable*, 26 October (available online: *https://thebristolcable.org/2020/10/the-problematic-past-of-the-merchant-venturers-wulfstan-to-colston/*, accessed 29 March 2022).

Stewart, H., P. Walker, A. Mohdin & B. Quinn 2020. Boris Johnson 'stoking fear and division' ahead of BLM protests. *Guardian*, 12 June (available online: *https://www.theguardian.com/world/2020/jun/12/boris-johnson-stoking-fear-and-division-ahead-of-blm-protests*, accessed 29 March 2022).

Taussig, M. 1999. *Defacement: public secrecy and the labor of the negative*. Stanford: University Press.

Traister, R. 2020. The poison of male incivility. *The Cut*, 24 July (available online: *https://www.thecut.com/amp/2020/07/aoc-speech-ted-yoho-new-york-times.html?__twitter_impression=true&fbclid=IwAR2hqV_9zPw3MG2U7fUYytVDZLvqKey9UvR4XM6GhP5eSImqFYkzmv562cs*, accessed 29 March 2022).

Turner, C. 2016. *Violence, law and the impossibility of transitional justice*. London: Routledge.

Tyler, K. 2012. *Whiteness, class and the legacies of empire*. Basingstoke: Palgrave Macmillan.

UK Government 2021. New legal protection for England's heritage. Press release, 17 January (available online: *https://www.gov.uk/government/news/new-legal-protection-for-england-s-heritage#:~:https://text/New/20laws/20to/20protect/20Englands/20cultural/20and/20historic/20heritage/20haveand/20explained/20for/20future/20generations*, accessed 29 March 2022).

Universities UK 2020. Tackling racial harassment in higher education. November (available online: *https://www.universitiesuk.ac.uk/what-we-do/policy-and-research/publications/tackling-racial-harassment-higher*, accessed 29 March 2022).

Wallace, E.K. 2006. The transatlantic slave trade in Liverpool and Bristol. In *The British slave trade and public memory*, 25-65. New York: Columbia University Press.

Wemyss, G. 2016. *The invisible empire: white discourse, tolerance and belonging*. London: Routledge.

YouTube 2020a. British protestors topple Edward Colston statue. 7 June (available online: *https://youtu.be/04NXGb1pA6g*, accessed 29 March 2022).

———— 2020b. Doula: Meet Cameroon's colonial statue toppler. 7 July (available online: *https://www.youtube.com/watch?v=e_P7oiSCB60*, accessed 29 March 2022).

Younge, G. 2021. Why every single statue should come down. *Guardian*, 1 June (available online: *https://www.theguardian.com/artanddesign/2021/jun/01/gary-younge-why-every-single-statue-should-come-down-rhodes-colston?CMP=Share_iOSApp_Other*, accessed 29 March 2022).

Temps irréconciliables

Résumé

Dans son *Denktagebuch* (*Journal de pensée*, 1950-73), Hannah Arendt a écrit que les actes qui ne pouvaient pas être pardonnés étaient au-delà du châtiment, donc hors de portée de la réconciliation. L'autrice de cet article y puise inspiration pour théoriser davantage et élargir le concept d'irréconciliation. Cet article combine matériaux ethnographiques et historiques, documents, articles de presse et rapports durant une époque d'irréconciabilité qui a vu Black Lives Matter, les débats mémoriels sur l'enlèvement des statues d'esclavagistes, l'histoire de l'esclavage au Royaume-Uni et l'idéologie « de l'harmonie » à laquelle font face des universitaires noirs, asiatiques et membres de minorités ethniques (« BAME ») au sein d'organisations liées à des discriminations de longue durée au Royaume-Uni. Elle avance des arguments pour le concept d'irréconciliation comme rempart contre l'impunité, contre un redressement des torts symbolique, « d'affichage », faisant par là écho aux mots d'Arendt selon lesquels « cela » (toute cause originelle d'injustice) « n'aurait jamais dû arriver ».

11

Action beyond intent: experiencing ir/reconciliation (Afterword 2)

SARA SHNEIDERMAN *University of British Columbia*

As I drafted this afterword in late summer 2020, two news stories that demonstrated the national and global significance of the relationship between 'reconciliation' and 'irreconciliation' unfolded in parallel here in Canada. One emerged locally at the University of British Columbia (UBC) in Vancouver, where I live and teach on the unceded territories of the Musqueam, Squamish, and Tsleil-Wa-Tuth peoples; the other in Montreal and on the federal level.

On 14 September 2020, UBC released its Indigenous Strategic Plan (ISP) and began planning for its implementation, making the institution 'the first university in North America to commit to implementing the United Nations Declaration on the Rights of Indigenous Peoples' as part of 'UBC Vancouver's response to the Truth and Reconciliation Commission's Calls to Action'.[1] Developed through a long-term consultation process with Indigenous and non-Indigenous faculty, students, staff, and community members, the document highlights the need to put 'truth before reconciliation', and once on the pathway to the latter, to keep the focus on 'meaningful reconciliation' through a plan to 'transform intent into action' as an ongoing process rather than a singular event.

At that time, I was still struggling to understand Canadian Prime Minister Justin Trudeau's excoriation of anti-racism protesters in Montreal who had toppled a statue of Canada's first Prime Minister just a few weeks earlier. John Macdonald is widely understood as a key architect of the Indian residential school system in Canada, among other strategies designed to effect the genocide of Indigenous peoples. As CBC reported, 'The Macdonald statue was toppled and decapitated during a protest calling on political leaders to de-fund police services – part of a wave of protests across the continent against excessive violence perpetrated by law enforcement against Black and Indigenous people'. Yet Trudeau himself invoked the logic of law and order to condemn these actions, saying, 'We are a country of laws and we are a country that needs to respect those laws, even as we seek to improve and change them, and those kind of acts of vandalism are not advancing the path towards greater justice and equality in this country' (Tasker 2020).

These parallel realities highlight the inherent contradictions of reconciliation as a form of politics as well as policy. Such contradictions were catapulted into the media spotlight again in May 2021 with the 'discovery' of the presumed remains of 215 children in unmarked graves on the grounds of the former Kamloops Indian Residential School in British Columbia. While the 'Calls to Action' of the Truth and Reconciliation Commission (TRC) included several points regarding 'Missing Children and Burial Information', the 2021 revelation at Kamloops was the result of research undertaken by the Tk'emlúps te Secwépemc First Nation at their own cost – not by the government. These circumstances served as a brutal reminder of the government's inaction, and led to social media amplification of long-standing claims that 'reconciliation is dead'.

As all of the essays in this special issue show, such forms of irreconciliation may be a necessary embodiment of reconciliation in action, beyond intent. As Noa Vaisman writes, irreconciliation refers to the 'ongoing active practice of vigilance against impunity and to the collective engagement with a living past'. Practices of irreconciliation not only can, but must, live simultaneously with practices of reconciliation to have hopes of making change within existing frameworks of governance. Yet the ongoing irreconciliation between intent and action may also provide a space for productive technologies of power and subjectification to operate. This may paradoxically work to strengthen structures of oppression through the processes intended to dismantle them.[2]

Irreconciliation and reconciliation; protesters, politicians, and bureaucrats: all are intimately entangled in the *longue durée* dance of structural transformation. A Prime Minister invokes the violence of law to protect the memorialized image of his forebear, at the same time as his government – and its institutions, for instance UBC as a provincial university – proceeds with implementing the 'Calls to Action' put forward by the TRC, which has been a core element of his political platform. As the UBC ISP architects wrote in the *Vancouver Sun*, '[I]t is our expectation that through this plan, the university will demonstrate how public institutions, not just governments, can play a critical role in upholding, advancing, and, indeed, implementing the human rights standards set out in the United Nations Declaration on the Rights of Indigenous Peoples' (Lightfoot, Ono & Moss 2020).

My invocation of 'structural transformation' here derives from the political application of Victor Turner's call to focus our 'attention on the phenomenon and processes of mid-transition' (1967: 110). By taking seriously how structure and transformation are experienced and expressed in discursive and material terms by citizens in so-called 'post-conflict' contexts, I understand specific legal mechanisms for reconciliation such as transitional justice as windows into understanding broader imaginaries of the ideal state and social orders in which people wish to live. In this way, my approach to ir/reconciliation prioritizes political agency and practice in the ritualized sense, rather than power, subjectification, and discourse in the Foucauldian or Derridean sense.

At the risk of giving Trudeau too much credit, perhaps his critique of protesters – whose toppling of statues embodies irreconciliation (as articulated by Mookherjee in this volume) – is a necessary tactic to enable the deep work of structural transformation embodied in institutional processes of reconciliation like UBC's ISP. The practices of the protesters themselves certainly push at the boundaries of this space. In other words, the affective power of publicly visible acts and words may provide political cover of sorts for the mundane everyday work of transforming intent into action within the institutional structures that govern our lives. In the best of all possible worlds, the results of such hard work can transcend their own already anticipated critiques.

These complex dynamics between affect, temporality, embodiment, and visibility are common themes across the four essays that I have been asked to comment upon. In Colombia (Clarke), Argentina (Vaisman), and Sri Lanka (Buthpitiya), we see how the affects of irreconciliation are embodied in gendered relationships where the ties of kinship call into presence those who have disappeared, demanding their 'visibilization' (Clarke) in ways that challenge official narratives of closure. In Mookherjee's description of the uncomfortable memorialization of slave traders and other figures complicit in the violent past of the global present, we see this relationship between visibilization and disappearance in inverted view: activists like those who toppled Macdonald's statue in Montreal want these icons to disappear, yet they remain painfully visibilized at the expense of those whom their actions disappeared. In this case, Mookherjee calls not for erasure, but for a shift in memorialization beyond the intended 'window dressing' of institutional messaging around BLM while following the action of 'due process' to condone long-term bullying and harassment of BAME staff. Instead of reproducing structures of oppression through the very actions of their proclaimed dismantling, she is calling for a meaningful acknowledgement of complicity in pasts linked to entrenched institutional practices of injustice.

In reading these essays together, we can understand the calls for visibilization of the disappeared embodied in the murals of Colombian activists, as well as the placarded photographs of Sri Lankan protesters, as conscious strategies to assert global relevance for what the state often strives to portray as localized grievances. State perpetrators attempt to foreclose global recognition of their wrongdoing by creating scapegoats: diasporic populations and other 'external' actors are blamed for fomenting protest, in a doubly violent move that disregards the agency of protesters. While it is ultimately the state and military that need to provide answers, why should they, who have been responsible for violence, become forever memorialized in stone as historical actors, when those who have suffered the consequences of their violence are erased? And how do we understand this question at the heart of irreconciliation as a globally significant one, although it may take different forms across place and time?

Strategies of visibilization such as those Clarke describes in Colombia or Buthpitiya in Sri Lanka invoke the power of what Allen Feldman calls the 'violent particular' (2004: 169), while at the same time seeking to universalize it for the purposes of global mobilization. Feldman identifies the tension in this double movement, as well as in our anthropological attempts to understand it comparatively: images of victims may become useful in global narratives of reconciliation when decontextualized from the local particularities of terror, but once deployed in this manner, they lose their power to embody necessary irreconciliations in their political particular. This begins to hint at the limits to comparative conversation under the rubric of 'reconciliation', a challenge that the theme of irreconciliation as articulated in this volume seeks to address directly.

This tension between particular and general, and the related challenge of situating multiple 'locals' within a shared framework for understanding ir/reconciliation, has framed my own personal experience of settling in Canada over the last several years.[3] My family and I arrived from the United States in mid-2014. In late 2015, during my first year as a faculty member at UBC, the final report of Canada's TRC was released. I knew little about this process or its history at the time. Rather, my professional life as an anthropologist had focused on Nepal, and I was then engaged in a second project about 'post-conflict' state transformation there,[4] in the wake of the 1996-2006 civil conflict between the Maoist People's Liberation Army and state forces.

Through my own lived experience, these two historical trajectories in Canada and Nepal began to overlap – often uncomfortably – as I watched Nepal's efforts to establish a TRC falter just as Canada's gained traction.[5] When I spoke with colleagues and friends here about Nepal's TRC and sought to place it in comparative conversation with Canada's experience, for the most part I received blank looks. There were many reasons for this, some to do with the difference in temporal scale between state-perpetrated violence in each case – a ten-year civil conflict in Nepal versus hundreds of years of settler colonialism-induced genocide in Canada – but also some to do with the way in which, as Buthpitiya's essay highlights, so-called Western liberal democracies such as Canada see themselves as essentially different from those elsewhere in the geopolitical global order like Sri Lanka or Nepal.

The temporal question requires further consideration. On one end of the timeline, although Nepal's civil conflict formally lasted for ten years, from the declaration of a People's War by the Communist Party of Nepal (Maoist) in 1996 to the Comprehensive Peace Agreement in 2006, the histories of state violence, labour and land exploitation, and marginalization on the basis of Indigenous, caste, and other identities that led to Nepal's conflict stretch back much longer. These dynamics were already in place as the era of settler colonialism began in North America. Nepal's 'nonpostcoloniality' (Des Chene 2007) neither absolves the contemporary Nepali state from the need to recognize its own history of internal colonialism, nor places it outside the ambit of global understandings of ir/reconciliation.

On the other end of the timeline, as I wrote about the politics of post-conflict in Nepal in 2014, little did I know that Nepal was not only 'post-conflict' but 'pre-disaster'. The massive earthquakes of spring 2015 then pitched the country into a whole new set of 're'-s: recovery, reconstruction, resilience. My own ongoing ethnographic work in Nepal seeks to understand post-conflict state restructuring in relation to all of these. If, as Vaisman proposes in this volume, irreconciliation is 'an agentive act of social reconstruction', how do we understand the relationship between social and material reconstruction when conflict and disaster intersect?

Further, the essays in this volume push me to ask: if we advocate irreconciliation as a necessary form of transformation, then what would irrecovery, irreconstruction, or irresilience look like? These questions are important in understanding relationships between contemporary states and their citizens as a whole, because they call into question the teleological assumptions baked into all of these putative processes of 're' starting something that never was that way in the first place.[6] The authors in this volume and their interlocutors provide ways to imagine forms of ambivalent agency (Buthpitiya) that may lead to material as well as social reconstruction – along different lines than that mandated by governments, whether through formal processes of reconciliation or reconstruction. In the research I have been conducting through a collaborative partnership about post-disaster reconstruction in Nepal,[7] we have learned that the ideal outcomes are usually hybrids – what may often be called 'compromises' in transitional justice legislation. By this I mean that the rebuilt houses that people are most satisfied with are those that blend government-mandated engineering best practices towards future seismic resilience with traditional Indigenous knowledge of

Journal of the Royal Anthropological Institute (N.S.) **28**, *179-186*
© Royal Anthropological Institute 2022.

building design. Could we apply this insight to ir/reconciliation as well, to suggest that both reconciliation frameworks in the formal sense, and practices of irreconciliation that push against them, must proceed in tandem?

This calls into question the idea that 'reconciliation' and 'irreconciliation' are opposites, framing them instead as simultaneously necessary counterparts. The contributions by Clarke, Vaisman, and Buthpitya hint at this by showing that irreconciliation is in a sense enabled by the structure of a formal reconciliation process. By contrast to these cases in Colombia, Argentina, and Sri Lanka, in Nepal the formal structures of reconciliation have never been fully established. This is in large part due to the long, drawn-out process of state restructuring which began in 2006, culminating in the constitution of 2015 and implementation of new political boundaries after local elections in 2017. Refusal may have different valences in different contexts. In some, the very premise of reconciliation may be refused, but in others, where the shape of the polity as a whole is in flux, a well-conceived and implemented legal-juridical framework for tackling impunity may be seen as a desirable element of a newly functional and compassionate state structure. In such cases, like Nepal, ir/reconciliation may be not about refusing reconciliation entirely, but rather about refusing to participate in poorly conceived formal processes that misrecognize the origins of suffering as somehow located outside the state.

The refusal of state forgiveness processes that Clarke highlights resonates with approaches to 'theorizing refusal' developed by anthropologists such as Audra Simpson and Carole McGranahan (see McGranahan 2016). However, such practices of outright refusal only seem to make sense in circumstances where there is something on the table to refuse at the collective level. What of a place like Nepal where the TRC was never fully implemented, superseded as it was by the logics of post-disaster reconstruction? Or in Bangladesh, where there is no intention of reconciliation (as Mookherjee explains in the introduction to this volume)? Instead there prevails a refusal to forgive that makes irreconciliation the norm, as the foundational violence of the war of 1971 has not been acknowledged in the first instance – making an apology inconceivable.

In such contexts, it may be more valuable or validating to practise what Clarke calls 'affective attribution', or visibilization of those who have been disappeared. On the one hand, we can see this as a refusal of reconciliation. On the other, we can also see it as a means of demanding such a process itself, for instance in the ongoing campaigns of women like Devi Sunuwar in Nepal to secure a legal process to prosecute conflict-era crimes like the murder of her daughter Maina in 2004 by known military perpetrators. In 2019, Sunuwar explicitly made her refusal clear by rejecting an offer from the army of financial compensation and a statue memorializing her daughter as long as they refused to fully prosecute all known perpetrators.[8] Such strategies of visibilization via refusal may be seen as practices of irreconciliation, but they can also be seen as strategies to call judicial and legal processes into existence in places where those formal frameworks remain flimsy. These efforts by many Nepali family members of the disappeared are represented photographically in a recent project titled 'The Empty Chairs' (Jia 2020).

Here in Canada, the practice of visibilization is also paramount in making policy-makers accountable to the TRC's calls to action, ensuring that intent is translated into action. We can see this in the ongoing campaign for justice for Missing and Murdered Indigenous Women,[9] as well as in artistic representations such as Cree artist Kent Monkman's travelling exhibit, recently on display at UBC's Museum of Anthropology, 'Shame and Prejudice: A Story of Resilience'.[10] Here a series of nine installations take us

Figure 1. Chapter V: Forcible Transfer of Children. From the exhibition 'Shame and Prejudice', Kent Monkman, Museum of Anthropology, UBC, Vancouver, Canada. (Photo by the author, 21 August 2020.)

through the often unspoken history that has produced modern Canada, visibilizing its disappeared along the way. Such multimodal work opens a space for intergenerational transmission and transformation. It was the wall of empty cradleboards from different First Nations, interspersed with empty outlines (see Fig. 1), that stopped me and my 10-year-old daughter in our tracks as we walked through Monkman's exhibit. Here, the affective horror fully surrounds visitors: of disappearance through residential schools, through generations of kin, a collectivity constituted through ancestral absence. Absence, presence, and the play of the past in the present visibilize ir/reconciliation in these words from Monkman: 'This is the one I cannot talk about. The pain is too

Journal of the Royal Anthropological Institute (N.S.) **28**, *179-186*
© Royal Anthropological Institute 2022.

deep. We were never the same' (Monkman 2017: 16). Such words resonate with the responsibility of creating a future for our children that can never be the same, yet is rooted in everything that has gone before. That is the work of ir/reconciliation.

Acknowledgements

I thank Sheryl Lightfoot and Mark Turin for their comments on this essay. Two reviewers also helped to improve it: one anonymous, and one self-identified as Allen Feldman. I am also grateful to Nayanika Mookherjee, Editor of this special issue, contributor Vindhya Buthpithiya, and the Editors of the *JRAI* for the opportunity to develop these ideas in conversation.

NOTES

[1] *https://indigenous.ubc.ca/indigenous-engagement/indigenous-strategic-plan/* (accessed 29 March 2022).

[2] I am grateful to Allen Feldman for clarifying this point in his comments as a reviewer of this special issue. In chapter 5 of *Archives of the insensible*, he builds upon the Hegelian notion of 'intentionalist continuity' to show how an overemphasis on intent in reconciliation processes can offer a perverse validation of the political subjectivity of perpetrators (Feldman 2015: 289). For further discussion of Feldman's work and its relationship to the arguments of this special issue, please see Nayanika Mookherjee's introduction.

[3] I use the term 'settling' intentionally, following Lowman and Barker's use of the term (2015) to emphasize how all 'new Canadians' are in fact complicit in the ongoing structures of settler colonialism.

[4] See Shneiderman & Snellinger (2014) for reflections on the limitations of the term 'post-conflict'.

[5] For scholarly work about Nepal's transitional justice process, see Robins (2012; 2014), Sajjad (2013), and Selim (2018). A recent wave of concern around the TRC's unfinished work emerged in early 2020, as described in media pieces such as K.D. Bhattarai (2020) and S. Bhattarai (2020).

[6] For reflections on this theme from a linguistic perspective, see Pine & Turin (2017), notably: 'The very use of the prefix "re" in words such as revitalization, rejuvenation, revival, and resurgence points to the undoing of some past action or deed'.

[7] See *https://elmnr.arts.ubc.ca/* (accessed 29 March 2022).

[8] Three out of four received life sentences, but the fourth was acquitted, and the army subsequently filed an appeal to the Supreme Court requesting annulment of the life sentences, which is still pending at the time of writing (*My República* 2019).

[9] *https://www.mmiwg-ffada.ca/* (accessed 29 March 2022).

[10] *https://moa.ubc.ca/exhibition/shame-and-prejudice/* (accessed 29 March 2022).

REFERENCES

BHATTARAI, K.D. 2020. Nepal's transitional justice process runs the risk of failing. *The Diplomat*, 25 August (available online: *https://thediplomat.com/2020/08/nepals-transitional-justice-process-runs-the-risk-of-failing/*, accessed 29 March 2022).

BHATTARAI, S. 2020. Victims unhappy as Nepal revives transitional justice process. Al-Jazeera, 13 January (available online: *https://www.aljazeera.com/news/2020/01/victims-unhappy-nepal-revives-transitional-justice-process-200113082330798.html*, accessed 29 March 2022).

DES CHENE, M. 2007. Is Nepal in South Asia? The condition of non-postcoloniality. *Studies in Nepali History and Society* 12, 207-23.

FELDMAN, A. 2004. Memory theaters, virtual witnessing, and the trauma-aesthetic. *Biography* 27, 163-202.

———— 2015. *Archives of the insensible: of war, photopolitics, and dead memory*. Chicago: University Press.

JIA, G. 2020. The empty chairs. *Nepali Times*, 28 August (available online: *https://www.nepalitimes.com/here-now/the-empty-chairs/?fbclid=IwARoauWdS2OrxQ-1niO-8pSoyMH5NxXwK6B7HMraVJTLk5sFeh3e9n66pbbE*, accessed 29 March 2022).

LIGHTFOOT, S., S. ONO & M. MOSS 2020. Opinion: UBC demonstrates that we all have a role in upholding the rights of Indigenous peoples. *Vancouver Sun*, 11 September (available online: *https://vancouversun.com/opinion/op-ed/opinion-ubc-demonstrates-that-we-all-have-a-role-in-upholding-the-rights-of-indigenous-peoples*, accessed 29 March 2022).

LOWMAN, E. & A. BARKER 2015. *Settler: identity and colonialism in 21st-century Canada*. Winnipeg: Fernwood Publishing.

MCGRANAHAN, C. (ed.) 2016. Openings and retrospectives: theorizing refusal. *Cultural Anthropology* 31: 3.

MONKMAN, K. 2017. *Shame and prejudice: a story of resilience. Stories from the memoirs of Miss Chief Eagle Testickle* (available online: *https://agnes.queensu.ca/exhibition/kent-monkman-shame-and-prejudice-a-story-of-resilience/*, accessed 28 March 2022).

MY REPÚBLICA 2019. Maina Sunar's mom declines army's offers of charity. 19 August (available online: *https://myrepublica.nagariknetwork.com/news/maina-sunar-s-mom-declines-army-s-offers-of-charity/*, accessed 29 March 2022).

PINE, A. & M. TURIN 2017. Language revitalization. In *Oxford research encyclopedia of linguistics* (ed.) M. Aronoff. New York: Oxford University Press. *https://doi.org/10.1093/acrefore/9780199384655.013.8*.

ROBINS, S. 2012. Transitional justice as an elite discourse: human rights practice between the global and the local in post-conflict Nepal. *Critical Asian Studies* **44**, 3-30.

———— 2014. Constructing meaning from disappearance: local memorialisation of the missing in Nepal. *International Journal of Conflict and Violence* **8**, 104-18.

SAJJAD, T. 2013. *Transitional justice in South Asia: a study of Afghanistan and Nepal*. Abingdon, Oxon: Routledge.

SELIM, Y. 2018. *Transitional justice in Nepal: interests, victims, and agency*. Abingdon, Oxon: Routledge.

SHNEIDERMAN, S. & A. SNELLINGER 2014. Framing the issues: the politics of 'postconflict'. *Fieldsights*, 24 March (available *online*: *https://culanth.org/fieldsights/framing-the-issues-the-politics-of-postconflict*, accessed 29 March 2022).

TASKER, J.P. 2020. Trudeau condemns destruction of Sir John A. Macdonald statue in Montreal. CBC News, 31 August (available online: *https://www.cbc.ca/news/politics/trudeau-statue-sir-john-a-macdonald-1.5706247*, accessed 29 March 2022).

TURNER, V. 1967. *The forest of symbols: aspects of Ndembu ritual*. Ithaca, N.Y.: Cornell University Press.

Index

abuse 70, 84; children 19, 86–8, 90, 91, 92; sexual 80, 81, 88; women 154

accountability 12, 13, 16, 22, 25, 26, 28, 29, 34–49, 69–73, 97–8, 99, 106, 107, 120, 128, 129, 131, 144, 148; and the state 130, 135, 138, 139, 142; as abjectness and ruination 44; as building the self 44–5; criminal 100; definition 35, 101; for violence 137, 140; legal 83, 96, 104, 105, 106, 111, 112,

acknowledgement, as sense of self 39–43

activism 12, 22, 24, 65–78, 98; in Argentina 105, 113; in London 68–9, 71–2; in Sri Lanka 118, 119; transnational 71, 75, 76

aesthetics 26–8; exhibitions 27; films 27; memorials 27

see also photographs; statues

Africa, and restorative justice 21; slavery 161, 163; structural adjustment 21; violence 80

Améry, Jean 36, 45–6, 107; *ressentiment* 45–6, 47, 112

amnesia 11, 12, 14, 26, 36, 165, 174; and amnesty 40; and photography 120; 'commanded' 36; historical 155

anger 39, 45, 46, 67, 98

apology 11, 12, 13, 14, 16, 22, 34, 36, 37, 39, 40, 47, 65, 67, 183; as speech act 12, 40; by Church of England 169

Arendt, Hannah 36, 51, 89, 98, 139; *Denktagebuch* 14, 153, 155

Argentina 16, 21, 22, 23, 24, 74; irreconciliation 103–17; National Pacification Act 105

atonement 22, 34, 35, 40, 45, 47, 123

Australia 13–14, 15

BAME academics 154–5, 158–60, 175, 181

Bangladesh 16, 22; 1971 war 12, 13, 24, 26, 69, 71, 72; Collaborators Act 69; genocide 11, 13; human rights activists 12, 22, 24, 65–78; international crimes tribunal 13, 17, 24, 26, 65, 66, 68, 73–4, 75; London activism 68–9, 71–2; People's Court 70, 71, 72; Sreeramshi Welfare Association 68, 74–6; war crimes tribunal 21

Bedouins 19

Bertelsen, Bjørn 7, 23, 50–64, 96, 97, 99

Black Lives Matter (BLM) 9, 11, 15, 23, 25, 153, 155, 156, 163, 164, 167, 173, 175; and institutions 156–60, 181